GOLD AND SILVER

The life and times of
Franz Lehár

By the same author
PRIVATE LIVES OF THE GREAT COMPOSERS
PRINCE OF VIENNA
etc.

GOLD AND SILVER

The life and times of
Franz Lehár

Bernard Grun

David McKay Company, Inc.
New York

Author's Note

Grateful acknowledgements are due to my friend Oliver Coburn, who showed his usual care, patience, and linguistic expertise in helping to prepare the English edition of this book under my supervision. I have also received much help and encouragement from Mark Goulden and Jeffrey Simmons of W. H. Allen and Co Ltd, London– and as always through the years from my friends Blanche and Eric Glass. Mrs Betty Marshall-Gordon has again taken her usual great pains in preparing the typescript. To all of them my deepest thanks.

B.G.

Gold and Silver

To Edith with love

CONTENTS

8   CONTENTS

List of Illustrations

All pictures are from the Lehár-Archives unless otherwise acknowledged

PART ONE

Threshold
1870–1904

I
THE PARENTS

At the Foot of Mount Altvater

The Lehars were glaziers, plying an itinerant trade in the north of Moravia, in what is now Czechoslovakia. Their home was the village of Lesnitz in the district of Hohenstadt, at the foot of Mount Altvater. The name Lehar can be traced back to the end of the seventeenth century in various parts in this area, spelt differently according to the language it was written in: Lehar in German, Léhar in Czech, Lehár in Hungarian. Its etymology is obscure.[1]

About 1770 Johann Lehar,[2] great-great-grandfather of the composer, settled in Brünnles, a small market town with a picturesque ruined castle, part of the estate of the Prince of Liechtenstein. In 1782 he had a son, also called Johann, and in 1808 this second Johann Lehar had a son called Josef. At the age of nineteen Josef married Anna Polach, six years older than himself, the daughter of a landowner in Schönwald near the Moravian town of Neustadt; she was one of fourteen children. A woman of spirit and purpose, endowed with a pleasant singing voice, she brought both prosperity and music into the Lehar family. Thanks to her considerable dowry, the young couple were able to buy a

---

[1] No one has found a satisfactory explanation for the origin of the name. Stan Czech in his Lehár biography (*Schön ist die Welt*, Berlin, 1957) tries to derive it from the Czech word *Lehárna* (a resting veranda in a clinic or hospital) or the Slovak word *Lekár* (doctor), but comes to the conclusion that this "does not quite add up to a real word Lehar".

[2] Born about 1750.

house in Schönwald, "No. 138", and established the J. Lehar Glaziery.

Of their three sons, only the eldest went into the family trade. He was the composer's uncle Johann, master glazier and joiner in Deutsch-Liebau, who came to Vienna at the age of seventy-three to bask in his nephew's fame. Lehar's mother[1] writes: "I gave him a warm welcome and entertained him well. He was with us in the box at the *Rastelbinder* (The Tinker), and wept for joy. Among other things he declared that your great-grandfather was a Frenchman. He had kept his papers. One document is even framed. He promised to send us the papers."

The papers never arrived. They were supposed to show that the family was founded by an officer in Napoleon's army, one Marquis Le Harde ("The Daring"), who was taken prisoner by the Russians in 1799, escaped, and on his way through Moravia took refuge in the castle of Brünnles. A peasant girl secretly brought him food; he married her, and she became the mother of his children.

There may have been a French officer at Brünnles in 1799 who had escaped from the Russians and was called Le Harde; but uncle Johann was certainly romancing. He must have known that the parish register showed the Lehars already in their second generation there; and his grandfather's glaziery at Brünnles was something he would remember from his boyhood. The story, however, was much repeated and reproduced. The composer's officer brother Anton readily believed it; the composer himself always expressed amused scepticism on the subject.

The two younger sons of Josef and Anna were called Anton and Franz. Anna wanted them to become musicians, and they were "apprenticed" to a town musician by the name of Heydenreich in near-by Sternberg, which (like all towns of any size in the Habsburg Empire) had its own orchestra or band. Anton later joined the army, rose to band sergeant, and eventually succeeded Heydenreich as musical director to the town of Sternberg. His brother Franz[2] was the father of the composer.

[1] In a letter to her younger son, Anton, in 1903.
[2] Born 29th January 1838.

Joybells Ringing

At the age of sixteen Franz Lehar Senior had finished his apprenticeship. He had become a competent violinist and horn-player, besides playing the piano, 'cello, double bass, clarinet, trumpet, trombone—and all the percussion instruments. Such versatility was often to stand him in good stead later on; and he kept it up. When celebrating the completion of thirty years in the army he could still delight comrades and friends with a musical selection arranged by himself, in which he performed as soloist on ten different instruments.

Heydenreich would have liked to keep his talented pupil in Sternberg as one of his musicians. But either the salary was not attractive enough or the old *Wanderlust* of the Lehars was stirring: Franz left home, and played his way through the country. In April 1855 he arrived in Vienna, capital of the Austro-Hungarian Empire and the seat of the Emperors. The previous year the young Emperor Franz Joseph I had married Elisabeth, the beautiful daughter of the Bavarian Royal house of Wittelsbach: the guns thundered out in joyful salute, the organ pealed; "the sharp wind, and Vienna's poisonous air", dissolved into radiant sunshine and the scent of lilac. "Above all heads a heaven of melody soared, a canopy of black-and-gold notes."[1]

The young man from northern Moravia earned his living at first by teaching music and playing the violin in dance bands. He also attended courses at the Academy of Music, studying musical theory and orchestration. In the autumn he found a position as horn-player at the Theater an der Wien.

His musical director was Franz von Suppé, who had by then been working at this theatre for ten years, writing overtures and incidental music, and in the evening wielding the conductor's baton. His huge figure, gleaming bald pate and massive beard had become a familiar landmark in Vienna's theatrical life.

The first news was arriving of the rise of Jacques Offenbach in Paris: the opening of his *Bouffes Parisiens*[2] and the success of the

[1] From the classic Austrian novel *Radetzky March*, by Joseph Roth.
[2] 5th July 1855.

first one-act operettas. Suppé felt instinctively that a new genre most congenial to his talents was being born, and that he might be the man to produce an amalgam of Gallic wit and Viennese *Gemütlichkeit,* to transpose the spirit of *bouffonnerie* into the Austrian emotional world.

By the time the first of Suppé's operettas, *Das Pensionat* (The Young Ladies' Finishing School), had its première at the Theater an der Wien,[1] Lehar Senior had long given up playing the horn in the theatre orchestra. He was called to the colours in the autumn of 1857, and was serving in the band of No. 50 Infantry Regiment, based on Vienna.

Between 1859 and 1866

A bad time was starting for Austria, a period of political and military entanglements from which the country emerged each time more seriously weakened.

The war of 1859 against Sardinia and France was fought by stupid generals, with demoralized troops and obsolete weapons. It lasted two months and fifteen days, and cost the Habsburgs Lombardy. Franz Joseph, Commander-in-Chief, lost 20,000 men at Magenta and Solferino, and "got to know the feelings of a defeated general".[2]

Lehar Senior was in the field at both defeats, and at the end of the campaign he was promoted to band sergeant. After the war he remained with his regiment in Venetia. Between then and 1866, Austria's next year of disaster, the Crown Prince Rudolf had been born,[3] two paladins of the old monarchy, Radetzky and Metternich, had died; Bismarck had taken over the reins of government in Prussia; and Franz Joseph's brother Maximilian had ascended the throne of Mexico.[4] Vienna had seen the foundation stone of the new Opera Theatre laid,[5] and the opening of its new boulevard, the Ringstrasse.[6] And in November 1860 an illustrious guest from Paris had arrived, M. Jacques Offenbach, to be fêted like a prince and have speeches of homage, flowers and laurels lavished

[1] 11th November 1860.   [2] Letter to Elisabeth, dated Verona, 26th June.
[3] August 1858.   [4] April 1863.   [5] 1861.   [6] 1865.

upon him. The short, slender *maître*, with his dark-brown sideburns and black-rimmed pince-nez on its long silk ribbon, had
started on a series of successes which included the Viennese production of sixty-five of his operettas.

The Emperor received him in private audience, the Hofoper
(Court Opera) commissioned him to compose a full-length work,
and wherever he appeared he was greeted with an ovation. One
evening, so the story goes, he entered the dining-room of the
restaurant Zum goldenen Lamm (At the Golden Lamb), surrounded by the usual circle of admirers. An elegant gentleman of
about forty with dark curly hair and sideburns not unlike his own
was sitting in a corner of the room. Offenbach left his circle and
walked over to the stranger. When he reached him he smiled and
held out both hands, exlaiming: "You must be Johann Strauss."

The catalogue of Strauss's works had already by then reached
op. 280. He invited Offenbach to sit down, offered him a glass of
wine. The two men chatted, and Jacques expressed his great admiration for Johann's waltzes. "But believe me," he said, "waltzes
and polkas, however charming, are not enough for a man of your
talent. You must make a big effort and write for the stage—
operettas!"

Strauss was diffident. He doubted whether he had sufficient
talent for the larger form, and then one must consider the difficulties of getting a libretto. "But I assure you," Offenbach persisted,
"that you have all the qualities necessary for success." He begged
Strauss to try, little knowing that he had helped create the Viennese operetta and the emergence of his own most formidable
rival.

Meanwhile, in the autumn of 1863, the 50th Regiment had lost
its bandmaster; Lehar, its band sergeant, applied for and obtained
the position, becoming at the age of twenty-four the youngest to
hold it in the Imperial Austrian Army.

Tantantara! Tzing! Boom!

The sound of an Austrian military band is one of the freshest and
most exciting instrumental effects in the whole realm of music. It

fired and inspired great composers from Haydn to Mahler; guided and led young Austrians to music; and remained, until the end of the First World War and of the Monarchy, a basic source of their musical sense and taste.

Like Austria itself, the band combined heterogeneous national elements: Viennese flutes, Hungarian trumpets, Bohemian clarinets, Alpine horns, Croat and Turk cymbals, tambourines and triangles—all welded together into a splendid kaleidoscopic unity.

'Tantantara! Tzing! Boom!" was W. S. Gilbert's version of the sound,[1] rendered by the German poet Detlev von Liliencron as:

> Kling-kling, bum-bum
> Und Tschingdada . . .
>
> With tramp and stamp
> And stamp and tramp,
>
> It bangs and booms and clangs and clashes,
> Glass of lamp and window smashes![2]

There are forty, fifty or sixty men doing the banging, blaring and warbling. The golden lyre flashes on their collars, the shining instrument in their hands. The band sergeant marches ahead of them, stiff and erect, left hand twirling the gold-edged drum-major's staff, right hand stroking now and then the ends of his moustache. At the side the bandmaster swings smartly along, by him and behind him all his boys, back to the kettle-drum player in the rear whose heavy instrument rests on the cart drawn by the regimental pony.

To provide the army with march music was the most characteristic but not the only function of the military bands. They also had to satisfy the demands of the town where they were stationed: they gave concerts on the promenades, in the squares and parks; played in the churches on Sundays and in theatres; and supplied the appropriate music for parades, receptions, balls and funerals.

The bandmaster had to be an all-rounder indeed in order to fill the bill satisfactorily; teacher, taskmaster, father confessor, civil

[1] In *Iolanthe*.

[2] *Die Musik kommt* (The Band Comes). Set to Music by Oscar Straus in 1901.

servant, banker, as well as versatile conductor, composer, arranger
and programme director, with a mastery of every style. His
social position, between the officer corps and the other ranks, was
delicate; his pay at best that of a major. It was provided out of
a regimental band chest, which was also responsible for obtaining
instruments, scores and so on; this depended on subsidies from the
War Ministry and fees paid to the band.

Most of the two or three hundred regimental bandmasters in
the Imperial Army led a precarious existence in the garrisons
between Bohemia and Bosnia, the Tyrol and Galicia. Only a few,
extremely talented and extremely favoured by destiny, rose above
this.

Of these few only Julius Fučik[1] achieved world fame, by his
Entry of the Gladiators. With its themes racing chromatically up
and down, its massive basses and the *grandioso triomphale* of its
trio, the march remains an ever-fresh masterpiece of its genre.
Nearly all the other Austrian marches had to be content with local
success in the Habsburg Empire, whereas a full dozen marches by
the American march king John Philip Sousa[2] became popular all
over the globe. It is hard to explain the reason for this, even admitting the unique magnetic power of Sousa's compositions.
Perhaps it was his good luck that his rhythms symbolized a youthful world approaching victoriously, as against the calm, slightly
melancholy, sauntering pace of the Austrians. Perhaps it was their
bad luck that the local idiom, the source of all their strength, was
in the last analysis not a universal one.

The Settlement

Three years after Lehár Senior's promotion, in June 1866, the
Austro-Prussian War broke out, and directly afterwards the
Austro-Italian War. The young bandmaster was in the field in the
southern theatre, saw the early Austrian victory at Custozza, and
was wounded in an attack on the village of Oliosi near Lake
Garda. The same night, by candle-light in a farm, he composed his
masterpiece: the *Oliosi March,* a fresh, unpretentious work with

[1] 1872–1916.　　[2] 1854–1932.

obvious Slavonic accents. It became one of the historic marches of
the Austrian Army, and was made the regimental march of the
50th Imperial Royal Infantry Regiment.

The victory of Custozza was soon followed by the fiasco at
Sadowa in Bohemia, which cost the monarchy 32,000 men. All
available army units in Italy had to be rushed to the relief of the
northern front. By the time the 50th Regiment arrived the war
was over; it had lasted thirty-eight days. Lehar and his band were
captured by the Prussians near Znaim in Moravia, taken to a camp
at Brno, and at the end of the war returned to Vienna.

The defeat accelerated the process of political change within the
Habsburg Empire: the "Dualism Settlement" with Hungary
(called *Ausgleich*), signed on 18th February 1867, created the new
Imperial *and* Royal Austro-Hungarian Monarchy.

The general pacification brought with it a cautious exchange of
civil servants and soldiers between the two countries. In the course
of this, in the late autumn of 1868, the 50th Imperial and Royal
Infantry Regiment, with its bandmaster, Franz Lehar, was transferred to the small Slovak town of Komorn in Hungary.

Komorn and the Neubrandts

Komorn (Komáron in Hungarian, Komárno in Slovak) lies at
the confluence of the Danube and the Váh, about forty-eight miles
north-west of Budapest. Its history begins with the Romans, who
built a fortress in the plain near it. In 1240 it was invaded by the
Mongols, in the sixteenth and seventeenth centuries it was besieged
by the Turks, and in the 1848 revolution the rebel general, Klapka,[1]
defended it successfully against Austria. In 1866 the gold reserves
of the Vienna National Bank were in its fort. After the First World
War it was allotted by the Peace of Trianon to Czechoslovakia.

The town is surrounded by cornfields, meadows and vineyards,
and has at its centre an old market-place with a fountain. The
mineral resources of the region—brown coal, clay and limestone—
are freighted in the harbour. The folk music of Hungarians,
Slovaks and gipsies can be heard everywhere you go.

[1] 1820–92.

Pride of place among Komorn's sons goes to the novelist Maurus Jokai,[1] the Hungarian Balzac, romantic and revolutionary, who wrote 350 books; his short novel *Saffi* gave Johann Strauss the material for his *Gypsy Baron*. Jokai's characters are the old Hungarian aristocrats, the corrupt small-town lawyers and golden-hearted ragamuffins, the spritely village beauties and flirtatious noble ladies, the merchants from the south, and the immigrant workers from Württemberg, Prussia and the Rhineland.

The story of the Neubrandts, Lehár's mother's family, sounds like a family saga by Jokai. Coming from Swabia and originally called Neubrandenburger, they soon became assimilated in Komorn, to the point of extreme Hungarian patriotism and hostility to Austria. Ferenc Neubrandt, Lehár's maternal grandfather, a soap-boiler by trade, wore the old Hungarian national costume all his life, talked only Hungarian, and brought up his children as Hungarians.

In 1835 he married Christine Goger, a farmer's daughter from the neighbouring village of Igmánd. Well off, energetic and intelligent, she brought him as dowry a handsome mansion on the corner of Nádorgasse, helped him to build up his business, and bore him five children. When the sixth was on the way the 1848 war broke out. Ferenc Neubrandt went to the front with Klapka's militia. The fine house was severely damaged during the battles for Komorn, and the family had to flee from the burning town into the fields. There, in a gipsy encampment, Christine Neubrandt, Lehár's mother, was born.

Ferenc's wife had taken the family savings with her, sewn into her petticoat. The Austrians threatened to shoot her husband unless she surrendered "every penny". To save him, she obeyed, and for the time being the Neubrandts' prosperity was over. An embittered and disappointed man, Ferenc retired from his business and became a recluse, living only for his delight in little Christine, whom he loved most fondly. He spent much of his time planning and carrying out minor improvements to the house, and while at work one day knocked a rusty nail into the forefinger of his left

[1] 1825–1904.

hand. He developed blood-poisoning, stubbornly refused to have his arm amputated, and died.

"My youth was certainly no bed of roses," Christine Lehár recalled half a century later;[1] "especially the years when I was a little girl." But now, true to the traditions of a Jokai saga, her mother, when all seemed lost, went into action. She had not forgotten her farming experience as a girl, and set up a as corn-chandler. In a few years the house in Nádorgasse was completely rebuilt, and the savings were back in her petticoat.

A Whirlwind Wooing

The 50th Regiment were received coldly and with reserve in Komorn. The inhabitants would not let officers or men enter their houses, and it was only after months of effort by conciliatory elements that a gradual rapprochement took place.

Even then, when Regimental Bandmaster Lehár (he accented the A in his name as a token of Hungarian assimilation) fell in love with Christine Neubrandt, and after a whirlwind wooing of four weeks married her, both sides were disapproving. A Hungarian girl and a soldier in the hated Habsburg Army who spoke scarely any Hungarian; an Austrian and the daughter of an anti-Habsburg revolutionary who could barely express herself in German: the prospects did not look bright. "It took the wife's unbounded affection for her husband," Anton Lehár wrote in his Memoirs, "to make the marriage a happy one".

"Speaking of it to us children, she was pleased to attribute it to the fact that our father was very like her own, in externals such as looks and gestures, and also in character and kindness. She often talked adoringly of Ferenc Neubrandt, the father who had been also her playmate and friend; and she carried over her feelings from father to husband. Although only nine years younger, she always looked at our father with a quiet respect, which had something in it of childish shyness. I never heard her call him anything but 'Father'."[2]

[1] Letter to Anton Lehár, dated Budapest 1898.
[2] Anton Freiherr von Lehár: Our Mother, Vienna, 1930.

The Lehárs had been married just over a year when a son was born, Franz Christian. It was Saturday, 30th April 1870, at 10 p.m. "The little chap really could have waited the extra two hours," the mother observed, when the midwife brought her the child. "The first of May would always have been such a fine birthday for him."

II
AWAKENING CONSCIOUSNESS

Migrations through the Empire

Franz Lehár was christened on Wednesday, 4th May, by the Chaplain of the 50th Infantry Regiment. The witnesses were the Captain of Militia in the near-by small town of Raab, "representing Frau Christine Neubrandt, née Goger", and the wife of the Lieutenant-Colonel commanding the regiment.

The baby's mixed antecedents, Czech, Moravian, Hungarian, Slovak, Italian and Viennese, made him, from the moment he first saw the light of day, the ideal *Homo Austriacus*. And any Austrian elements he did not inherit at birth he soon picked up as a *Tornisterkind*—a knapsack-child.

Regiments were sometimes transferred to meet political requirements, sometimes as reward or punishment.

With the father's different stations the mother's cooking recipes altered, and so did the schools, schoolfriends, manners and linguistic habits of their young. The changes of garrison meant moving from dozens of officers' billets, taking all their furniture with them: pianos, sewing-machines, prams, carpets, family pictures, cooking utensils, uniforms, clothes, shoes—and with the children, as it were, in the knapsack.

The Lehár household had to go through this process twenty-two times in the coming years. From Komorn they went to Pressburg and Ödenburg, then to Karlsburg and Klausenburg in Transylvania, to Vienna, Prague, Budapest, Kronstadt, Sarajevo: all over the Empire. Lehár's cosmopolitanism, his flair for languages, and the bravura with which he incorporated folk-song elements into his music, can easily be recognized as an effect of these frequent migrations. If to the Viennese he always seemed a Viennese, to the Hungarians a Hungarian, to the Czechs a Czech, to the Poles and Slovaks a Pole and a Slovak, this was not only because he had a virtuoso ability for so appearing; in his youth he had learnt also to *be* "all things to all men".

After Franz the Lehárs had six more children: Anton, Marie, three who died as babies, and the late-born Emmy. The eldest remained mother's favourite, she his idol. A photograph from 1875 shows him as a chubby mother's darling snuggling close to Mama. The right hand rests on her knee, the left in Napoleonic style on his little tummy. Forehead, mouth and ears reveal a strong personality in miniature; the light-brown hair is curled upwards, the wide eyes look out loftily on the world. Mother and son both wear the same small white collar, he with a saucy bow, she with a golden brooch. Her position is erect, perhaps rather too stiff for a woman of twenty-seven; a fashionable watch-chain dangles from her black-frilled silk dress, which is closed right to the neck; the hair has been freshly curled—but one lock has strayed over the forehead on the left, as if to make her look less matronly.

A picture of the Regimental Bandmaster from the same time aims to stress the martial rather than the artistic element in his appearance. The chin, like the nose, is thrusting, the gaze stern and resolute, the moustache vigorous. Yet the melancholy eyes and long hair are expressive of the artist, the well formed-ears and powerful back of the head suggest the musician.

Lehár Senior took for granted his son's musical talent: "He would only have talked of me as an infant prodigy if I had been unmusical! When I was no more than five, he was very ready to find fault with me. He thereby fulfilled the most important precondition for artistic achievement: harsh and stern criticism, which is most essential just where the possession of talent might lead to less thoroughness."

Lehár's musical aptitude was lovingly cherished and cultivated by his mother. While his father brought the first violin home, and started violin and piano lessons, before the little boy could read or write, she sang him the old songs of the Komorn region. While his father insisted on systematic training, she listened entranced to his fantasies on the piano: when he picked up melodic sequences, discovered major and minor triads or experimented with sound combinations in bass and treble.

Besides his elementary aptitude, the five- and six-year-old already revealed a vigorous will and a precocious astrologically conditioned Taurian obstinacy. He could not yet pronounce the difficult consonant R in his Christian name, and had to convert the "Franzi" to "Lanzi"; but his cry of command "Lanzi wants!" often rang through the house. Lanzi wants some white trousers, Lanzi wants a drink of lemonade, Lanzi wants a ride on the tram—and Lanzi wants to go to the big concert in Klausenburg Cathedral!

For weeks his father had been talking of how the world-famous Franz Liszt would be coming to conduct his Oratorio *Christus*; how all the musicians in the town counted it an honour to take part, and he himself would be there as second violin-player to pay homage to the Master.

The Liszt renaissance in Hungary during the seventies was a direct result of the Dualist Settlement. The State approved funds for an Academy of Music in Budapest, and appointed Liszt as its head.[1] In the search for gifted teachers and pupils, the newly fledged Royal Councillor travelled round the Hungarian cities. Wherever he went he was offered the traditional salt and bread, with the red Szezgard wine which was known to be his favourite. He gave recitals, conducted, made speeches—and enjoyed being fêted. Klausenburg was one of the towns he visited.

Lanzi sat on Mama's lap behind one of the high cathedral pillars, drinking in the *Christus Vincit* and *Pater Noster*. He had never imagined there could be anything like this. Till then music for him had meant Papa: Papa's band, Papa's programme—the *Poet and Peasant* Overture, a Donizetti medley or a Strauss waltz. Here was something extraordinary: a strikingly handsome white-haired man, sending these magical sounds through the great church. A prince, before whom the regimental commander stood to attention, the Mayor bowed deeply, and whose hand Papa kissed

[1] Hubay, Dohnányi, Bartók, Kodály and Kálmán were later among its show pupils.

respectfully. So there were musicians above Papa, artists everyone must treat with deference . . .

"In my childish soul the consciousness awakened for the first time, that music, 'basic form of all the arts', is more than mere entertainment, or earning a living; that God has given it for the lifting up of hearts, to exhilarate and to comfort; that the musician's profession serves Man's affirmation of life and joy in life."

The First Motifs

Christine Lehár looked further ahead than her husband. She was well aware that in his profession there was no permanent family home; yet the children must grow out of provincialism, must emerge from "the knapsack", go to good schools: she insisted on a move to a capital city.

Lehár Senior got himself transferred to the 102nd Infantry Regiment at Budapest, and Lanzi became a pupil at the grammar school there, run by Piarist monks. The good Fathers tried patiently to instil in him the elements of geometry, algebra and physics, but without much success; he got very good marks for singing, but in other subjects was "adequate" at best. As he said himself: "School work just didn't interest me." But he was all the more attracted by the composition class at the Academy of Music, which he was allowed to attend externally because of his father's position. Many years afterwards he still remembered with gratitude a Professor Istvan Tomka who taught there.

Grandmother Neubrandt was living in Budapest, well off and still very active at seventy. "She was a physically imposing woman," wrote Lehár,[1] "and everything about her bespoke toughness and endurance. Even when Mama was fifty, she would not have dared address her mother by the familiar 'Du'. If you wanted to ask Grandmother anything, you did it very cautiously and nervously Any instructions she gave were followed blindly, no one would dream of opposing her."

Towards Lanzi the old lady's heart melted. Grandson and grandmother grew into friends, playmates, allies: her house in

[1] In a newspaper article, *My Youth*.

Rakoczy Square became his second home. "It was filled with valuable old Viennese furniture. In the courtyard there was a small garden, leading to a well which was painted green. There were pretty beds of rosemary and thyme, carnations and mignonettes. The gravel paths were lined with empty mineral bottles, their necks dug into the ground. High rose-trees, which my father had bought and planted himself, were supported by stakes with red, white and green glass bowls on them. But by the garden wall stood the arbour, with lime trees and wild vines all round it. There I found my first love: the first motifs for the operas and operettas of my life."

He was eleven, a tall boy with clever eyes, smart in appearance. When Mama dressed him up in velvet trousers with buckled shoes, he wore a wide, loose cravat, a showy watch-chain, and a rather incongruous bowler hat. Such elegance could only mean there was a young lady in the offing.

She was a Budapest girl from the flat in the courtyard of the Neubrandt house. He sat by her side in the arbour and pressed her hand. "We looked into each other's eyes. I was boundlessly happy. Till Grandmother came. She tore us apart. I wept bitterly. I went on crying, and wouldn't stop, until my mother saved the day. She gave me a four-kreutzer piece to buy the little girl a bag of sweets. But the fickle thing shared my present with a rival: both got tummy aches from it, and I wrote my first song. . . ."[1]

[1] The quotation is in Lehár's own handwriting. So are all the other musical quotations in the book—except for the printed ones. The two lines above the music say: "The song has been lost. The beginning I can still remember. It goes like this."

So Lehár's op. 1 refers not to Mama (as tradition has it) but to
the anonymous young lady from the garden flat, and was written
when he was eleven, not six. In later life he remembered exactly
where he had picked up the verse: "Someone advised my mother
to read a lot out loud and to declaim, if she wanted to perfect her
German. Thus I often heard poems from her. '*Ich fühl', das ich tief
innen kranke . . .*' (I feel I am ailing deep inside me)—I liked that
particularly and it stuck in my mind. I'm not sure I knew what it
meant, except that I realized 'ailing' was something sad." The tune
sounds like the echo of a Komorn gipsy song, entwined with the
major-minor piquancies which soon became so characteristic of
his harmonic style.

Papa looked through the composition, and decided that musically the boy was getting right out of control. Mama was anyhow
displeased at the way he had lately been neglecting his German; so
Lanzi was packed off to Sternberg in Moravia, to his Uncle Anton,
the town's Musical Director.

There he first had to go back to the town's primary school;
what a humiliation for a boy from the Budapest Grammar School!
After school hours his uncle took him in hand: two hours' piano
practice a day and two hours violin practice; then harmony exercises, homework, copying. The day was hard, and—this was the
hardest thing—Lanzi was alone: without Mama's love and care.
He set his teeth, mastered his curriculum, and became independent,
ambitious, stern towards himself.

In July and August uncle Anton gave him his first practical
orchestral experience. All summer Sternberg's Musical Director
functioned as conductor of the twelve-man spa orchestra of Bad
Ullersdorf. The sufferers from rheumatism and arthritis who
during the 1882 season sought healing in the sulphur springs of the
Moravian market town, took little notice of the boy violinist; but
he enjoyed all the more the morning, afternoon and evening
concerts. For the future master melodist and orchestrator, it was a
valuable period: the simple programme pieces of the band
sharpened his ear for the well-formed *cantilena*; from the limitations of the tiny orchestral combination grew his amazing skill in
instrumental economy; at the second-violin desk in Ullersdorf he

got to know the delights of being a musician. There was no longer any doubt as to what he wanted to become and should become: neither for him nor his parents. His father had three Academies of Music in mind. Vienna was the obvious choice; but you had to be fourteen before you were allowed to sit the exam for that. Budapest? Lanzi would have liked to become Tomka's pupil, but the scholarships and free places were all taken, and without them any prolonged course was out of the question. There remained Prague; and Prague became one of the great pieces of good fortune in Lehár's life. The Böhmische Landes-Konservatorium (Academy of Music for the Country of Bohemia) opened its gates to the twelve-year-old boy—who passed his entrance exam brilliantly—and gave him a six-year course free. (Principal subject violin, subsidiaries piano and composition.)

To help with board and lodging he also received ten kreutzer a day pocket money.[1]

Praga Regia

Prague—that meant the world-famous hundred towers, the bronze cupolas gleaming in the sun, and the dark corners of the old town; the mighty silhouette of Hradčany Castle, the Alchemists' Lane, and the Town Hall Clock with the Twelve Apostles. A synthesis of reality and fantasy, a "golden net of poems, hundreds of sagas and stories", sang Liliencron, a medley of Gothic, Renaissance, Baroque and Romantic, the symbiosis of German, Czech, Austrian and Jewish cultures. Eternal Prague, *zlatá Praha*, Praga Regia!

When the young Lehár arrived, Prague seemed like the Sleeping Beauty newly awakened, coming to full consciousness of her beauty and importance; but far away on the horizon the day was dawning (as in Kafka's terrifying prophecy),[2] "when the city will be smashed to pieces by a giant's fist".

In 1881 the new Czech Národní Divadlo (National Theatre) opened with Smetana's *Libuše*—only to burn down not long afterwards. Within four weeks the nation had collected the money for a new building, which was soon erected as an imposing home for

[1] Present value about 1s. 6d.   [2] In his short story *The City Arms*.

music and poetry. Six months later Smetana died[1] in the Bohemian Provincial Asylum. On the day of his funeral the theatre rang with laughter at his masterpiece, *The Bartered Bride* (*Prodaná Nevěsta*).

At the Neue Deutsche Landestheater (New German Theatre) the twenty-five-year-old Gustav Mahler was soon to make his appearance as conductor; and with him at the rostrum Lehár gained his first crucial impressions of Mozart, Beethoven and Wagner. To Mahler's musical purity and integrity Lehár owed the high artistic standards which remained with him all his life.

The young Academy student walked down Wenceslas Square to the Příkopy. He looked longingly at the butchers' and bakers' full windows, and at the theatre posters. On the Charles Bridge he saw the statue of valiant Johannes Nepomuk, Patron Saint of Bohemia, and of the Saviour on the Cross with the words in Hebrew "Thrice Holy" in gold letters round his head. On Sundays he would go upriver on the steamer to the Vltava Rapids, or walk to the Villa Bertramka at Smichov, where in a single inspired night Mozart wrote the Overture to *Don Giovanni*.

Besides the artistic standards that he learned from Mahler, Prague gave him three other things for life: a perfect knowledge of the Czech language, the Prague-German accent with the sharp double-S sounds and slightly singing intonation, and the melancholy of Slavonic melody, as the poet Rilke heard it:

Mich rührt so sehr
Böhmischen Volkes Weise,
Schleicht sie ins Herz sich leise
Macht sie es schwer.[2]

"Know what, my lad? You should write music!"

Ten kreutzer a day didn't take you far in Prague. It meant living on watery soup, dark rye bread and dripping, practising the violin

[1] On 12th May 1884.
[2] Bohemian song
Stirs my deepest feeling
Into the heart soft stealing,
Makes the heart long.

in dirty, ice-cold rooms, washing your own shirts and underwear. Mother helped out, sending now and then some salami, a cake, or a few coins she had saved from the little bags for each day into which she divided the housekeeping money on the first of every month. "It was out of the question (declares Brother Anton) to empty one of the bags before its day. Mother was a splendid saver. But she very readily and willingly used what she had saved if it was for her children." When she came unsuspectingly from Budapest to visit Lanzi, she found him thin as a skeleton. From pride and defiance he had never written home a line about his pauper's existence. She tidied him up, looked for a better board and cleaner lodging, and persuaded Papa to give him one and a half florins a month extra.

At Christmas he brought home to his parents a new composition: the piano piece *Christmas Spirit*. "After we children had sung *Stille Nacht* hand in hand in front of the lighted tree, I presented my opus to Father with thumping heart, sat down at the piano and played it. Mother, brother and sister clapped loudly. But Father took me by the hand and led me to the Christmas tree. He carefully unwrapped three thick green music books from tissue paper and gave them to me. They were the vocal scores of *Carmen*, *Faust* and *Lohengrin*, for which I had been yearning for ages. They aroused in me the first desire to compose for the theatre myself one day, to write a vocal score myself—and perhaps even see it printed: youthful dreams which began to be realized through the rare mixture of seriousness and encouragement that greeted my first musical efforts in my parents' house. 'Emulate the masters,' said Father, 'and you'll make your way!'

"I put the scores by me in bed on the pillow: the sounds from the three green books wove themselves into my blissful, boyish dreams; and no child in the whole world was happier that evening than I."

No child was happier the following year, when someone in the War Ministry at Vienna had the splendid idea of transferring the 102nd Infantry Regiment from Budapest to Prague. This meant that in the crucial boyhood years Lehár was spared the dirt, drudgery and humiliations Brahms, Bruckner and Puccini had to endure; it meant reuniting with the family, a home, an ordered life and Mama's cooking.

For his brother Toni it meant friction and protracted arguments. Father had decided that his younger son, too, should go to the Academy of Music and become a musician; but the younger son rebelled. Perhaps after all a drop of daring Le Harde blood had somehow come into his veins: he insisted on becoming a soldier, and in the end his parents were left with no alternative but to find him a place in Vienna's Military College. Anton Lehár had taken the first step on the career which was to make him officer, general, Knight of the Order of Maria Theresa, and Baron.

Franz devoted himself to studying, practising and enjoying music. The head of the Academy was the violinist Anton Benne-witz, a friend of Dvořák's, one of Smetana's chamber-music partners, and teacher of a whole generation of Czech violinists. Lehár worked a full six years with him, and six years also in the composition class with Josef Foerster.

Prague's musical firebrand in those days was the composer Zdeněk Fibich,[1] Modern, internationally minded and in his musical idiom far in advance of his time, he had a magical attraction for the young musicians in the city. Lehár took private lessons with him. Bennewitz found out, expressed his disapproval and brought the strayed sheep back into Foerster's flock.

To cheer the boy up, the Academy head introduced him to Antonin Dvořák, then in his mid-forties and at the peak of his European fame. He was much loved in Bohemia, and everyone smiled over his idiosyncrasies: that he lived with his wife and six children in a two-room flat, wrote his orchestral scores on the kitchen table, had a strange passion for railways and stations, would go off every day to the Franz Joseph Station, and have lively chats with the booking-clerks, guards and porters.

The meeting with Dvořák meant for Lehár contact with music in its full earthiness—in contrast to the academic music he was taught at the Konservatorium. His original shyness gave way to an unaffected openness, the Master's dispassionate attitude to one of eager concern. The boy's Academy compositions were analysed

[1] 1850–1900.

at the piano: two sonatas, a *Scherzo*, a *Capricioso*, and the *Sonata à l'Antique*, which was published ten years later and brought the composer his first fee, thirty florins.

(It was not, in fact, quite the first: a few months earlier a well-known Prague tailor had come to his father asking Bandmaster Lehár if he would be so kind as to write a gavotte which the tailor could dedicate to his lady love, and would he accept a smart bespoke suit in payment? Lehár Senior passed on the commission to Lehár Junior; the composition was delivered; but the suit turned out to be old, turned and altered. Papa was furious, but Franz laughed. "You know, to be honest, the gavotte wasn't quite new either—an altered March and a turned Polka!")

Dvořák expressed satisfaction, often delight, at Lehár's compositions. "*Viš co, hochů* (he advised), *povĕz housle na hřebik, a piš hudbu!*" ("Know what, my lad? You should hang up your fiddle and write music.")

Lehár Senior warned his son against "high-flown ideas". "Just try to master your instrument properly first," he admonished. "A good violinist is never lost, he can always make a living, but a composer . . ." It seemed as if he hesitated to go on: ". . . after all, what did I ever earn in the end with all my composing, the marches and everything? A mere pittance."

So the boy sacrificed "in vain" (as he later admitted) hundreds of hours of nightly practice: "It cost me ten years of artistic creation."

Brahms came to Prague to visit his friend Dvořák, and Lehár played before the great man. He was given a visiting-card, which he was to present in Vienna, together with his youthful works, to the music theorist Eusebius Mandyczewski, Archivist of the *Gesellschaft der Musikfreunde* (Society of Friends of Music). It said:

The enclosures provide further recommendation.

J.B.

Mandyczewski never received the card. The autograph was far too precious for Lehár to pass on. Fifty years afterwards he still showed it proudly to friends visiting his private museum on the top floor of his house in Theobaldgasse, Vienna.

In the middle of 1888 the Prague period came to an end for the Lehárs. Papa had never really felt quite at home with the 102nd. Now he heard that his first regiment, the 50th, was being transferred to Vienna and wanted to have him back. So he put out feelers in the direction of his old comrades. Franz was eighteen, and at the end of his Academy studies. Mother knew she could no longer be much use to him—and she guessed how much the young cadet Anton needed her in Vienna. So the knapsack was packed once again. But before they left, one more big event took place.

On Thursday, 12th July—at ten o'clock in the morning!—in Prague's Rudolfinum Concert Hall, the Academy's instrumentalist students "took their finals" in the form of a public concert. It lasted over four hours, and gave the students a chance to show their abilities.

Bandmaster Lehár in full uniform, the sword-knot on his sword, sat in the front row with his wife. During the concert Franz, accompanied by the orchestra, played Max Bruch's *Violin Concerto in G minor*. He earned the applause customary on such occasions, and received a leaving certificate which spoke highly of his industry and his talent, and emphasized how well he had "matched up to all the demands made on him".

In the same week he signed his first contract—as first violin (salary 150 marks a month) at the Vereinigte Theater (Allied Theatres) of Barmen-Elberfeld in Germany's Rhineland.

III
SCHOOL OF PRACTICE

Barmen-Elberfeld

The year 1888 was for Germany the Year of the Three Emperors. William I died, and his son Frederick III, already dangerously ill, began "in courageous quiet devotion" a reign which lasted only ninety-nine days. On 15th June, after Frederick's death, William II became *Dei Gratia Imperator Germaniae* at the age of twenty-nine. Wearing the flowing purple cloak of the Order of the Black Eagle, surrounded by soldiers in uniforms from the time of Frederick the Great, by chamberlains, ministers and pages, he sat enthroned in the White Hall of Berlin Castle and read the proclamation: ". . . I am resolved to keep the peace with everyone—as far as it lies in my power . . ."

The age of Kaiser Wilhelm had begun.

At the end of August, Lehár arrived in Barmen-Elberfeld, entering Germany for the first time. The Allied Municipal Theatres were under the direction of the able and honest Emil Gettke at whose theatres the eighteen-year-old first violin was an important person, especially as he was soon made leader of the orchestra. He had snapped up the position, which was not particularly attractive, for two reasons: so as no longer to be a financial burden on his parents, and to become his own master. Now he had to rush continually to rehearsals of operas and concerts, doing the orchestral hack-work, glossing over the mistakes of mediocre conductors, calming any fits of temperament among the players—and all for a salary only just enough to live on.

"Write music, my lad!" Dvořák had bidden him; and Father's

"A good violinist is never lost!" was still ringing in Lehár's ears. But to write music one needs time and leisure, while to practise the violin every day after playing for hours in the orchestra was really too much for him. That the drudgery proved a blessing in disguise was due to Lehár's nature and talent. "In this school of practice he was obliged to learn the repertoire, the tricks of the theatrical trade, the concert literature, above all how to listen to and write for an orchestra . . . The sound of an orchestra trained his musical colour sense; revelling in violin solos, he became a living study for his own *Paganini*—for craft and again craft is the treasure-house of creative spirits."[1]

To a certain extent, no doubt! In some circumstances it may become a morgue. Father had regained his old position with the 50th, and asked whether Franz would like to become his first violin; the bed, so to speak, was made up for him. Mama wrote of sister Marie's awakening beauty, of brother Toni's progress, of the untold musical opportunities of the capital, and of the house in Schützengasse which had been acquired with Father's savings and Grandmother Neubrandt's help.

Lehár felt he was beginning to stagnate after a year in the Barmen-Elberfeld routine, and also that he must extricate himself from a love affair in which a blonde thirty-six-year-old singer at the Municipal Theatres had entangled him.

So he plucked up his courage, went to Gettke, told him about Father's offer, and asked for his release. The Director looked at him benevolently: should a suitable substitute be found, he would be ready in the circumstances . . .

Lehár kept a look-out in Vienna, Budapest, Prague—in vain. "So I decided on a breach of contract, the only time I ever did."

In November 1889 he left Barmen-Elberfeld "under cover of darkness", telegraphing to his father from Cologne station: HAVE BOLTED STOP SEND ENLISTMENT FORM TO BARMEN AT ONCE.

This form was an order signed by the appropriate authorities to present oneself at a certain time and place for medical examination with a view to enlistment in the army. It compelled Gettke to

[1] Ernst Decsey: *Franz Lehár*, Munich, 1930.

acquiesce, protected Lehár from a charge of breach of contract, a fine—and ended the affair. After taking his military oath and having a brief "drill" period, he found himself first violin in his father's band with the rank of corporal.

A short epilogue to the Barmen-Elberfeld days concerns the singer with whom Lehár had been on intimate terms, and who (according to Decsey) had "gradually taken over a guardian's role, unobtrusively mothering her beloved, that is, and protecting him from dissipation". A fortnight after the young man's arrival in his parents' house, she turned up there, not to assert her rights but to "hand the boy over". Mama was grateful but embarrassed, Papa—still the dashing officer for all his fifty years—deeply moved.

Her departure may have gone off according to the rules of future Lehár finale scenes. Perhaps she even spoke words like those of Maria Elisa to Paganini at the end of the operetta, though they were probably in a less high-flown romantic vein: "You have fled; I could bring you back by love or force. But . . . I release you . . . go! Go out into the world, bless it with your art . . . Farewell!"

A New Trio

The soldier sitting on Lehár's left in the band was a cheerful, plump youth of barely seventeen: Leo Fall. His father, Bandmaster of the 9th Infantry Regiment stationed at Olmütz, had sent him to Lehár Senior, asking his colleague to look after the boy in Vienna, supervise his studies at the Academy of Music, and let him—as a new recruit—earn a few kreutzer pocket money in his band. Lehár Senior little knew that he had two future Croesuses of melody under his baton.

The boys had both been "knapsack-children"; they shared, too, a boundless delight in making music, and a terrific drive to get on. It was natural enough for Fall to take Lehár to the home of Edmund Eysler, his fellow student in Professor Robert Fuchs's counterpoint class. The new generation of the Viennese operetta had met—except for Oscar Straus, who at that time was just leaving his home in Vienna in order to study with Max Bruch in Berlin.

In 1890 the classic Viennese operetta was fading out. Although its three great masters were still alive, it was some years since their last successes: Suppé's *Boccaccio* in 1879, Millöcker's *Gasparone* and Strauss's *Gypsy Baron* in 1884. Their flagging creative power led to the rise of three gifted novices, Ziehrer, Zeller and Heuberger, but also to the infiltration of the genre by amateurs. Besides bankers, there were racehorse-owners, gentlemen of private means, businessmen, lawyers, journalists, and music-teachers, all hoping to draw the winner in the great lottery. Artistically, morally and commercially the operetta had reached its nadir.

While ephemeral pieces occupied the stage at the Carl Theater and the Theater an der Wien, young Lehár and Fall were playing their fiddles at garden concerts (and now and then by kind permission of Bandmaster Lehár, conducting the opening or concluding march!). Gathered round Eysler's upright piano, they studied the scores of exciting new works like Richard Strauss's *Don Juan*, or played over to each other their own compositions: Eysler offered fragments from his grand opera *Zrinyi*, Fall his settings of verses by modern poets, and Lehár his first waltz, *Liebeszauber* (Magic of Love).

At the end of the year the trio broke up; they did not come together again till fifteen years later. Fall Senior left the service to lead a small orchestra of his own in Berlin, for which he needed Leo. Eysler's parents went broke, so the son took a beggarly post as a piano-teacher. Lehár had differences of opinion with his father and military superior. Eighteen years afterwards he said in a newspaper article: "Possibly Father saw me as a danger to himself. Anyhow he said to me one day: 'See if you can get on a bit, look for a position of your own.' I went and looked for one, and although there were forty or fifty candidates I obtained the post of Bandmaster with the 25th Infantry Regiment in Losoncz (in the northern part of Hungary), at 60 florins a month, plus 17 florins for billets! At twenty I was the youngest Bandmaster ever appointed in the whole army, beating Father's record by four years."

Losoncz

The new regimental bandmaster—fluffy little moustache, pomaded hair parted down the middle, narrow-waisted tunic from the best military tailor in Vienna—remained for the next three and a half years the sensation of Losoncz. "You look like a Prince!" cried Mama admiringly, when he came to say good-bye wearing his new outfit for the first time. "Like the Archduke Otto!"[1] echoed the beauties of Losoncz.

Their leader was the young Baroness Vilma Fries, daughter of the Regimental Commander of the 25th—Lehár's "rosy adventure on the threshold of his new sphere".[2] He had no inkling of the methods and hazards of giving singing lessons, but was commanded by her father to train the voice of the seventeen-year-old young lady.

"My embarrassment was considerable," he recalled, "but orders are orders, and there was nothing to be done about it. Admittedly she didn't learn singing with me, but by the second lesson she was already singing a song, *Vorüber* (Gone), which I had composed for her. She went on singing it until she became hoarse. With some alarm I recognized that by my singing method I might completely spoil what little vocal powers she had. So we agreed that she should pretend to be ill until I was forgotten as singing teacher."

The image of young Vilma Fries soon faded, against that of another passionately loved lady of the regiment, the Countess Rosa Cabrian, who wrote the words of the earliest of all Lehár waltz songs, *Möcht's jubelnd in die Welt verkünden!*—I'd joyful to the world proclaim it! (After forty years the composer would still show slight embarrassment when the name of one of the ladies was mentioned, or the conversation turned to the subject of his Losoncz production.)

Vienna was a metropolis, Prague a great city, Komorn a small

---

[1] The Archduke Otto was the nephew of the Emperor, brother of the heir apparent, Archduke Franz Ferdinand, and father of the future Emperor Karl. He was the black sheep of the Habsburg family, the idol of all Vienna's aristocratic ladies and ballet girls.

[2] Maria von Peteani: *Franz Lehár*, Vienna, 1950.

town—Losoncz a village. It had a pretty old church, an officers club, and 9,000 inhabitants, soldiers, local officials, shopkeepers—landowners; and in the surrounding country several manor houses But despite all this it remained a village in appearance, with its whitewashed single-storey houses, muddy streets, herds of swine and dung-heaps: a drowsy village which only came awake on Saturday evenings for the band concert in the main street. The programme of Lehár's first concert, on 11th October 1890, contained waltzes, marches, Flotow's *Stradella* overture, a fantasy on works by Verdi, selections from *Lohengrin* and *The Mikado*—and a *Persian March*[1] by Franz Lehár Junior. An unadventurous programme, it gave little indication of the fiery spirit which now took over the organization of musical life in Losoncz.

The Church Music Guild was induced to perform Haydn's *Creation* under his direction, the Chamber Music Society to rehearse new works by Brahms and Dvořák, in which he himself played. In the mornings he drilled his band at the barracks; in the afternoons he trained civilians to play in symphony concerts. He would plan the programmes a whole year ahead, and make new easy arrangements of pieces too difficult for them to perform. Where he detected musical inclinations, he encouraged them; where he could not see any, he created them. With all the enthusiasm of his youth he fired the spirits of the inhabitants, until the sleepy town found itself at the centre of an explosion of music.

Everyone exploited the young man's talents, while he grew weary—and gradually got into debt. Mama admonished her "thoughtless darling" to thrift. "Well, that was easy in Vienna," he wrote back, "I could get by there on my money, but that was just thanks to you . . ." To improve on his meagre pay, he arranged medleys of operatic music and folk-songs, adapted classical scores, and tailored favourite musical pieces for military bands. His drawing-room compositions from this period bore conventionally romantic titles, such as *Heart's Greetings, Coral Lips* and *Catkins*; the violin works which he wrote to perform himself in the officers' mess were given names like *Hungarian Song-Sequence*

---

[1] Later expanded to a *Scène Fantastique*, renamed *A Tale from the Arabian Nights*, and published as op. 3.

or *Hungarian Fantasy*. His Regimental Commander accepted with a handshake the dedication of the *Baron Fries March*, Fries's successor that of the *Colonel Pacor March*. Music publishers in Vienna and Trieste began to show an interest in Lehár's work. (The *Fries March* appeared later under the title *On the High Seas*.) They paid five florins for orchestral arrangements, but only two florins for his own compositions.

Cavalleria and all that

At the beginning of May 1891 a mammoth concert took place in Vienna's Sängerhalle (Choral Hall) in honour of Johann Strauss. Composers, singers, conductors and instrumentalists came from all over Austria to pay him homage. At the end of the programme, to the general delight, he conducted his just-finished waltz, *Gross-Wien* (Great Vienna), op. 440. Then the deputations proceeded on to the platform: speeches and presentations were made, and the evening reached its climax when two spick-and-span regimental bandmasters marched up, came smartly to attention, saluted, and presented a huge laurel wreath to the man of the day. One of them was Karl Komzak of the 84th, the other Franz Lehár Junior of the 25th. Strauss thanked them, much moved, and shook hands with both. Though none of the 3,000 audience could have guessed, it was a historic moment: the Waltz King and his Crown Prince were facing each other for the only time in their lives.

"I can still see him before me," Lehár recalled half a century later, "with tinted pitch-black hair and moustache. He was obviously tired and frail. But the moment he went up on to the high rostrum, he suddenly changed. After the first bars of his waltz he was already beginning to move gracefully with the rhythm. One had the impression of dance motions. Tremendous applause filled the vast hall, the orchestra was drowned by the cheers. This is my vision of Johann Strauss before he died—a true Waltz King, honoured and appreciated by his Viennese subjects."

A year later Lehár was again in Vienna. He wanted to say goodbye to his parents, who were moving with the regiment to Sarajevo in Bosnia, and he wanted to see the Italian opera companies performing at the International Exhibition for Music and the Theatre.

Never did he forget the overwhelming impressions he received then. *Cavalleria* and *Pagliacci* thrilled him, although he had been familiar with their music for months. In *Mala Vita* he discovered the exuberant melodist Umberto Giordano, and Ciléa's romantic brigand opera *La Tilda* continued to have a powerful effect on him long after he was back in Losoncz.

He plunged headlong into writing music for a play, *Der Kürassier* (The Cuirassier) by Gustav Ruthner, a local railway clerk —only to recognize after a few weeks the hopelessness of the venture. So he suggested to an officer friend, Lieutenant Rudolf Mlčoch, who shared his enthusiasm for Ciléa's opera, to write "something similar". Mlčoch had a reputation in the regiment as an ardent and talented *littérateur*. He had just read in the papers of an attack on a French honeymoon couple by Sicilian bandits, and blended ideas from this actual event with themes from *La Tilda*, from an old penny-dreadful *Rinaldo Rinaldini*, and from Körner's play *Hedwig the Robbers' Bride*.

The result of all this, the one-act opera *Rodrigo*, had a novelletish libretto, hashing together several incompatible plots, and was musically a mixture of well-tried ingredients from *Mala Vita*, *Pagliacci* and *Cavalleria* (there was even a *Preludium Religioso*). The central figure was the beautiful Donna Angela; just engaged to the noble Rodrigo, she is abducted by the fiendish Fernando, and agrees to become his sweetheart if she may first say good-bye to her knight. The brigand foolishly gives his consent, and has to watch her, stabbed to death by her beloved, expiring with the words: "A thousand thanks!"

The *Cavalleria* craze had meanwhile reached unprecedented dimensions. People who had never before been in an opera house rushed off to see it a dozen times. Music critics argued about its faults or virtues: some saw its composer, the twenty-eight-year-old Pietro Mascagni, as a liberator from Wagnerian ideas, others deplored the fact that a generation brought up on Wagner could not distinguish between masterpiece and mediocrity. Eduardo Sonzogno, the opera's publisher, rubbed his hands: in 1883 he had had the happy idea of starting an annual competition, the *Concorso Sonzogno*, for an Italian one-act opera. It ran for seven years before, and fourteen years after *Cavalleria*, without producing anything approaching that success. But this did not deter the music-loving Duke Ernst II of Saxe-Coburg from establishing just such a prize for a German one-act opera.

Lehár submitted his *Rodrigo*; but it did not even gain a favourable mention. (Admittedly Puccini's first opera, *Le Villi*, had suffered the same fate: it was returned to him from the *Concorso* without a word of acknowledgement or comment.)

The results at Coburg were pathetic: the first prize went to *The Rose of Pontevedra* by the Styrian composer Joseph Forster; the opera was first produced in Gotha in July 1893, but taken off after a very short time.

For Lehár's future, however, the episode had two positive consequences. The failure of his hastily written and none too legible score taught him in future to prepare his manuscripts with the utmost care. And twelve years later, when his librettists were looking for two names that sounded right for the Merry Widow's and Danilo's home country, he remembered the Rose who had snatched the prize from him, and suggested a change of "a" to "o" which would coin the new country of Pontevedro. His suggestion was accepted, and thus Forster's opera acquired, after all, its modicum of immortality.

An Officers' Club Incident

Lehár's parents felt quite at home by now in Sarajevo, and he heard from Mama that his sister Marie, little Mariska, idolized by all, had become engaged to a Lieutenant Adolf Bessaraba; the wedding would take place as soon as the young couple had saved up the surety prescribed by the War Ministry for officers getting married. Brother Anton would be passing out shortly from his cadet school and starting his military service. Mama was anxious to have him in Sarajevo.

"Where there are four people to feed," she wrote to Anton, "there's plenty for a fifth to eat too. You can stay with us as well, so that you don't have any money worries. We live very modestly here, of course, but very agreeably. You could share all that with us. A nice cup of coffee to start you off. Mid-morning refreshments with Father. A good lunch with me. Then we read in the drawing-room until you both go to the barracks. After that we go for a walk if it's nice weather, and in the evening you play a game of cards with Dolfi[1] and Father until supper. Then the Vienna paper arrives, and you get another cup of tea. What do you say?"

Toni said yes. But Franz, stranded in his "one-horse" town in northern Hungary, had mixed feelings about this idyll: he despised it, and he longed for it. The brief meeting with Johann Strauss had left behind a certain dissatisfaction, the failure with *Rodrigo* a certain unruliness. As time went by the soldier with unblemished record became guilty of negligence and insubordination, the polite and respectful young man grew aggressive, irritable and unpleasantly arrogant. At the end of January 1894 the incident took place which ended with his leaving both Losoncz and the service.

It was during a Saturday-afternoon concert in the officers' club. Lehár had conducted for two hours, and finished with two or three solo pieces on the violin; then he handed the baton to his band sergeant and retired to the table of a younger fellow officer. Five minutes later a waiter stood before him: the Staff Major would like him to return and play on. Affronted, Lehár poured out all his spleen: "Tell the Major that if he wants to say anything to me he should come himself." To send such a message by a waiter, informing a superior officer of one's refusal to carry out an order—it was the ultimate sin against all military tradition.

The Court of Honour which met next day could not help finding against the Regimental Bandmaster, despite the sympathy they felt for him and despite the absurdity of the incident. He was instructed to apologize to the senior officer, but refused to do so. Instead, he offered his resignation to the Regimental Command. The Colonel tried to mediate, the Staff Major was ready to wink an eye; Lehár, however, had made his decision.

On Tuesday, 27th February, he conducted his farewell concert; on Wednesday afternoon half the Losoncz garrison and civilian

[1] Bessaraba.

population gathered at the station—with the regimental band at their head—and Lehár boarded the train, his destination Sarajevo.

Pola

He did not stay long. In the past three years his name had become known in interested circles, and offers of positions as conductor or orchestra leader came in from both German and Austrian provincial theatres. An attempt to find a place in Budapest proved unsuccessful, but while he was staying there he made his first acquaintance with the music of Puccini. The Royal Opera put on *Manon Lescaut*, then a little over a year old, in its first production outside Italy; Lehár was enthralled by its terrific melodic power, elegance and freshness. Here, he felt, a new style of lyric drama had been found, superseding the robust realism of *Cavalleria*, a style which might be a signpost for himself.

Back in Sarajevo his father came home one day and told him about Pola. The only Naval Band in the Imperial and Royal Navy was stationed at this port: it was looking for a new Bandmaster. Lehár Junior went there, was tried out conducting the 110-man orchestra, and engaged on the spot. It was an artistic, military and financial advancement such as he could never have thought possible after the way he had left Losoncz.

A month later the young German Emperor paid a visit to the naval fortress. He was at his most charming, distributed orders and compliments, visited the officers' club, and listened in high good humour to the Band's programme. The concert lasted for almost four hours, and the Bandmaster had to send off three times for new music. The same evening the Admiral in command of the base handed him a card saying:

To Bandmaster Lehár

6/4/94

Philipp Count Eulenburg

Royal Prussian Ambassador

in Vienna from May onwards

full of admiration

for your excellent performance

The next day Lehár was summoned to the Admiral, who informed him, on behalf of the German Emperor, that His Majesty expressed the highest possible satisfaction with him, and he should be prepared to receive an order.

As soon as the decoration was on his tunic, he had himself photographed, displaying for the first time his smart, dark-blue uniform, also a striking new moustache, pulled out four inches at each end. The family in Sarajevo took due note of the splendid metamorphosis.

At Pola, owing to two extremely powerful influences, Lehár's artistic stature began to develop very strongly. It is surprising, indeed, that Commander Felix Falzari and the composer Antonio Smareglia never met each other, although they both lived at the same time in this same small town, were contemporaries, and had each fixed his eyes on young Lehár as his protégé. Perhaps they were too different in character and upbringing ever to have become intimate, and perhaps Lehár was too shrewd to introduce them—in case they should ever become allies to his disadvantage. Smareglia was an Istrian, a composer of the Ponchielli school, and one of the rare species of enthusiastic Italian Wagnerites. He introduced Lehár—still under the sway of the Mahler interpretations—to the scores of *Tristan* and the *Ring* cycle, and Lehár repaid this by honouring the *grande operista* as man and artist throughout his life. (In 1924, when he heard that Smareglia, completely blind and in precarious financial circumstances, was still living in Pola, he became the old man's generous "anonymous well-wisher".) Of Smareglia's operas Lehár loved *Cornelius Schutt* best. Its colourful crowd scenes and fresh dances doubtless found an echo in *Kukuschka*. He never forgot the great second-act finale, in which the artist Schutt gives up his idyll on the land, and tears himself from the arms of his beloved, to follow his friends into the town: twenty-three years later Lehár succeeded in transplanting the identical scene into a work of his own, *Where the Lark Sings*.

While Smareglia was an Italian through and through, Commander Falzari, although born in Venice, was a fanatical "professional" Austrian: an officer, poet and gentleman. He opened Lehár's ears to the new literary tones coming from Vienna—

Schnitzler, Bahr, Hofmannsthal—and he read the young Band-master his own poems: "The eternal song of parting sounds", "What greets my eyes . . .", "The crimson ramblers bow with scented bloom". Lehár set seven of them to music in a song-cycle, *Waidmannslieder* (A Hunter's Songs), op. 26.

From there to *Kukuschka* was only a short step.

Kukuschka

On a steamer trip round the Dalmatian islands Falzari talked to Lehár for the first time about George Kennan and his Siberia book. Kennan was an American journalist who had been sent by the Western Union Telegraph Company to the eastern provinces of the Tsarist Empire, to supervise the building of a new telegraph line. He stayed there six years, and described the bleakness of the landscape, the pitiless weather, the creeping apathy among the people—from the first rays of the spring sun and the first cry of the cuckoo: the signal for these wretched folk to run away, live in the open in the woods, and to wander in endless columns from the mines in Kara to Lake Baikal—to freedom.

The cry of the bird, "General Cuckoo's command", became for Lehár the opera's *Urlaut* (primal sound or inspiration). All through his life as a composer it was always the *Urlaut*, a sound, a picture, a scent, a character or a situation which attracted him to a libretto or an idea for a libretto, which released the inspiration, ordered him to work. His analytic memory allowed him years afterwards to think of most of these moments of first impulse: Sou Chong's entry into Lisa's drawing-room in *The Yellow Jacket*, the Slovak boys marching off in *The Tinker*, Hanna's enticing waltz-wooing of Danilo in *The Merry Widow*, the scent of the perfume *trèfle incarnat* in *The Count of Luxembourg*, the hypnotic tone of Jozsi's fiddle in *Gypsy Love*, the Alpine landscape in *Endlich Allein* (Alone at Last), the spring magic in *Frederica*. All were germ-calls for future growth and unfolding.

Falzari had soon suggested a plot: the soldier Alexis loves Tatiana, daughter of a Volga boatman. He defends the boatman by force of arms against the Circassian Sacha and the village elder.

Franz Lehár, senior,
1875

Christine Lehár with
Franz,
1871

Franz Lehár,
1881

Praga Regia

Lehár in Pola,
1894

Lehár and the Band of the 26th Infantry Regiment, 1899

Franz Lehár,
1900

The Viennese operetta-café Dobner, 1902

Princess Pauline Metternich-Sandor, 1920

Louis Treumann (*Danilo*) and Mizzi Günther (*The Widow*), Vienna, 1906

Joseph Coyne (*Danilo*) and Lily Elsie (*The Widow*), London, 1907

The Lehár family in Ischl.
Franz, Emmy, Mama,
Anton, Anton's wife,
1906

Juli 1906

Lehár with Leo Stein and Victor Léon, 1908

George Edwardes—
The Guv'nor,
1908

George   Graves,
1908

Banished to the goldmines for life, he there meets Sacha as his warder. It is spring: "Loud rings Kukuschka's recruiting song, and penetrates into our prison night . . ." The noble-hearted Sacha helps his former rival to escape. Tatiana appears and follows her beloved into the steppe, and to death in the snow. ("The astonishingly well made glittering snowfall," remarked a Leipzig paper after the first performance, "was a surprise for the audience's eyes.")

A Russian opera was a bold undertaking for a non-Russian composer of the time.[1] But the Slav elements in Lehár's musical make-up reacted very strongly to the material: the Volga landscape, the atmosphere of the steppe, and the tragic love of Alexis and Tatiana—so like that of Des Grieux and Manon Lescaut.

Work on the opera was interrupted after a month by an order from naval headquarters: a squadron of Austrian ships were to attend the opening of the Nordostsee-Kanal (between the North Sea and the Baltic), with the Naval Band and its conductor included. It was the only long sea voyage Lehár made in his life, and the longer it lasted, the more impatient he became. They went from Pola to Marseilles, Morocco, Gibraltar, Lisbon, London, Holland and Hamburg—their destination.

Once back in the home port, Lehár had started eagerly on *Kukuschka* again, when a letter from Mama brought the news of the death of eighteen-year-old Mariska, that "ethereal creature scarcely destined for the harsh realities of life". Father took the blow hardest of all. "He finds it very difficult to keep at his work," Mama wrote, "a man who has never known weariness before." The bereaved couple decided to leave Sarajevo, which had become so sad a place for them all, and go to Budapest. The old gentleman had been invited there by the 3rd Infantry Regiment to serve out the last months before his retirement.

Meanwhile the son, having finished composing his opera, started on his first large-scale orchestration. Long afterwards, at

[1] Russia at that time had not produced any opera of note since Borodin's *Prince Igor* (1882) and Tchaikovsky's *Queen of Spades* (1890). It was seven and eight years after *Kukuschka* that Italy showed two operas set in Russia, Giordano's *Siberia* (1903) and Alfano's *Resurrection* (1904).

the time of *Frederica*, a story was told in Berlin of the master orchestrator Lehár. A young composer, during a rehearsal of his new operetta, was told that a passage in the score sounded harsh and would he please reorchestrate it? He agreed to this, asked for the band parts to be collected, promised to work on it "and come back with the revisions tomorrow". "What's that?" cried the producer, Alfred Rotter, from the orchestra stalls. "Collected? Work on it! Tomorrow? I saw Lehár rehearsing yesterday; he orchestrates on the spot, from his desk, by word of mouth!"

The technique of this orchestration "by word of mouth", improving on a sound on the spot during rehearsal, was something Lehár had learnt in Pola when orchestrating *Kukuschka*. He was amazingly lucky, of course, to have a complete orchestra at his disposal to experiment with. Number by number he listened to what he had written, making full use of the whole orchestra to try out new effects and variations. In Pola he became the absolutely assured orchestrator, who could afford to retouch his scores "by word of mouth".

The progress of the work and the appearance of some prospects of success brought Lehár back to the irritability and restiveness of his Losoncz days. The Viennese publisher Hofbauer was interested in *Kukuschka* and wanted to print the vocal score; Leipzig's Municipal Theatre made it known that they would like to give the opera its first production. It did not take the composer long to make up his mind.

Without obvious cause, and against the advice of both Smareglia and Falzari, he gave up his post, one of the most desirable musical positions in the whole Austro-Hungarian armed forces. "I'm not cut out to be a military bandmaster," he informed his parents; "I've too much pride for that." And: "Won't you forgive your child if he at last shakes off his servitude? I can't serve any longer. I want to be free—since the hour I made this decision, I have felt like a man reborn. At last liberated! I am happy. The time is coming when you will understand me."

For his father, who had spent his whole life contentedly in the army, the time of understanding never came. "When you study him, you get quite alarmed," Mama reported to Toni, now at

Kronstadt, a garrison town in Transylvania. "It's incredible that a healthy person should not have more self-discipline . . . He gets up at eight in the morning. Has his bath. Reads the paper. Then he has breakfast. Works for barely half an hour. Refreshments. Then he reads again. A bit of work. Lunch. Then he sleeps till four. Shower. Works quite without spirit. Sometimes he'll write all night. Then he gets an attack of cramp in his fingers, has nightmares and wakes up with a terrible headache. There are times when he doesn't do any work at all. Everything's got to come to him of its own accord. He dreams of riches, but he'll get a bad letdown there. That he's been feckless you can imagine. He's sold his piano and the violin, and his debts!—he's spent everything . . ."

No one who knew the well-groomed, punctilious Lehár, the super-conscientious worker, the respectable property-owner, will recognize him in this pen-portrait by his mother, written in 1896. The contract-conscious composer is even harder to spot in his negotiations with the publisher Hofbauer. "We don't know whether he has signed an agreement with him or not," Mama complained. "Franz thinks all that unimportant."

In fact, Franz did not want to talk about anything before it was settled. He waited till after an audition with Staegemann, manager of the Leipzig Opera House; only then, when everything had been brought to a happy conclusion, did he inform his parents about the première, now fixed for the 27th November. And with great pride he handed Father the printed vocal score of *Kukuschka*.

Good-bye to Father

Old Lehár studied his elder son's work "most thoroughly", as he told Anton. "There is very fine music in it . . . I hope confidently for success." Then he poured out his heart: "Whether Franzi is capable of exploiting his success is another matter. He thinks after a good success the money will roll in. Which naturally is not the case, that's just where the businessman has to get going, and at that he's the clumsiest person I've ever come across, like a small child. He could stay the winter with us, of course, but he feels too cramped in our house, our life is too simple for him—he's used to throwing out of the window the money he's never had, but not to spending it the way he should, oh no—it's merely for putting on fine airs, which gets him cheated on all sides. Other people will always be fed, while he makes a fool of himself. One shouldn't think only of oneself, but you'd have to have a super-fluity to give money away like that."

The première took place on the date fixed. Anton arrived from Transylvania to attend it, and—being impecunious—without a return ticket. Lehár's excitement knew no bounds, especially as, shortly before the curtain went up, the oldest stage-hand slapped him on the back benevolently and predicted a great success. ("As a theatrical novice I didn't suspect that he said this to every author, every young actor or singer; and I proudly gave him ten marks. After the performance I met my brother at the supper to which I had invited him, to celebrate the première. But I ate nothing myself and pretended I wasn't at all hungry. What I had left after the princely ten-mark tip wouldn't have been enough for us both anyhow.") All his life Lehár remembered the final ovation—"with five curtain calls!" as he would always add.

The opera *Kukuschka* is no masterpiece. Its book, though interesting for its setting, remains thin in plot, unoriginal in characterization, poetically rough. The music is highly respectable for a man of twenty-six, even if it follows in the wake of pre-Puccini *verismo*, and although for us today its harmonic tricks appear as rather ineffective "gimmicks". But the melodic line remains pale and faceless; the early signs of Lehár's future in-dividuality show only in the choruses, ballet sequences and Russian dances. Their essence can be found again in the *Tsarevich* score thirty years later: matured, moulded, clarified.

The reviews were without exception friendly. "For theatrical and operatic effects," said the *Leipziger Neueste Nachrichten*, "Lehár in his first work for the stage shows more skill than many who can look back on longer practical experience, as can be seen from the effective construction of several of the scenes . . . without doubt a considerable success." The *Dresdener Zeitung* went so far as to state that "for nobility and sensitivity Lehár's music could worthily adorn the saga of Tristan and Isolde or other great stories. Distinguished talents are indicated . . . Lehár possesses creative genius, and thinks and feels with a passionate musical sense."

For the time being, however, the original production brought only a single meagre result: the Königsberg Municipal Theatre put on the opera—but took it off again after four performances. Disappointed and without means, but determined not to give in, Lehár returned to his parents' house. "Like a true artist!" Mama wrote to Toni in desperation. "Tie askew. *Fledermaus* cape. Without rings, without watch-chain, without tie-pin. 'What do you think of the success?' were his first words. Luckily I found the right thing to say in time, 'Congratulations', for I couldn't take my eyes off the crumpled clothes. And then we were off. 'Oh, you'll see soon!', 'You always refused to believe in me!'—and more in the same vein. On the 8th comes the postman, bringing fifty-one florins in royalties from the first two performances. Now he has to wait a month for the next account. That's the first big success! Franz has got himself forty-one florins. He gave me ten. He spent 170 florins in Leipzig and pawned everything. Will it be like this everywhere his work is put on, that he spends three times as much as he earns? Is that an artist's envied lot?"

"Harsh words," commented Anton, who understood his brother, even though he was unable to help him. He made excuses, too, for Mama, realizing her bewilderment and the fact that it was only Franz's youthful wildness she saw, the circumstances attending his struggle, not the strength of his aspirations and his art. All the parents wanted was to see their eldest son back in the army. He hesitated at first, then recognized himself that the opera-dream was over—and put on the Imperial and Royal uniform for the third time.[1]

There was a position as Regimental Bandmaster of the 87th waiting for him in Trieste; but soon he had to face a humiliation far worse than when as a Budapest grammar-school boy he had to go to an elementary school in Sternberg. For the regiment was transferred to Pola, and Lehár, well remembered there from the

---

[1] Altogether (with three interruptions) Lehár served twelve years as military bandmaster in five garrisons.

Kaiser's visit and from squadron cruises, had to return to the old "Tantantara! Tzing! Boom!" of march music.

Father gradually went into a decline. He could still carry out his duties, but only just, and had to do without any outside earnings, keeping the family on the eighty-florin surety. "And yet we are content in our comfortable warm room," wrote Mama. "I work hard. We are without a maid. Everyone does his job, and is economical. For me the first day of the month is the same as the last. That is a good feeling to have. Sometimes there are things I would like to get. But my daily 'little bags' say no."

On New Year's Day 1898 Lehár Senior, after twenty-one years' service, applied to be retired, on the 31st March. At the same time he proposed "with all due submission" that his son Franz, Bandmaster of the 87th Imperial and Royal Infantry Regiment, should succeed him. The made-up bed was waiting once more.

At the end of January the old man marched out on a church parade at the head of his band, not in his fur but in a gay light coat. The same evening he had a shivering fit; his temperature rose: the doctor diagnosed double pneumonia.

The sons kept watch alternately by his bed, and Anton has described the last hour: "Franz had relieved me a little while before, I was lying in a doze. Then I suddenly heard sounds, as if from another world. Quite soft and hesitant at first, then ever louder and more powerful. Franz was sitting at the piano saying good-bye to his father . . . I crept to the door, and saw the dying man's ashen face. His eyes were wide open, looking towards the next room, from which my brother's *Kukuschka* fantasies were streaming forth. I saw my father following each bar, his features becoming more and more transfigured. He who had served only music all his life now experienced the fulfilment of his artistic longings in his son. The music from the next room grew more and more mighty and passionate. My father tried to sit up just once more, then sank back inert. I rushed to Franz—'Our father,' that was all I could say. Never again have I heard my brother play like that. And we knew God's grace accompanied our father right to the last hour; after an industrious and harmonious life— a peaceful death."

IV

FLASHING SPARKS

Hunt for a Libretto

On 1st April 1898 Franz Lehár took up his dead father's position. His heart, however, was with the *Kukuschka* rehearsals at the Royal Opera. "It was accepted there," he recalled, "only through some guile—but in the theatre the direct route is not always the best. In the last weeks of his life my good father went every day to the café frequented by the manager of the Opera, Julius Káldy, to ask His Omnipotence to put on my work. All that was in vain, and yet it was accepted. Help came from Raoul Mader,[1] then Káldy's *repetiteur*. He went to the blackboard at the side of the stage and chalked up: 'Thursday 9 a.m. rehearsal *Kukuschka*.' The effect was amazing. Káldy read the announcement and, to save his authority, had the parts given out, concealing his pique. Father couldn't help smiling when the manager said to him in the café with a patronizing air: 'Well, Herr Lehár, you'll be pleased with me now, eh? When I take something in hand, it always works out right!'"

Now Father was dead. But a Budapest success, for which he had hoped so fervently, might still change the fate of the opera, and thereby of its composer. The success failed to arrive. Again there was applause, curtain calls and friendly reviews—that was all. Except for an aftermath which involved the sanctified person of Franz Joseph I in the *Kukuschka* proceedings.

An appalled Mama wrote to Toni: "A terrible thing has

---

[1] 1850–1926, Hungarian conductor and composer, later the manager of the Wiener Volksoper.

happened to Franz. How shall I tell it to you, an officer, without blushing? To put it briefly, there happened to be a Court banquet the day of the première. The Corps Commander, Prince Lobkowitz, mentioned to the Emperor that an opera by a Budapest military bandmaster was being put on. The Emperor asked which regiment. The imperial parade was next day. Franz didn't come home till two in the morning, when he said to me, 'I don't know, shall I turn out or not?' Then we went to bed. Franz didn't turn out. At the parade the Emperor asked to see the bandmaster who had written the opera. Franz doesn't care a fig about all this!"

(Ten years later, at another Court banquet—in Ischl—the Emperor was told that Lehár's *Merry Widow*, acclaimed everywhere, had now taken by storm the Imperial summer residence in the Salzkammergut. "Lehár . . ." said Franz Joseph thoughtfully. "Isn't that the young man who didn't turn out on the parade in Budapest. . .?" He still remembered the Regimental Bandmaster's breach of duty.)

Mama's letter to Toni also remarked that "everyone's congratulating Franz, he's getting invitations everywhere, and above all the Herr Direktor Mahler of the Wiener Hofoper wants to talk to him." This was not quite accurate! It was Lehár who wanted to talk to Mahler, to persuade him to come and see *Kukuschka* in Budapest. He sent him a telegram:

URGENTLY REQUEST YOUR HONOUR'S PRESENCE AT PRODUCTION MY OPERA WHICH I SHALL CONDUCT MYSELF STOP FATE OF MY WORK IN YOUR HONOUR'S HANDS STOP YOUR HONOUR ALONE CAN DECIDE ITS FUTURE STOP FRANZ LEHAR.

In his struggle to get it performed in Vienna, Lehár gained an influential ally in the critic Ludwig Karpath. Karpath had met the Lehár brothers fifteen years earlier on a steamer trip from Vienna to Budapest, but had lost sight of them since then; he renewed his acquaintance at a performance of *Kukuschka*.

"Franz informed me that he had submitted his opera to the management of the Vienna Opera. I was at that time seeing a good deal of Gustav Mahler, who used to talk to me about all that was going on at the Opera House. One evening he asked me if I knew a certain Herr Franz Lehár. When I said I did, he told me that Lehár, of whom he had never heard before, had submitted the opera *Kukuschka* to him, and that he had already read the libretto. 'If the music is as good as the book,' he added, 'I shall probably put the opera on.'

"I was delighted at the future prospects opening up for the young composer, and hastened to let him know of the conversation. Yet, though Mahler liked the libretto, he was not all that pleased with the music—he hadn't found in it the mature signs of a recognizably great talent. In fact my urgings were of no avail, he didn't take the work."[1]

Lehár held Hofbauer responsible for the disappointments over *Kukuschka*, accusing him of stinginess, obstinacy and inefficiency. The truth was that the publisher had lost interest in his business: he was in financial difficulties, and had to engage in lawsuits to obtain capital. He sued the Budapest Opera for arrears of royalties amounting to 300 florins—whereupon Káldy took off *Kukuschka*, which was in any case not proving very profitable.

Furious, Lehár abrogated his publishing contract and refused to allow Hofbauer any further handling of the opera. At the same time he offered to buy the available music material: vocal scores, band parts, individual numbers, and all the copper plates. They reached agreement on an immediate payment of 1,200 and a subsequent payment of 300 florins.

The money came from Mama, who took out a mortgage on the house in Schützengasse. "All for the two of you!" she wrote to Anton. "I have done my utmost . . . So now Franz is a publisher himself and his joy is great." It became even greater when the well-known music publisher Emil Berté promised to take *Kukuschka* up and get the famous Max Kalbeck to work over the book. Kalbeck was two years revising the Lehár opera, and eventually secured it a production at the Wiener Volksoper, following a further rejection of it by Mahler at the Hofoper. So it was put on again, with the title changed to *Tatjana*, ten years after

[1] Ludwig Karpath, *Begegnung mit dem Genius* (Encounter with Genius), Vienna, 1934.

its Leipzig production (and a year after the première of the *Merry Widow*).

Julius Korngold, the well-known critic on the *Neue Freie Presse*, sat in stern judgement on *Tatjana*. "This opera," he declared "is, to be frank, only a goodish run-of-the-mill work": written "before our delightful composer had brought to the tired rhythms of the Viennese dilettante operettas the lilting briskness of South-Slav dances"; and "before he was condemned to operetta hard labour in the goldmines of the Theater an der Wien". After commending a few agreeable passages in the score, the notice ends: "But what can be done by isolated blossoms of melody in view of the work's basic weaknesses? 'The blossoms were—snow', in our view, surveying the opera with the dying Tatjana."

The few performances at the Volksoper closed the career of *Kukuschka-Tatjana*. They were followed by a provincial production in Brno, and—over thirty years later, at the composer's special request—a broadcast on Vienna Radio.

The winter of 1898-9 was for Lehár a time of emptiness, dissatisfaction and indecision. The life of a military bandmaster with its unrewarding monotony, the need to cringe before superiors and shout at inferiors, was a burden to him. The material poverty he lived in, and longed to escape from, made him doubt whether his will-power and fighting spirit were a match for his ambitions. Were his talents big enough to produce an opera of his own which would rival the successes of the period, *Hänsel und Gretel*, *Evangelimann* (The Evangelist) and *La Bohème*? It became clearer to him with every day that his road lay in the direction of the operetta, that he might even be the man to overcome the prevailing emptiness of the genre—and restore it to life. But the first and most important problem to solve was the crucial question of a libretto.

In the Otthon Club, where literary and artistic Budapest was at home, he became that most pathetic of all musicians, a composer hunting for a libretto. Tragic or comic opera, operetta, musical comedy or farce: anything would do so long as he could set it to music. But the authors who usually plied so nimble a pen were not forthcoming; and after *Rodrigo* and *Kukuschka* Lehár felt no urge to collaborate again with his fellow officers in the regiment.

Karpath encouraged him to try for a transfer to Vienna, to settle down there and make contact with operetta circles: conducting a military band would help him over the first difficult period. Lehár agreed there was something in this. He had heard that the 26th Infantry Regiment and its well-known band were just being transferred to Vienna. So once again he sent in an application, was auditioned, and engaged on the spot. He made one condition in his contract: that he did not have to accompany the regiment on any change of garrison.

Mama was only too pleased to leave Budapest with him, "to see he has an orderly household". "I would like your advice," she wrote to Anton, "as to whether I shouldn't prevail upon my mother to let me move to Vienna." Grandmother Neubrandt, aged eighty-nine, was still the undisputed head of the family. She gave her consent—and a small subsidy.

Amidst the Thunder

"The wonderful, inexhaustible, magical city"—this was what the poet Hugo von Hofmansthal called the Vienna of the dying century: the Vienna of the grand Opera Balls and the little love affairs, the Vienna of Alexander Girardi and Katherina Schratt. Girardi was a delightful comedian, the reincarnation of all the city's great old jesters, and in the young Court actress Schratt every Viennese woman fancied she could see herself as she was, or would like to be.

After a command performance one day Katherina was invited to take tea with the Emperor and Empress, and Franz Joseph was seen in animated conversation with her. As a result Elizabeth herself made discreet arrangements, bringing her husband in touch with a new soulmate: a role that she herself had been unable to fill for him, since the night of Mayerling, when her beloved son Rudolf committed suicide.

In September 1898 Elizabeth was assassinated on the Geneva Embankment, and the Emperor remained alone amidst the gradual dissolution of his empire, the thunder of national and social schisms, and the tragic accumulation of misfortune.

"The reign of the Emperor Franz Joseph I," an old official at the Viennese Court used to say, "really lasted only until the death of Johann Strauss"—a statement as perceptive as it is controversial: Johann Strauss died seventeen years before the Emperor, on a sunny day in June 1899. Four years earlier his librettists Zell and Genée had both passed away in quick succession. ("They arranged even that in pairs," commented Girardi.) The year 1895 also saw the death of Suppé; and on the last day of the old century Millöcker died, too, as if to symbolize the end of the classical era of the Viennese operetta.

But perhaps it really ended with Heinrich Reinhardt[1]—unless he is considered to have introduced the modern era. His first operetta, *Das süsse Mädel*[2] (The Sweet Maiden) ran for 200 consecutive performances. The unpretentious score revealed the arrival of a fresh and lively style: all it needed was a Master to widen, ennoble and magically transform it.

On 1st November 1899 Lehár arrived in Vienna. He was exactly twenty-nine and a half, wore a smile of assurance, a big moustache like the German Emperor's, and four glittering orders. "My whole aim and purpose," he let it be known, "is to make a name for myself." And with a pertinacity from now on characteristic of him in everything—all signs of Mama's dreamy "true artist" gone—he set about achieving his ambition.

Individuality Breaks Through

Parades, marches, receptions, garden concerts, dances, funerals: the old round of duties started again for Lehár, only this time twice as strenuously, and under the eyes of all Vienna. The 26th Regimental Band, made up of Czech and Hungarian musicians, was soon the talk of the town, and to be heard everywhere; in the Prater cafés, outside the Imperial Palace, at the skating rink, at society balls. The programmes remained light, and became modern as if adapted to the demands of a big city's population.

"We'll see to it that you enjoy your playing again," Lehár pro-

[1] 1865–1922.   [2] Première was at the Carltheater on 25th October 1901.

mised his men. One of them[1] recalled that "a glorious, unforgettable time started. We had to slave away at rehearsal after rehearsal, but we always felt a real eagerness to work; for a real magician was standing up there, sending flashing musical sparks into our inspired hearts."

From another voice[2] we hear of Lehár as the idol of the women. When he was a young student, Hans Müller, who afterwards wrote plays for the Burgtheater and the libretto of Benatzky's *Weisses Rössl* (*White Horse Inn*), took a girl friend into a garden restaurant where the 26th were playing. "The young military bandmaster, a slim, sturdy, shortish, fair-haired Hungarian with glittering metal braid on the sleeves of his tunic, had already looked eagerly at Anna quite often while conducting. He kept blushing like a schoolboy caught in the act; but as soon as I turned round, he laughed, shrugged his shoulders apologetically, and—according to the custom—exchanged his baton for the fiddle, to pay homage to the unknown girl, with a specially sweet and fiery Tokai *cantilena*. It can be imagined how Anna watched this spellbound, how she sat rapt between desire and fear."

Tokai cantilenas and occasional "homages" apart—Lehár never lost sight of the chief aim of his heart and mind: the libretto he needed. (If only he had sensed that Hans Müller, the young writer sitting in his audience, was working on a collection of short stories, *Book of Adventures*, the nicest of which, *Nux the Prince Consort*, was soon to supply the basic idea for Oscar Straus's *Waltz Dream*!) In the three or four years still ahead of Lehár before he reached his goal, he had to go through the grim final stages of a young composer's career. Through lack of suitable collaborators, his production sank to a level unworthy of him, lower even than that of the amateur operetta manufacturers.

Of two small musical comedies, *Fräulein Leutnant* (Miss Lieutenant) and *Arabella, die Kubanerin* (Arabella, the Cuban Girl), little is left, and if in the Lehár waltzes of those days[3] there is still

1 Otto Römisch, soon himself a well-known Austrian military bandmaster.
2 Hans Müller-Einigen: *Jugend in Wien* (Youth in Vienna), Vienna, 1948.
3 *Ohne Tanz kein Leben* (No Life without Dancing), *Mädchenträume* (Girlish Dreams), *Stadtparkschönheiten* (Park Beauties).

no spark of individuality to be found, in the march *Jetzt geht's los* (Now We're Off), the title is really borne out:

In Liliencron's words, "it bangs and booms and clangs and clashes". And if you try, you can hear in it the herald of a new gold-and-silvery age of melody.[1]

Princess Metternich

Pauline Metternich-Sándor, one of the most famous women in Europe, took a hand in Lehár's career in her sixty-sixth year, just as she had done earlier in the careers of Wagner, Liszt, Gounod, Mahler, Offenbach and Strauss. Her grandfather was Metternich, the Chancellor, her father the Hungarian daredevil knight Count Moritz Sándor, her husband Prince Richard Metternich, Austrian ambassador in Paris.[2] Her first great days were in the Second Empire of Napoleon III, her second in the *fin de siècle* of Franz Joseph I.

"She is not beautiful—and was never young," they said of her in the *Tuileries*; "but she is *chic*—and that's the worst of all!" Her most intimate women friends were the beautiful Empress Eugénie, and Thérèse, even more beautiful, the most impudent of café *diseuses*: so Paris called Princess Metternich "*la belle laide*". Among men her best friends were the Rothschilds, Königswarters, Wertheimsteins and Todescos: so in Vienna she was called *Notre Dame de Zion*. She was tall, very slim, vivacious and disarmingly frank; had great flashing eyes, a bulldog face and a merry laugh. To the unfailing dismay of her suite she smoked

[1] All quotations from Lehár's music are reprinted by kind permission of the Lehár family and Lehár's publishing house, Glocken-Verlag Ltd.

[2] Pauline's mother was Leontine Metternich, the Chancellor's daughter by his first wife, Eleonore von Kaunitz. Richard was the Chancellor's son by his second wife, Antoinette von Leykam—and so Pauline's step-uncle.

thick Havana cigars, went boar-hunting and originated the most
bizarre women's fashions. One of her "charming *toilettes*",
according to Count Crèneville,[1] was made up of a "small bouquet
in front—and nothing behind". At the première of Offenbach's
Grandduchess of Gerolstein[2] she appeared in a tight-fitting dress
with a train, thereby causing a sensation and bringing the crinoline
fashion to an abrupt end.

Joseph Bayer's delightful ballet, *Die Puppenfee*[3] (The Fairy
Doll), came into being as a result of one of her casual suggestions;
another of these was responsible for the first visit to Paris of the
Vienna Philharmonic orchestra under Gustav Mahler. It is a
historical fact that the first production of *Tannhäuser* in Paris was
due to her enthusiasm and pertinacity. The première[4] created a
famous scandal, for the audience greeted it with howls and
whistles. She was so furious at this that she broke her ivory fan in
two; which caused almost as great excitement as the opera and its
rowdy reception.

In the days of the Paris World Exhibition of 1867 she gave a
ball to introduce Johann Strauss into international society and
Napoleon and Eugénie danced to the strains of his waltzes.

Eight years later, at the Paris première of Strauss's *Indigo and
the Forty Thieves*, the Princess applauded so vigorously that she
almost fell over the rail of her box into the stalls. By that time the
Second Empire was no more, and Pauline, confident that she
could take with her some of the Parisian *joie de vivre*, returned to
Vienna.

On Whit Sunday 1885 she arranged at the Prater a "fiacre
festival", the first of the charity galas which throughout a generation delighted Vienna and brought in hundreds of thousands of
florins to charitable institutions. From early morning onwards the
whole city, led by the Court, went out in all sorts of carriages,

1 Count Franz Folliot de Crèneville-Poutet, Adjutant-General and Lord
Chamberlain of Franz Joseph I.
2 12th April 1867.
3 From 1888 till the destruction of the Vienna Opera in March 1945 *The Fairy
Doll*, with over 700 performances, remained the theatre's most-played piece.
4 18th March 1861.

landaus, fiacres, or on foot into the wide meadows. People sat on the grass or in the restaurants. There were flags, lamps, garlands, confetti, horse-races, boat-races, merry-go-rounds, a great battle of flowers, bands, clinking glasses and laughter right into the night.

The following years brought a "Japanese Cherry Blossom Festival", a "Festival in an Old-Viennese Garden Restaurant", a "Spring Festival in a Futuristic Village", a "Mars Festival", a "Nile Festival". But the Princess found it too long to keep her public waiting from one May to the next, so she started her January Balls, glittering spectacular affairs, always the climax of the Season.

The ritual never changed: at nine o'clock the electric chandeliers of the Sophiensäle (Sophie Hall) blazed on, trumpets blew a fanfare, hurrahs sounded from the vestibule, and the Princess entered *en grande toilette*. Behind her marched the patronesses— over a hundred in number; then came the patron of the evening, one of the imperial Archdukes. The ladies curtsied, the gentlemen bowed: presentations on the raised platform, champagne in the boxes, throngs on the dance-floor. The orchestra broke into the "Name Waltz", the Ball had begun.

The Name Waltz

The Viennese custom of naming waltzes after balls and balls after waltzes, which goes back to Lanner, Johann Strauss the Elder and their contemporaries, was highlighted by Strauss the Younger; for Lehár it became the starting-point of his popularity.

When for the 1902 Carnival, after a "White" and a "Red" Gala Evening, Princess Metternich planned a "Gold-and-Silver" one, she was reviving the old Name Waltz custom. She summoned the young Bandmaster of the 26th Regiment, told him of her idea and gave him the commission. "Well—now you sit down and write something specially fine," she concluded the audience. "A waltz to make you famous in a night!"

"So I did sit down," Lehár recalled many years later, "and looked for something specially fine. I also thought I'd found it—

but it didn't make me famous—at least not on the night of the Gold-and-Silver Ball: Thursday 27th January . . ."

The Sophiensäle was flooded in gold and silver, the ceiling a silvery grey like the sky, with golden stars glittering down from it. The boxes were lined with gold and silver trinkets, and between each of them stood golden fan-palms, trunks shimmering in the silver light of arc lamps. The ladies had dressed in keeping with the character of the evening, gold and silver could be seen in all variations: subdued, shaded, gleaming, glistening. The Princess herself was wrapped in a long wide cloak shining with gold, studded with silver spangles.

According to tradition, the Name Waltz was always played first as a concert piece, with introduction and coda. After the conducting composer had received the applause, and the Archduke had ceremonially taken the floor with the Princess for the Ball's opening, general dancing began.

With the Gold-and-Silver Ball it was not quite like that. "As soon as the first theme sounded, people already began chattering, laughing and dancing. At the end there was isolated clapping, one single encore was called for—and that was all. I kept out of the Princess's way that evening . . ."

The press reports next morning contained no information about the first performance of the waltz. Only the *Neue Wiener Tagblatt*, after speaking of the "almost alarming crowds in the hall" and the "authentic Gala Ball proceedings of the most elegant kind", mentioned that the Bandmaster, Franz Lehár, had dedicated to the evening's patroness a "new waltz".

Nobody could guess that the evening's failure would turn into a world success; least of all Lehár himself. "I didn't even try to offer the rights to the big music-houses. The publisher Chmel bought the whole thing, lock, stock and barrel, for fifty florins. I accepted, and was quite convinced that the 'gold-and-silver' episode was finished."

It was not. Chmel had excellent business contacts with the famous old publishing house of Bosworth & Co. in London. Bosworth had just come back from a business tour in America, and knew how very much they were on the look-out there for new Viennese waltzes. He took charge of *Gold and Silver*, and the first reactions from music shops and bandleaders showed him at once that he had a "hit" on his hands.

Towards the end of the year, while *Der Rastelbinder* (The Tinker) was being rehearsed, Lehár received first reports of a *Gold and Silver* success in England and America, and how it was spreading continuously over Europe. At first he wouldn't believe it, but when he got letters and telegrams of congratulation from strangers in Paris, Berlin and Moscow, he knew there was no further need to keep out of the way of his patroness: the piece *had* made his name famous.

The end of the Metternich story cannot be told without sadness. In 1906 the Princess celebrated her seventieth birthday with her fiftieth entertainment. Until 1914 occasion followed occasion, then the great Pauline faded out of the news, and when the monarchy collapsed she was a living legend of Vienna. Her fortune had melted away, her income sunk to nothing: to keep alive, she had to sell mementoes of her great days, including the famous carriage in which she had ridden through the city for a generation, to a newly rich butcher. The hardships of the time did not rob her of her bearing or her wit, and every week there was a new Metternich *bon mot* going the rounds of Vienna. The last of these concerned the fashionable dances of the postwar period. During a ball in the Konzerthaus the old lady of eighty-five peered at the dance-floor and observed with a smile: "In my time, to do this sort of thing you went to bed."

Since Johann Strauss's *Emperor Waltz*, no one, not even Strauss himself, had written a waltz that could rival *Gold and Silver* for sweetness, intensity and rhythmical vigour. Here theme joined hands with theme, form grew out of inspiration, harmonies blossomed from melodies. As the title of the composition might provide the motto for Lehár's life, work and character, so the swelling richness of the six motifs here united may stand as a symbol of his whole musical style: of strong feeling and passion, of melancholy and dash, softness and suppleness, sensuality and tenderness, gaiety, elegance and beauty.

The introduction opens like the jingle of coins, before coming to rest with a harp *arpeggio*. After that it passes, by way of wood-wind *staccati* and string *legati*, to the first hint of the later *scherzando* theme, which seems to be singing quite distinctly: "Gold and silver, gold and silver!" Falling cascades on the strings lead to the glorious main motif:

Like the starry sky at the ball, the noble melody extends in a single thirty-two-bar curve, soaring upwards and descending again, from its first G to its last C. Then the contrast: skipping, fresh, light-hearted; until the waltz recalls for the first time its bitter-sweet amorous mission—and directly afterwards its name. While the flattering third-harmonies of the fifth motif suggest Lehár's bow to the Princess's Viennese present, the sixth and last[1] sounds like a reminiscence of her Parisian past. The coda, in a minor variation of the *scherzando*, seems to treat gold and silver as the root of all evil, has a brief laugh (a Wagnerian quatation from *Rhein-gold*), then returns *a tempo* to the main waltz, and *prestissimo* to the jubilant end.

The vibrant final chord of a development of the waltz over eighty years is achieved. It started with Weber's *Invitation to the Dance*, and carried the noblest blossoms of all $\frac{3}{4}$-time music. In the six fascinatingly beautiful themes of the *Gold and Silver* waltz, a young master presents himself to the world for the first time; and the light music of the new twentieth century pays homage to the palmy days of Old Vienna. Full of drives and desires, deliriously in love and then ethereally weightless, this flood of noble harmony sweeps past us, as if to give a hint of all the joy still ahead which we can expect from Lehár's inspired pen: the musical component of the lines which the young Hofmannsthal wrote as prologue to Schnitzler's *Anatol*:

. . . behind a yew-tree wall
Sound violins and clarinets . . .

---

[1] Lehár took it from a song, *Die arme Näherin* (The Poor Seamstress), which he had written years earlier.

And they seem to come flowing
From the graceful amoretti,
Who sit round on the terrace
Playing the fiddle or winding flowers . . .

With Open Ears

Soon after the "Gold-and-Silver" Ball rumours were heard that
Lehár's regiment were to be transferred to Raab in Hungary. He
wrote to Headquarters and asked for the position to be clarified.
With a reference to the wording of his contract of service, he
stated that in case the garrison were moved he would with great
regret have to resign. On 16th February 1902 he conducted for the
first time in the Theater an der Wien—where his father had started
his career forty-seven years earlier. The occasion was the golden
wedding of the popular Archduke Rainer, and the 26th Regiment
played old historic military marches. During the interval Wilhelm
Karczag, the new manager of the theatre, talked to the young
conductor, complimented him, and invited him home: "My wife
and I have been wanting to have a chat with you for a long time.
You know, don't you?—she's also from Komorn."

The wife was Julie Kopacsi, the most delightful and dynamic of
all the leading ladies of operetta who ever left the Hungarian for the
German stage. Karczag himself was eleven years older than Lehár.
Originally from Szolnok in Transylvania, he had been a journalist
and writer in Budapest, until 1894, when he came to Vienna as his
wife's manager. She made a successful début in the musical farce
Die Brilliantenkönigin (The Diamond Queen), and during the next
three years toured America and Russia. At the time of her and her
husband's return the Theater an der Wien had reached the lowest
ebb in its hundred-year history; for seven months the stage was
empty. Karczag, optimist and gambler—whose gambles often
came off—did not take long to make up his mind, and quickly
overcame all obstacles. In Karl Wallner, who put 160,000 crowns
at his disposal[1] and Emil Steininger, an official in Vienna's muni-

[1] The Austro-Hungarian currency had meanwhile been converted from *gulden*
(florins) and *kreutzers* to *kronen* (crowns) and *heller* (pennies): one florin (100
kreutzer) was exchanged for two crowns (100 heller).

cipal administration, with a strong theatrical and commercial bent, he found the ideal helpers for his advancement. They started without any definite artistic programme, but simply with the vague idea of "restoring the theatre to its former glories", and of making the great Girardi the centre of their repertoire.

After his first, very enjoyable visit to the Karczags, Lehár found himself engaged to take over as Musical Director of the theatre from 1st July. In March the 26th Regiment left Vienna, and he stepped out of army uniform for the last time. The last two years had made him a well-known and well-liked Viennese personality. In the beginning of May he received a most opportune offer to conduct in *Venedig in Wien* (Venice in Vienna) at the Prater until he took up his post at the theatre.

"Venice in Vienna" was a famous place in the Prater given over to exhibitions and entertainment. From the turn of the century till the beginning of the war the city's inhabitants and visitors flocked there every summer. For an entrance fee of 60 heller, they could revel in the atmosphere of a make-believe Venice: cross the bridges over small canals, glide in imported gondolas with imported gondoliers, eat Venetian specialities in *locande* and *trattorie*, and see the latest international operetta novelties in the charming summer theatre. The sound of music was everywhere: Italian, Tyrolean, Hungarian music, music for brass bands and mandolin orchestras, waltzes, polkas and marches.

Lehár with a forty-five-man orchestra provided his usual programme. In the pavilion nearby Sousa's band were playing under the baton of their founder and leader. Having them in such close vicinity was doubtless another important factor in Lehár's development as composer and cosmopolitan. He heard Sousa's well-known marches[1] in their rousing, virile, original orchestration, conducted by the composer himself. He heard them, as from his boyhood on he had heard all music important to him, from Komorn folk-songs to *Tristan*: with open ears.

Listening again and again, he became aware of the possibilities which Sousa's bold extension of the march form offered to all light music, and to his own talents. How skilfully he exploited this

[1] *Washington Post, Stars and Stripes Forever, Liberty Bell, El Capitan.*

awareness is shown by the distance between the utility music he had written till now (*Gold and Silver* apart) and the music for the stage that he now began to produce.

His career as conductor in the Theater an der Wien started as agreed—and ended abruptly three months later. The story of this turbulent time is the story of the definite rise of the operetta composer Franz Lehár.

V
FINDING HIS FEET

Two Irons in the Fire

The failed libretto-stalker from Budapest's Otthon Club found new hunting-grounds in the Viennese branch of the quasi-masonic organization called "Schlaraffia". This had started in Prague as a round table of painters and actors, and in the four decades of its existence had grown into an international fraternity of the arts, artists and patrons.

According to their custom, Lehár began as a simple *Junker* (page) then became Squire Franz, and in a lifetime's membership as *Ritter Tonreich* rose to the highest honours in the brotherhood. The friendships he made on his travels through a Schlaraffian universe lasted for life—with poets, musicians, journalists, theatrical people and *cognoscenti* of the arts. One of these was the Viennese business-man Friedrich Schmiedell, brother of the actor Emil Norini, and a friend of the popular author Ottokar Tann-Bergler, who was an intimate of Girardi's. Tann-Bergler knew that Girardi cherished a naïve desire to add more to the host of different professions he had "adopted" in his parts: stock-breeder, donkey-driver, diplomat, pasha, watchmaker, painter, flautist—to name only a few. He was now anxious to appear as a piano-tuner!

So in the middle of March 1902 Lehár, Norini and Tann-Bergler sat down together, deliberated, and agreed to turn the tragic situation of *Le Maître de forges*[1] (The Ironmaster)—the unconsummated wedding night—into a farcical one, and make it

[1] This play by Georges Ohnet was for many years one of the mainstays of the Burgtheater's repertoire.

into an operetta libretto, with a piano-tuner as hero. Karczag was informed of the plan; the idea appealed to him. Girardi was to reappear in the Theater an der Wien at the beginning of October in the new Ziehrer operetta *Der Fremdenführer* (The Tourist Guide); and the management were on the look-out for further parts for him to play.

What Karczag, Norini and Tann-Bergler did not know was that Lehár had a second iron in the fire: for several weeks he had been working on a libretto by Victor Léon.[1] Am imperious character, forty-three years old, stocky but agile, with tousled black hair falling over his forehead, Léon was considered the ablest man in the Viennese operetta business, as well as the most important and successful.

Fifteen years earlier, when he was a small-part actor with ultra-modern ideas on writing for the theatre, he had found favour with the ageing Johann Strauss. The Waltz King invited him to collaborate, and immediately after *Gypsy Baron* wrote music for a book by Léon, *Simplizius*. But, as often in later years, inspiration deserted Léon when it came to developing his brilliant ideas and high-flown theories; he could not convert them into theatrical reality, and this failure became obvious with his first product. *Simplizius*, which started as a bold and intelligent conception, sank in a morass of mistaken-identity situations. The operetta expired, according to the critic in the *Extrablatt*, "of acute softening of the libretto".

It is one of the oddities of the profession that this work never-theless established the librettist as a talent of the first rank, a man of drive and ability. Twelve years and eight failures later Léon at last lived up to the name he still had, with the triumphs of Heuberger's *Opernball* (Opera Ball) and *Wiener Blut* (Viennese Blood)—a charming posthumous arrangement of Strauss melodies.

Right from the outset Lehár had looked on Léon as the favou-rite among his prospective librettists: the friend of the big music publishers, chief producer of the Carltheater and herald of a new era for the operetta. The young composer sent him the vocal score of *Kukuschka*, assuring him in an obsequious letter how happy he would be if "the Master would be so kind as to entrust him with

[1] 1859–1940.

an opera libretto to write the music for". The answer was quite a time coming; when it did, it contained the usual polite flourishes, with Léon's regret that owing to further commitments for years ahead he was not in a position to meet Lehár's wish. A fortnight afterwards, to his great surprise, Lehár received a second letter: Léon was still not interested in an opera; should the *Herr Kapellmeister* settle on an operetta, however, he might pay him a visit— "and in the very near future, please!"

The *Herr Kapellmeister* had already "settled on an operetta" long ago. He made his way to the suburb of Hietzing, stopped a moment outside Léon's villa in the Wattmanngasse, breathed deeply, then rang the doorbell.

"I was not at home," Léon wrote to him many years later, describing the scene. "Lizzy received you. She was the first person you spoke to in my house. It was she who welcomed you in, who discovered you. When I arrived, I found you in lively discussion with her. You had that smile on your lips all the time which you still have all the time today: three quarters charm, one quarter irony. A *mixtum compositum* which makes you one quarter interesting, three quarters attractive. Lizzy's face glowed. And I saw that all your four quarters had produced a tremendous effect on her."

Lizzy

Lizzy Léon at fifteen was the female archetype of young Vienna's modern girl at the turn of the century: clever, pretty, alert, sport-loving, flirtatious, thrilled by Mahler, Schnitzler, and the new school of painting called the *Sezession*. She was full of enthusiasm for anything exciting, glamorous, new, wherever she found it: for the Graf Zeppelin and the great actor Kainz's Hamlet, for the new Mercedes motor car and the American cake-walk, for Maeterlinck, Marconi, Monet—and for Bandmaster Lehár of the 26th Regiment.

At home the *Now we're off* March was something she constantly played on the piano, hummed, whistled or yodelled. When the post brought *Kukuschka*, she had made her father listen to the music, executed by her and accompanied by continual cries of enthusiasm.

During the two and a half years since *Viennese Blood*, Léon had had another run of bad luck, with six more failures. To be honest he would have had to admit that he needed a young composer with fresh ideas, just as the young composer needed him, the experienced librettist.

At their first meeting Lehár received a complete operetta book: *The Club Baby*. The dedicated libretto-hunter would have liked nothing better than to set to work on the spot with the libretto king. But after the first reading he knew already that Léon was trying to sell him stale goods: an old-fashioned *vaudeville* without inner music, warmth or spirit. He made his opinion known, and the author, impressed by the young musician's initiative and magnetism, came out with a second work.

With a lordly gesture he handed the novice the first scene of *Der Rastelbinder* (The Tinker); Lehár should write music for that as a trial piece. A week later, after listening to the first numbers, the old professional knew he had found an important new composer.

Lizzy's enthusiasm had succeeded in forging one of the most successful alliances in the history of operetta. Lehár owed his rise to her, her father gained through her the most important partner in his career. Two years later she brought to the Wattmanngasse another composer with operetta ambitions: Leo Ascher, son of a worthy umbrella-maker. Léon wrote for him *Vergelt's Gott* (God Bless You For It), but this was not very suitable for Ascher's specifically Viennese talents. It was only years afterwards that he found the libretto to provide a real success.[1] For the second time Lizzy's flair had been right, though this time without particular benefit to her father.

In 1910 she married Hubert Marischka, whose star was beginning to rise in the firmament of Viennese operetta, lived with him in great happiness, but died in tragic circumstances at the age of thirty, shortly after the birth of a son.

Turbulent Weeks

Something beyond Lehár's expectations had come about: he was

[1] *Hoheit tanzt Walzer* (Her Highness Dances). See p. 141.

working simultaneously on two operettas, to be produced at two different theatres and printed by two different publishing houses. It was in some ways a welcome and desirable situation for him, but it obviously had its pitfalls and complications as well.

Having no idea that his musical director was writing a work for the rival Carltheater, Karczag had accepted the Lehár—Norini-Tann-Bergler opus *Wiener Frauen* (Viennese Women) for the Theater an der Wien. He had fixed the première for Christmas, cast Alexander Girardi in the lead, and with the purchase of the copyright for the operetta had created the basis for this new venture—the Karczag Verlag, music and theatrical publishers.

Without any idea that his protégé was working with other librettists on an opus for Karczag, Léon had offered *The Tinker* to the Carltheater. He had also fixed the première for Christmas, cast the up-and-coming Louis Treumann in the leading role, and was negotiating to buy the copyright of the operetta with the highly respected publishing firm of Josef Weinberger.

The first explosion occurred at the beginning of August when Wallner at his regular table in the operetta café Dobner heard of the *Kapellmeister*'s double game. He rushed into Karczag's office, demanding that Lehár should be reprimanded and if necessary dismissed. Karczag did not take it too tragically. He admitted that a member of his staff had a duty to be loyal, but on the other hand he didn't want to fall out with an important man like Léon. Steininger put in a good word for his fellow Schlaraffian, but Wallner remained adamant. The deceiver should be called to account and disciplined.

Lehár fought with all his resources for his second runner. He denied any dishonourable intention, insisted on his artistic freedom, tried for a friendly solution, asked for retrospective permission: Wallner replied to each proposal with "Impossible" "Out of the question!" or "Unfavourable to us!"

The Theater an der Wien had for months been looking for an opportunity to score off the Carltheater. Now Wallner saw his chance, and *The Tinker* could serve as scapegoat. In vain Lehár tried delaying tactics: how was he to inform Léon of the new situation—when, where? Wallner had his plan ready. He picked up the libretto: "Now, straight away, at the Café Dobner!"

Léon was sitting at his regular table there. He had heard by bush telegraph of what was happening at the Theater an der Wien. When he saw his young collaborator creeping miserably through the revolving doors behind the manager, he knew what was up. The ensuing brief scene was played by the three men concerned in mime, without dialogue. Wallner went up to Léon and threw the book down on the table. Léon, with a characteristic movement of his right hand, pulled his silk handkerchief out of his breast pocket, with his left hand felt for the monocle in his eye, and cleared his throat. Lehár smiled ('three quarters guilt, one quarter embarrassment") then followed Wallner, already on his way out again.

For two nights the composer reflected on the situation: the Theater an der Wien here, the Carltheater there; the much-loved Girardi here, the gifted Treumann there; his assured job here, uncertainty there. He re-read the books first of *Viennese Women*, then of *The Tinker*: there, hollow cardboard figures, here living people; there the empty *vaudeville* rhythms, here the melody of his youth at Komorn.

Suddenly he came to a decision—and asked to be discharged from his association with the Theater an der Wien. "But *Viennese Women* belongs to us!" Karczag insisted when he said good-bye— a fine burying of the hatchet. Lehár shook hands with him gratefully, then set off for the Wattmanngasse. This time Léon himself opened the door: "I've been waiting for you!" With that he gave Lehár back *The Tinker* libretto. Feeling completely confident of the result, he had already entered into negotiations with the "*Herr Rat*" for an advance on the publishing rights.

The "*Herr Rat*" (Imperial Councillor) was Josef Weinberger,[1] owner of Weinberger's, doyen of Viennese music publishers, friend of Strauss, Millöcker and Suppé and founder of the Viennese Society of Authors, Composers and Music Publishers. When Léon brought him *The Tinker*, with the music not yet written, the project appealed to the great man's flair and to his generosity. Lehár received a contract, with an advance of 1,000 crowns, payable in

---

[1] 1855–1928.

three instalments: 400 when signatures had been exchanged and 300 each on delivery of the vocal score and on the day of the première.[1]

He now had only one wish: to get out of the hurly-burly of cafés, theatre management and publishers' offices—and down to work. Somebody told him of an idyllic spot called Markt Hals near Passau in Bavaria, and of the friendly Möginger Inn there. The summer tourists were gone, so it would offer him the necessary peace and quiet. The only thing Lehár asked was whether there was a good piano there.

The Absolute Monarch

Rehearsals for *Viennese Women* started in the Theater an der Wien in the middle of October, and were dominated by the personality of the spell-binder Alexander Girardi, then fifty-two and idolized by the whole of Vienna. "The popularity you enjoy," Johann Strauss had once written to him, "is a quite natural consequence of your achievement. Nothing was given to you on a plate; all the affection and recognition you have attained was won by your industry and artistic dedication." Said Hermann Bahr: "It would not be so remarkable that every actor, even in the smallest provincial theatre, when he wants to be irresistible, should adopt Girardi's common-Viennese and yet appealing voice, quivering with excitment, and his innocently cynical gestures. But there is really no longer any young man amongst us who could flirt with his girl without automatically copying Girardi."

It is hard nowadays to imagine the full extent of his popularity. For four decades the big question exercising the minds of most of Vienna's inhabitants was not "Who will be the next Prime Minister?" "Will there be a war?" or "When do we get the electric tramway?"—but "What is Girardi's next part?" Personalities like Charlotte Wolter, Sonnenthal and Kainz remained the grandees of the Viennese theatre, respectfully admired; in the affections of the public, Girardi was its absolute monarch.

[1] The statement that Weinberger then acquired from Lehár all his rights in *The Tinker* for 1,000 crowns is completely unfounded.

Lehár had so far only seen him act four or five times, and like everyone in Vienna had duly marvelled. Now he studied the musical construction of the Girardi operetta, the phenomenon of his mastery of diction, his skill in enlivening the tone through the words. He composed for Girardi the title waltz of the operetta, yet he still felt the score was missing a last decisive number: the sighing, plaintive, sentimental song to which Girardi and his audience had a prescriptive right.

In Lehár's hands it became un-sighing, un-plaintive, un-sentimental: witty, light and sharp: the *Nechledil March*.

The première was on 21st November. Next day in their references to Lehár the papers spoke of "a new talent, finding his feet, guided by a true musical sensitivity, representing a handsome gain for the operetta"; of "the most welcome appearance, after a long gap, of a musician who knows how to write operettas". The critics hailed Girardi as the "incomparable, enchanting, consummate artist", whose "virtuosity and gaiety" had again produced a master performance. The libretto came out less well, and "with the best will in the world" they could not "shout 'bravo' for its writers". Nevertheless, "the house proved very enthusiastic", "the first-night audience went into raptures"; there was "tumultuous applause".

On the 19th December the operetta was performed for the twenty-fifth, on 14th January for the fiftieth time; thirty-six provincial theatres took it; in Berlin it appeared under the title *Die lieben Frauen* (The Dear Women), in other German theatres as *Der Klavierstimmer* (The Piano-Tuner) and *Der Schlüssel zum Paradies* (The Key to Paradise). In the end it had run for sixty-nine performances at the Theater an der Wien, nothing overwhelming for those days, but quite a respectable figure all the same.

In the Front: Nechledil

Considered with a critical eye two generations later, *Viennese Women* seems more the end of a former glory than the beginning of a new one. Though a good deal better than the mass of operettas of those days, it certainly does not compare with outstanding works of the genre like *Opernball* (Opera Ball). Its significance, as the Vienna critics perhaps recognized at this early stage, lies solely in the fact that with this piece a new master of "noble gaiety" set out on his conquest of the world.

Viennese Women has nothing of Offenbach's timeless topicality, the ingenious fantasies of Gilbert and Sullivan or Strauss's abundance of lovely melodies. The book fails to give a powerful impetus to the music, the music lacks coherence with the book. It is not, in fact, really an operetta at all, at best a *vaudeville*.

The plot concerns the beautiful Claire, who was in love years before with her piano-teacher, Willibald Brandl: not so much for his personal charm as for a waltz song which he could sing irresistibly. Willibald went off to America, and Claire hears he has been drowned. Now she is to marry the wealthy Philip; but just as bride and groom are starting on their duet traditional in such cases, they hear the tinkle in the next room of a piano being tuned—and the old waltz song. Claire knows that Willibald is alive, and runs away from her Philip. The last two acts drag on laboriously from one farcical situation to the next, until at the end she and Philip come together again, while Willibald finds consolation in Claire's maid Jeanette.

Lehár's score has little brilliance except for its one highlight. The mammoth overture, for years a staple item for bands in parks and restaurants, was built to the scale of Paul Lincke's overtures, then so popular. But the attempt misfired in the theatre, and thereafter he confined himself in his operettas to brief introductions merely giving the atmosphere. Among the waltzes, *Schöne Rose* (Lovely Rose), on which Claire's longing turns, is the weakest. Two others are pleasantly conceived, without achieving the elegance of *Gold and Silver*.

All the composer offers otherwise is unpretentious, limited and cheap: except for the Nechledil March.

> When in the front I march through town,
>   My staff I gaily twirl,
> Ring-ding, tara, diddledum,

The windows left and right come down,
A thrill for every girl,
Ring-ding, tara, diddledum!

Then the trio tune is heard, a B flat major scale rising in triumphant exhilaration:

In continual new variations, swelling again and again to new climaxes, the glorious tune marches ahead, now in firm harmonies from the brass, now in skipping wood-wind passages; now entwined with cheeky semi-quavers, now without any contra-puntal trimming—in brilliant, unadulterated perfection: the per-

fection which united old man Sousa's zip of young America with
young man Lehár's dash of old Vienna.

Security a Mask

If to conflict nations run,
    I don't say when or where,
Just to show what can be done,
    The time and place is there.
So peace twixt Czech and German comes about,
With each discordant shout completely faded out!
In proud salute my head goes smartly round,
At the band's harmonious sound!
Accord once more—as ne'er before,
All the feuds and grudges gone,
Arm in arm we're marching on.

Nechledil's well-intentioned ideas, in the third verse of his
song, for solving the problem of the different nationalities within
the Habsburg Empire, proved difficult in harsh reality to put into
practice. The Czech and German, also the Hungarian, Serb, Pole
and Italian, did not want to march on arm in arm; *their* aim was
separation from Austria and the Habsburgs.

Vienna, admittedly, attracted them as much as ever. Brothers
and cousins who had moved to the capital sent their family at home
exaggerated reports about the possibilities there, the gracious
living and the wealth. Of course, you had to start from the bottom
as a cobbler's apprentice, salesman or pedlar; but even the very
poorest could within ten years reap the fruits of their industry and
adroitness. Many went back to the provinces in their new affluence,
others became "hundred per cent Viennese". In the whole
monarchy there was no greater German, Czech, Ruthenian or
Jewish city, no greater garrison town or trading centre. Nowhere
was the process of assimilation made so easy and pleasant for the
immigrants.

New motor cars whizzed along the wide boulevards, and
revellers in the Grinzing taverns listened with splendid complacency

to singers who told them the dear old Almighty must be Viennese, and the heart of a true Viennese His masterpiece. Smart society met at the Sacher Restaurant and Demel's *Patisserie*; fashionable ladies sat on the terraces of cafés in huge cartwheel hats and dresses stopping just above the ankle. Stefan Zweig, writing about the city of that time, long after it had vanished, spoke of "the golden age of security". Was the security real, though—or only a mask for instability?

The old Emperor knew his Empire was not the best of all possible empires, but he believed it was best for Austria to accept the *status quo* and in the Voltairean sense "cultivate her own garden". Nevertheless, when a Swiss university professor told Franz Joseph: "Your charm has converted me to monarchism", the Emperor replied: ". . . and when I was visiting Switzerland recently, I found everything so perfect that I could almost have become a republican!"

He was seventy (and still "riding furiously at the head of his cavalry") when the rift occurred with Katharine Schratt and he was left completely solitary. This new loneliness coincided, symbolically enough, with the early symptoms of disintegration in the high Austrian style of living—symptoms which passed almost unnoticed and unsuspected amidst the cosmopolitan colourfulness of the Empire.

The Stop-gap

Lehár did not like the title *Der Rastelbinder* (The Tinker), for three reasons: it was old-fashioned, it was insipid and it was anti-Austrian. The Slovak tinkers who went from house to house in Vienna, mending broken pots and pans and begging for scraps of food at back doors, were an adornment, he felt, neither to the imperial capital not to their own land. He admitted that they made effective characters for the musical stage; but why rub the audience's nose in them right at the start?

Léon remained adamant, insisting that the title was ageless, striking and in the best Austro-Hungarian traditions; and he proved right.

As producer he was at his most gifted, ingenious and also most approachable. Long before the rehearsals started, long before Lehár had even seen the book, Léon's friend and assistant producer, Julius Wilhelm had pointed out to him a fatal weakness in it: the brilliant first act was followed by a good second and a wretched third. Wilhelm suggested cutting out this third act, bringing the operetta to a happy end with the second, and preceding the first with a prologue which would show the charming tale of the children's engagement. Léon quickly recognized the advantages of Wilhelm's suggestions. He adopted them and gave them dramatic form. Through masterly musical handling of them, Lehár showed him how wisely he had acted.

The managers of the Carltheater were sceptical, however, on the subject of Léon's enthusiasm. They called *The Tinker* a "children's pantomime", and saw it as a stopgap which would serve until *Madame Sherry*, the operetta on which they had set all their hopes, was ready.

A bad setback occurred when Louis Treumann,[1] portraying Wolf Bär Pfefferkorn, the onion-pedlar, returned his part to Léon: good friends had warned him that it was a mistake to play a Jew in these anti-semitic times: Treumann said he could only appear if the part were altered to make Pfefferkorn a Slovak peasant. Léon knew his theatre people, and at once brought into action his well-tried powers of persuasion. There were romantic leads by the dozen on the Viennese operetta boards, he told the would-be deserter, but only one who could sing and play character parts as well—Treumann.

The Tinker was saved, and Treumann took a leap forward in his career of success. Reactions to him varied greatly: some admired his rather extravagant elegance, others found his affectation repellent or irritating. But whether he was considered a Don Juan figure or a conceited clown, people were continually and passionately talking, writing and arguing about him everywhere.

His co-star Mizzi Günther,[2] who played Suza, came via Prague to the summer theatre at "Venice in Vienna"; from there she was

[1] 1872–1942.   [2] 1879–1961.

called to the Carltheater to play the title role in *The Geisha*. Her beauty and vivacity, combined with an unusually melodious soprano voice and the sharpness of her acting, made her the great operetta *prima donna* of her time, the most seductive blonde in the city. Arthur Schnitzler captured her enchanting personality in one sentence when he said: "If you wanted to set up a statue to the Viennese operetta, it would have to have Mizzi Günther's features."

On Saturday, 20th December, four weeks after the première of *Viennese Women*, *The Tinker* was performed for the first time. Its success was spontaneous, unmistakable and genuine. Mama Lehár sat with her twelve-year-old daughter Emmy in a box, and had the happiest Christmas of her life. The show was interrupted by tumults of applause, such as had not been heard for years in a Viennese theatre: they went on from Treumann's entrance song right till the last finale, and were still raging twenty minutes after the curtain came down.

The reviews were lukewarm. The liberal newspapers didn't care for the "farcical character" of Wolf Bär Pfefferkorn. The atmosphere surrounding him aroused age-old inferiority complexes; the laughter produced by his cheerful wisdom was found embarrassing. Léon was berated for sentimentality, and charged with having "let his composer down". Lehár came off better. The press conceded that he was at home "in Vienna, in the world of the waltz rhythm", and "revealed the fortunate hand of a fine musician in a long series of splendid marches, polkas and quadrilles". The tender minor-major colours of the score, though intuitively felt by the audience, remained unnoticed in the reviews.

It was eight years since Johann Strauss, in his Serbo-Croat *Jabuka* had last tried to introduce new folk-lore elements into operetta music. Now came Lehár, the great musical internationalist, whose melodic excursions were to take him and the Viennese operetta round the world. With every performance the songs from *The Tinker* grew more popular; their continually increasing popularity kept bringing new audiences to the old theatre. Meanwhile Josef Weinberger was working with inspired energy to get the operetta shown on other stages; by the beginning of the autumn season of 1903 there was scarcely a theatre in central Europe which did not have *The Tinker* in its programme.

Poor *Madame Sherry* did not get its turn until ten months later; and then only because the theatre managers, with various members of *The Tinker* cast taking a holiday, felt obliged to put it on as a stopgap. They had to take it off again very shortly, when it was generally rejected. That was not the end of the story, however. The American producer George W. Lederer saw *Madame Sherry* at the Carltheater, bought the rights and produced it in New York. Not caring for the original music, he commissioned a new score from his musical director, Karl Hoschna; and with the sixteen indestructible bars which Hoschna added as "Every Little Moment", *Madame Sherry* became in the end a success after all— one of the greatest successes of the American musical theatre before the First World War.

Molto con Brio

Viennese Women is average, *The Tinker* perfection: a bravura achievement in words and music, which—although it never attained world success because of the local limitations of its subject—need not fear comparison with any of the masterpieces of its genre. Victor Léon's book could serve as a model. The juxta-position of Slovak and Viennese elements in the story offers the author splendid opportunities for character-drawing, for humour and melancholy, the composer for rewarding melodic contrasts in colour. The three settings—the village square in Trenczin, the ironmonger's shop in suburban Vienna, and the barracks of the Austrian Lancers—breathe good sound theatrical air.

The characters, without exception fresh, effective and authentic, are dominated by the main part, the freshest, most effective and authentic of them all, Wolf Bär Pfefferkorn. He sells his onions— but is not doing well at all. Yet he is not too poor to do people a good turn now and then. Every year (so *The Tinker* story relates) the boys from his village are sent out into the world to peddle their mousetraps and children's toys. To make them remember their home, however, even when far away, each of them must be betrothed to a village maiden. So it is with Janku and Suza. But as Janku has to set out on his travels without means, Suza begs a silver florin for him from Pfefferkorn, who gives it gladly because:—

> It's simple as all that, my child, and you should never forget,
> The interest comes from doing good, your profit true from that.

In the orchestral introduction and in the four numbers of the prologue, a composer of individual stamp can be heard unmistakably and with three glittering facets: Lehár the melodist, dramatist and orchestrator. What does it matter that from time to time a thematic reminiscence can be heard, of Dvořák, Millöcker or Lortzing? A sure sense of the theatre is revealed in every bar, and everything is wrapped in an orchestral sound of rare delicacy. Where the Viennese Lehár of *Gold and Silver* and *Now We're Off*, does not yet break through, he apologizes—on behalf of the story, as it were—for keeping us waiting. It won't be long now!

To return to the story, twelve years have passed since Janku left Trenczin. He is now living in Vienna, the indispensable assistant to Herr Göppler in his ironmonger's shop, and a "hundred-per-cent Viennese". Suza and his native village are long forgotten: Janku loves Mizzi, his master's daughter. Pfefferkorn, who has meanwhile become a successful businessman—the silver florin has borne interest—remembers the childhood betrothal and is determined to make a match of Suza and Janku. He brings the girl from Trenczin to Vienna, but learns that Suza, too, has long ago found someone else: the Lancer, Miloš Blacek, son of the squire of Trenczin, who is doing his military service in Vienna.

Pfefferkorn is surprised to hear of the new arrangements, still thinks he should bring Janku and Suza together, and causes general confusion. In the last act it is, of course, dissolved—to the strains of an unadulterated Lehár march: "*Kamerad von Numm'ro vier!*" (Comrade from the good old Fourth!)

The Tinker score is a musical portrait gallery of the types encountered by Lehár the cosmopolitan during his boyhood travels through the Habsburg Empire: the Slovak peasant, the lower-middle-class citizen, the dashing officer in the Lancers—and the Viennese girl in love. He had absorbed their inner melodies, reproduced them *molto con brio*, and clothed them in an orchestral garb of intoxicating colours and irresistible sounds.

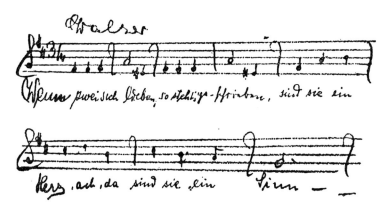

Now he was no longer just a promising composer. The promise was redeemed; but another three years were to pass before its complete fulfilment.

Attempt at an *"Offenbacchiade"*

To solve the problem of a successor to *The Tinker*, Léon called in Leo Stein,[1] his friend and co-librettist of *Viennese Blood*. Clever, able and cultured, a dramatist of great technical ability and delicate taste, Stein had originally studied law at Vienna University, afterwards becoming a railway official. He started writing drawing-room comedies, and an acquaintance with Richard Genée, librettist of the *Fledermaus*, led him to the operetta. For Lehár he put forward the Amphitryon story: the "Long Night at Thebes", during which Jupiter—*Der Göttergatte* ("The Husband God") as well as father of the gods—goes on amorous adventures with Mer-

[1] 1861–1921.

cury in the guise of the General Amphitryon and his servant Sosias, seemed to Stein an extremely promising subject for an operetta.

The revival of Offenbach's idea of mythological travesties was a continual temptation for later operetta. Paul Lincke had written a *Venus auf Erden* (Venus on Earth) and a *Lysistrata*; Oscar Straus was engaged on a burlesque of the Nibelung saga.

Lehár—as Léon must have seen—was the most unsuitable composer there could be for a burlesque-satirical musical comedy. Was the shrewd librettist trying to subdue his protégé's inclinations towards sentiment, to guide him back to hilarity, and with him the whole genre?

If Léon cherished any such intentions, he had not reckoned with Lehár's obstinacy: "Lanzi didn't want!" Much as he admired Offenbach's works musically, they remained alien to him as products for the stage. Even before *The Merry Widow*'s world success proved it to him, he had realized that his type of operetta must be based on the heart, the emotions and, the passions, not on wit, flirtations and impudence.

There may be two reasons why he decided nevertheless to write music for the *Göttergatte*: he wanted to keep Léon as partner, especially in collaboration with Stein; and he felt that thanks to his melodies the lyrical sections of the libretto would push into the background the comic and satirical ones. But Léon and Stein were not willing to abandon the idea of an *"Offenbacchiade"*: from the outset there were arguments, and eventually compromises which could hardly prove beneficial for the eventual product.

The première in the Carltheater[1] was received with respectful interest. Mizzi Günther as Juno-Alkmena had the success of the evening; Treumann was Mercury-Sosias. There were over forty performances, then a quick revision, and a dozen more. But Lehár retained his affection for the *Göttergatte* score a long time.

Taken separately—if this is at all possible with a collaboration for the musical theatre—both book and music are delightful; unfortunately they do not fit together. The work of Léon and Stein reveals taste, skill and a sense of what an *Offenbacchiade* should be. The dialogue is wittier, the lyrics neater, than was usual

[1] 20th January 1904.

in operettas; and the whole thing leaves an impression of civilized enjoyment.

Lehár contributed a few lively marches and a most inspired waltz:

Valse lento

"Delightful melodies," one critic declared, "which we welcome with special pleasure because they disdain all the crude 'Tantara Tzing Boom', insinuating their way into the ear through their fresh rhythm and attractive fluency." Melodies which—it must regretfully be said—missed their mark nevertheless because they bore very little relation to the merits of the book.

The Predecessor

With Lehár's next operetta, *Die Juxheirat* (The Mock Marriage), there was not much mark to miss in that respect. The music had no opportunity anywhere to rise above its libretto by Julius Bauer,[1] a cheap and inept farce.

It is reported that during the première of *Viennese Women* a gentleman in the stalls stood up clapping loudly and shouting towards the stage: "Bravo Lehár! That's the coming man!" This piece of ostentation contributed quite a lot to the success of the evening, especially as it turned out that the shouter was a theatre critic, the editor-in-chief of the *Wiener Fremdenblatt*, a man called Julius Bauer.

Bauer felt himself to be the accredited official jester of contemporary Vienna. People laughed at his jokes over the card tables in the cafés—especially when these were directed at someone else. In his younger years he had done his best from an editor's chair to win favour with the operetta composers of his day; and at last through Millöcker and Strauss collaborations achieved his long-desired connection with the *métier*. Now he found Lehár in receptive mood, still affected by the internal disputes during the work

[1] 1853–1941.

on *Der Göttergatte* and the lack of enthusiasm shown for it. Léon and Stein were reluctant to start on a new piece; Bauer's story, weak though it might be, had an up-to-date air because of the American background; and Girardi (as Bauer had wisely arranged in advance) was ready to play the lead in the Theater an der Wien. Moreover, three hundred provincial theatres were waiting to add a new Lehár to their repertoire, good, bad or indifferent.

Meanwhile, unchanged since the old knapsack days in her intelligence and modesty, Christine Lehár watched her son proudly and lovingly. She had aged prematurely and often felt tired and sick. "I don't know why I sometimes get so worried," she wrote once to Anton; and another time: "I eat the same simple supper as I used to, when we were all rather poor." From a holiday at Graz she reported: "Last week we were at the Municipal Park. The band played Franz's *Nechledil March*. Great applause from everyone, and I was happy." On her fifty-fifth birthday she had herself photographed for her children: "Think of me sometimes. Forgive me for not going to the hairdresser first and dressing up specially. But I want to remain a plain, simple woman. Just as I always was, no different. My pride are my children, and will remain so, with God's grace, till my last breath."

The Mock Marriage was performed for the first time on 22nd December 1904, with Girardi in the leading role as a chauffeur. It was not a success, and after endless quarrels with Karczag and Wallner led to the star's departure from the Theater an der Wien. With some justification he considered it beneath his dignity to do a monkey dance and sing Bauer's completely idiotic lyrics. Perhaps he realized that Lehár's style, the style of the new operetta and the new Theater an der Wien, was not his. He did appear there briefly once more in an Eysler operetta, but stuck to his decision to leave.

Lehár's score for *The Mock Marriage* contained no number of any merit. But how could the clumsy transvestite farce, with its Lesbian undertones, have had an inspiring effect? How could audiences be interested in the story of a widowed, man-hating American millionairess, who undergoes a mock marriage to a man she believes to be a woman in disguise, when it is really a man dressed as a woman?

In the press notices there was no mention of the book's stupidity or the music's poverty of ideas. The critics, on the contrary, spoke of their colleague's "nice plot, worked out in the best musical-comedy style"; and of his composer's "waltz and polka-themes, now slow and lilting, now robust and tingling".

It was no use. *The Mock Marriage* was taken off after thirty-nine performances, and no one suspected that Selma Brockwiller, the "mock-married" widow of Newport, Rhode Island, U.S.A., was the immediate predecessor of that other widow, the Parisian-Pontevedrin Hanna Glawari, who was to delight the world only a year later.

INTERLUDE

Fragments of a Mosaic
Saturday, 30th December 1905

Some Higher Cause

Every period, every social order, since the genre started, has produced its own great comic opera or musical comedy. The real triumphs of light music for the stage occur only when creative inspiration goes hand in hand with an understanding of the age. Thus *The Marriage of Figaro* heralded the approach of the French revolution; the *Mastersingers* reflected the complacency of the German bourgeoisie in the middle of the nineteenth century; the Vienna of the *Gründerjahre*, that prosperous time around 1870, came to new life in the *Fledermaus*, the French "Second Empire" in *La Belle Hélène*.

The Merry Widow is no exception; it strikingly proves the rule. From tiny fragments, sometimes clear and sometimes hidden, it forms the perfect mosaic of the time when it appeared, when perhaps it had to appear inevitably as an effect of some higher cause.

How did the world look on Saturday, 30th December 1905, the day when it was first performed at the Theater an der Wien?

Bloodstains in the Snow

Over Christmas it had been dull and unnaturally warm for winter. There was rain in Vienna and Berlin, mud on the streets in Paris, London was wrapped in yellow fog. Only in St Petersburg the sun shone brightly over the frozen snow, as if to wipe out the traces of blood on it.

In the small audience room of the Winter Palace, Nicholas II listened indifferently to his Prime Minister's report. Street fighting had stopped, Count Witte declared, the revolution was liquidated, thanks to the Cossacks' swords and whips; the members of the Socialist Committee, including the ringleader Trotsky, had been arrested. There was martial law in Moscow, Odessa and Kharkov. St Petersburg, where a little while ago 140,000 people had marched in protest, demanding a change in the Constitution and equality for all before the law, was now quiet. The number of victims could not at the moment be established, but in the hospital morgues alone there were over a thousand unidentified bodies. The Government begged His Majesty to win back the nation's confidence in the throne by tempering justice with mercy and stopping reprisals on the part of the military authorities.

Concluding his statement, Witte bowed deeply. The Tsar looked at him coldly: it was not for the throne, he said, to win back the nation's confidence, but for the nation to win back the throne's confidence. He gave a dismissive nod, left the room without a word, and strode past the guard through long corridors to his private suite. A year of disaster was ending: political assassinations, strike disturbances, peasant revolts, naval mutinies, ignominious defeats in the Russo-Japanese war, the terrible haemophilia of the young Tsarevich—where was the light?

In the quiet of his study he picked up his diary, and felt a sudden gleam of hope. "We have become acquainted with a man of God," he noted, "the monk Gregory from the region of Tobolsk . . ." (Six years later this monk, Gregory Rasputin— mystic, charlatan, libertine and miracle-worker, who had alleviated the Tsarevich's haemophilia—was ruling Russia from the Imperial Court, and leading it towards the abyss.)

In the evening the Tsar went to the Maryinsky Theatre with the Tsarina and the four little princesses, for a private performance of *Hänsel und Gretel*. He enjoyed it in untroubled serenity.

At the Meridian

William II spent the evening at the Berlin Hofoper, watching a performance of Leoncavallo's *Roland of Berlin*. By him in the box sat his bosom friend, Prince Eulenburg.

The opera had been written on commission from the All-Highest and dedicated to the Emperor "in deepest veneration and gratitude". It was designed to glorify the house of Hohenzollern; but the public did not like it, and all the patronage of the Court could not prevent a failure. "Now they'll become more polite again towards the German composers," wrote Richard Strauss, Imperial Director of Music, to his father in Munich, when the Leoncavallo craze had died down. His opera *Salome* had received its première in Dresden three weeks before. "All this modern stuff is not much good!" was His Majesty's verdict. "And Strauss is one of the worst. *Salome* will do him an awful lot of harm." ("Anyhow, thanks to the harm I was able to build my villa in Garmisch!" the composer remarked in his memoirs.)

The era had reached its meridian, and Germany stood before the world as "the strongest economically, best administered and worst governed country in Europe".[1]

It was said that William won hearts everywhere he went, but his chief of general staff, added: "Provided he doesn't stay too long!" Privy Councillor Holstein at the Foreign Office called his way of leading the State "*politics à l'operette*", and Bismarck declared: "He would like every day to be his birthday."

The cordon of sycophants round him saw to it that his ego was continually inflated. Generals kissed his gloved hand, and Court preachers proclaimed his divine right. The world, however, had stopped taking him seriously and the people sang disrespectfully to the toot-toot of his motor horn: "For all our cash!"

Yet one of his more objective observers in later years felt that he was "the expression of the overwhelming majority of his subjects, the champion and executor of their ideas, the representative of their view of the world: most Germans of the Wilhelmine era were nothing but pocket editions, reduced copies, miniatures of Emperor William".[2]

All the same, at the general election of 1903 it proved that a

[1] Friedrich Stampfer (1874–1957), Member of Parliament and editor-in-chief of the socialist newspaper *Vorwärts*.

[2] Egon Friedell: *Kulturgeschichte der Neuzeit* (*Cultural History of Modern Times*), Vol. 3, Leipzig, 1927.

third of all the electors rejected his regime. The process of disintegration began. It was not long afterwards that the cobbler and
ex-convict Wilhelm Voigt raised as "Captain of Köpenick" his
extremely personal protest against Wilhelmine authorities and
uniforms. The world rocked with laughter, in which—be it said to
his credit—the Emperor himself joined.

He was to laugh on the other side of his face, however in, 1908,
the year of the Harden lawsuit which involved his friends and
advisers in a scandal of global proportions. Seriously compro-
mised, William II kicked out his past clique, only to let a new one
form. His wise uncle Edward in England called the Harden affair
"the greatest folly in the history of the Hohenzollerns". Till then,
perhaps; an even greater one was reserved for 1914.

Pomp and Circumstance

The London *Times* of 30th December 1905 reported that the
stock market was firm, though money was short in the City, and
that the courts had reprimanded a motorist who drove through
London at the crazy speed of twenty miles an hour. In the political
section one read that the suffragette cry of "Votes for Women"
could be heard increasingly often at election rallies; in the theatrical
section, that Mr Bernard Shaw's new comedy *Man and Superman*
was playing at the Royal Court Theatre; in the musical section
that on New Year's Day Schubert's *Unfinished Symphony*
would be performed at the Queen's Hall with Mr Henry Wood
conducting; and in the advertisement section that a spoonful of
Eno's Fruit Salts, followed by a short walk in the bedroom, would
banish any morning depression caused by constipation.

One thing *The Times* did not report was that King Edward's
health showed a steady deterioration and that he had spent a tired
and depressed Christmas in the castle at Sandringham. The bad
weather had robbed him of the pleasure of duck-shooting; his cigar
tasted flat; whist and golf bored him. He saw the Great War
approaching, and could do nothing to stop it. Four years and four
months later he was to die peacefully.

His people, who had always sung in his honour the refrains of

Elgar's *Pomp and Circumstance* marches, mourned him like an old uncle, and nine monarchs accompanied his coffin.

A sixteen-year-old in the funeral procession reflected forty years later[1] how soon afterwards many of those who marched with him departed from the scene: the King of Denmark died; his brother, the King of Greece, was murdered; the King of Portugal lost his throne, and the heir to the Austrian throne was assassinated at Sarajevo. "Before the convulsions unloosed by that insane act subsided, three great Empires lay shattered; eight and a half million men were dead; and the principal architect of Europe's tragedy, the German Emperor, had become the lonely wood-chopper of Doorn."

Flashlights

For France the middle of the first decade of the new century was a time of cultural vigour and bitter political strife. Its great writers of the day were Proust and Anatole France, its great musician Debussy its great painters Cézanne and Renoir, its great sculptor Rodin.

The Dreyfus Affair had brought the country to the brink of civil war, and after the Captain's vindication the old *anti-Dreyfusards* found a new field for their machinations in the long-standing struggle between Church and State. France was again split into two opposing camps: the clericals and the anti-clericals. In these days a young lawyer from Nantes, Aristide Briand, started his political career. His skill allowed the separation of Church and State to become part of the Constitution without the Church being humiliated. It could not stop the spread of a modern political extremism with a modern mystique and brutality.

Like flashlights on the darkness of the future came the first reports of the *camelots du roi*, those private, half-uniformed storm troops, organized from rowdies, cranks and desperadoes of the radical Right, who attacked their adversaries and broke up rallies by brute force: forebears of the brown, red, blue and green shirts so soon to appear.

[1] The Duke of Windsor in *A King's Story*, London, 1951.

Wild, Picturesque, Exuberant

On 6th September 1901 William McKinley, twenty-fifth President of the United States, was shot dead in Buffalo while opening an exhibition. His office went to the Vice-President, Theodore Roosevelt; and with him America took on a new face. In journals like *New Republic* and *New Democracy* the "new idea" of the "new harmony" in the "new State" was developed; the "new society" radiated "new energies" and a "new spirit". "It appears to the visitor," remarked an English newspaperman, "as if the whole country were caught up in an endless whirl of new telephones, cameras, electric bells, motor cars, lifts and music-machines."

Wild, picturesque, exuberant and melodramatic, "Teddy" Roosevelt was already well known as a lawyer, naturalist, author, politician, cavalry officer and historian, before he started his campaign against corruption, for the cleaning up of America's public life. Some hated him as arrogant and ambitious, for others he united all the virtues, moral and intellectual. By trying to get rid of the worst social contrasts, he contradicted the commonly held view that in America there was one law for the rich, another for the poor. No President before or after him so enjoyed his office. He laughed on reading in a paper that it was his greatest mistake to try to be bride, groom *and* parson at a wedding. He laughed even more when another paper called him and the German Emperor the two "omniscient, omnipotent authorities on everything obvious".

Leaving the White House in January 1909, he was to devote the last ten years of his life to writing and science. Hailed everywhere as one of the great personalities of his age, the ex-President made a triumphal progress through Europe: in Paris, Berlin and Oxford he gave addresses to politicians and students; and in Christiania, on receiving the Nobel Peace Prize, he submitted his idea for a league of nations.

In the Palace at Vienna he said laughingly to the old Emperor:[1] "In me, Majesty, you see the first head of state who lets himself be photographed with his mouth open yelling into a megaphone!"

[1] In April 1910.

To which Franz Joseph answered in resigned tones: "And in me, Mr Roosevelt, you see the last head of state of the old school!"

Half-measures

The twilight of the Habsburg monarchy had begun: the last decade of that cultural, economic and historical unity which, to transfer Voltaire's famous remark, "if it didn't exist would have had to be invented".

Austria's peoples—fifty-one millions and twelve nations living in nineteen countries—were at odds with each other almost all the time; and within each group there were Catholics, Protestants and Jews, and Social Democrats, Liberals and Clericals, in mutual conflict. All that held together this shaky old organism, and left it still functioning in the year of grace 1905, was the legendary figure of the seventy-five-year-old Emperor. At the age of eighteen he had started a regime which lasted from the Crimean to the First World War, from the Californian Gold Rush to Charlie Chaplin, from the first safety match to the first gas-mask.

At one time or another the Emperor's subjects included Marshal Radetzky and Sergeant-Major Josip Broz of Agram (later Marshal Tito); Giuseppe Sarto, son of a postman in Venetia, later canonized as San Pio X; the painter Segantini of Arco; the writer Franz Kafka of Prague, and the producer Max Reinhardt of Pressburg; the adventurer Trebitsch-Lincoln, who managed to become a British M.P. and an oil millionaire, ending as a monk in a Buddhist monastery; and Ahmed Bey Zogolli, who ruled Albania for eleven years as King Zog I; the editor of the *Neue Freie Presse* in Vienna, Dr Theodor Herzl, who dreamed his dream of a Jewish State; and a boy at school in Linz, Adolf Hitler.

Every Austrian schoolchild knew the Emperor was fond of boiled beef, slept on an army camp-bed, got up at four in the morning and performed his ablutions in a wooden tub. (There was no bathroom in the *Hofburg*, Schönbrunn Castle, or the villa at Ischl.)

For the more critical among his subjects he was a tired old man, weighed down by his duties, unobjectionable but intellectually insignificant, an obstacle to all progress. Outside the Army List he never read a book, and he totally ignored new inventions like typewriters, lifts, telephones and motor cars. His taste for being independent of advisers, and his consequent refusal to delegate, made Austrian politics a morass of sloppiness and indecision.

His heir apparent, the Archduke Franz Ferdinand, worried more than any other Austrian about the monarchy's future, and thought more intensively about a constitutional solution. Owing to the death of the Crown Prince Rudolf, Franz Ferdinand had become the second most important man in the monarchy.

When he was forty he fell in love with the thirty-two-year-old Countess Sophie Chotek. As the Choteks were considered of inferior birth, and the heir apparent insisted on his choice, the Court lawyers drafted a plan for a morganatic marriage.

On 28th June 1900 Franz Ferdinand gave his solemn promise to recognize unconditionally the restrictions imposed by his action and to exclude from the succession "any children that by God's grace should issue from the marriage". He had exactly fourteen more years to live—to the day and hour—and never in that time did he forget the humiliation he had suffered. His Vienna residence, the Belvedere, became the seat of a shadow government, which fought against the prevailing shifts and compromises, against the political complications that grew more and more overwhelming, against the whole Empire's decline.

The curse of the Habsburgs, according to Franz Grillparzer,[1] the great dramatic poet, was "to go half-way, with acts half carried through, and with half-measures to dally undecided". Franz Ferdinand was not a man for half-measures. If the monarchy was to survive, he argued, its dualistic Austro-Hungarian basis must be transformed into a federal state comprising all its peoples —with the United States of Greater Austria as final objective.

His memoranda were noted by the Emperor—and pigeonholed. The Austrian style of muddling through and using delaying tactics on vital matters did not stop even for the heir apparent.

[1] In his tragedy *"Ein Bruderzwist im Hause Habsburg"*, II, 2 (A Fraternal Feud in the House of Habsburg).

With growing impatience he waited for his time: he knew it must come, though it was a long time coming.

Splendid Advances

While the general Austrian malaise grew, those with drive and originality withdrew from statecraft—into the arts. That was where the revolution took place for Austria's renaissance. The splendid advances made here produced a new approach to art, led by the author and dramatist Hermann Bahr. The *art nouveau* movement which spread all over Europe, reacting against traditionalism, found its Viennese expression in the *Wiener Sezession*. Klimt and Kokoschka gave "the age its art, the art its freedom".[1] Adolf Loos shook off the pompous style in architecture, and the *Wiener Werkstätte* (Vienna Workshop) called for the incorporation of art into the whole of human life. Young Vienna was represented in the world of letters by Schnitzler, Hofmannsthal, Peter Altenberg; and the scores of Gustav Mahler and Arnold Schoenberg mingled the pains of parting with the joy of new birth.

Thus in the dying monarchy on the Danube political and cultural developments ran in different directions, towards opposite destinations: one to disintegration, the other to world fame; one dragging on from crisis to crisis, the other sweeping from achievement to achievement; one symbolized by the Emperor's confession that he found himself "mentally declining",[2] the other by Hermann Bahr's cry of triumph, "Friends, the weather is changing!"[3]

An Average Year

The year 1905 was not one of those which light up all the future like a flame. It might be considered an average year, but nevertheless there was a great deal of ferment taking place, social, political, cultural: it was a year of continuing change.

Old ideas were sinking, new ones coming to the surface. Thought processes, morals, aesthetic and scientific attitudes were altering; people had taken on the aspect of the young century.

[1] Motto of the *Sezession*.   [2] Letter to Katharina Schratt, 11th March 1902.
[3] From Bahr's essay, Expressionism.

The decisive thing, however, was not that the first sleeping- and dining-cars were whizzing over the rails, or that the first omnibuses were filling the main streets, the first cocktails being drunk; but that with extreme rapidity all such phenomena were becoming accepted as normal and natural.

Only two years earlier the Wright Brothers had seemed like magicians when they stayed in the air for twelve seconds with their flying-machine;[1] four years later Louis Blériot would be crossing the channel by air.[2] Mr Rolls and Mr Royce in Manchester were just tinkering with their new kind of motor; soon their car would become the symbol of luxury and comfort. The first telegram had just been sent round the world in six hours; and already the wireless transmission of speech and music was turning into a reality.

1905! People lived in rooms overcrowded with furniture. Ladies wore clothes of plush velvet lined with satin, gentlemen frock coats with high stiff collars.

Lefcadio Hearn's books about Japan gained a wide readership, and in Vienna every number of Karl Kraus's satirical journal *Die Fackel* (The Torch) was eagerly absorbed. Sarah Bernhardt held French theatregoers in her thrall, Ellen Terry and Eleonore Duse those of Britain and Italy.

Maeterlinck's play *Monna Vanna* was hotly discussed, so was Siegfried Wagner's opera *Der Kobold* (The Goblin). A new Italian conductor, Arturo Toscanini, was reaching his peak; so were the Italian tenor Enrico Caruso, the Russian bass Chaliapin, the Spanish 'cellist Pablo Casals, the Viennese violinist Fritz Kreisler— and the most fascinating of all ballerinas, Anna Pavlova.

Names, images, echoes . . . only a few, the loftiest and most important among them, today still valid symbols of the age, while most of the others have faded away, sunk into oblivion.

The Merry Widow, operetta in three acts, book by Victor Léon and Leo Stein, music by Franz Lehár, which never claimed to be lofty or important, remained the reflection of its period. Chiefly, no doubt, owing to its exuberant and rousing score, but perhaps

[1] On 17th March 1903, in Kitty Hawk, North Carolina.
[2] On 25th July 1909.

also because in its content it sublimated "world history à l'operette" into "operette à la world history". Because toasts here dissolved in *chansons*, and mass demonstrations in vocal ensembles. Because castles turned into little arbours, the head of state suddenly appeared as "silly, silly cavalier", and the suffragette as siren of the ball. Because concern with scientific and technical problems made way for the study of women, women, women; the *Pomp and Circumstance* march for the waltz of silent lips and whispering violins. Because, in fact, all melancholy and solemnity turned triumphantly into sparkling exuberance.

On the Way Home

Ludwig Karpath had breakfast at the Café Dobner, read the morning papers and smoked a fat cigar. The previous evening he had inquired at the Theater an der Wien when the dress rehearsal for the new operetta was taking place, and learned that it was tomorrow morning at ten. He looked at his watch, paid, and walked over to the near-by stage door.

A strange sight met him there. The furniture of what looked to him like a cheap night-club was being unloaded from a small cart: gold tables and chairs, lamps with painted lamp-shades, bulbs fixed on glass, paper lanterns. Karpath shook his head and went up the creaking dark wooden staircase to the management offices.

His reception was not in accordance with his expectations nor with his position as first music critic of the *Neue Wiener Tagblatt*: through the open door of the inner sanctum the voice of Director Karczag boomed at him: "What are you doing here?"

"I wish to attend the dress rehearsal!" Karpath announced haughtily, his dignity offended.[1] "Nothing doing!" Karczag waved a dismissive hand. "Public not admitted to dress rehearsal."

"But, Vilmos, old chap," protested the critic, "am I public?" (They had both started in Budapest years earlier as local reporters on the same paper.)

"Public or not, we can't do with you today. Clear out!"

[1] Karpath's own description of the scene in his Memoirs.

"Can't do with *me*?" Karpath lost his temper. "You know what *you* can do? You can . . ." He stormed off. On the stairs he felt someone clutching his arm.

"It was Lehár (he related) imploring me in the most urgent terms to stay in the theatre, he would soon put things right. I told him I refused to take favours from theatre managers, and hurried towards the exit. But now Karczag was there: 'The dress rehearsal doesn't start till twelve thirty, let's go for a walk now, then to my flat for refreshments. But first apologize for what you said!'

"I did as I was bidden, and we strolled around, ending at Karczag's flat. The food was brought at once, for by then it was half past eleven, and Karczag naturally wanted to get back to the theatre. 'You know, it was Léon,' he told me, 'who as producer didn't want anyone in the house, least of all a critic. We've spent nothing on dresses and décor.' (Here Karpath remembered the gold tables and paper lanterns outside the stage door.) 'We haven't done enough rehearsing, everything's at sixes and sevens—one can't risk the presence of newspaper people. But we'll try to keep the operetta going until we've rehearsed thoroughly for another show . . .'"

Then he asked Karpath to avoid unnecessary scenes, and to sit in a corner of the dress circle. After the first act he crept over to him: "Well, what d'you think?"

"I think you're all utter fools. What I've heard so far is excellent, and if it goes on the same way . . ."

"I must tell Léon at once!"

Karpath was brought down in triumph from the dress circle and given a seat in the front row of the stalls. Lehár winked at him from the conductor's desk at the end of each number, and looked "highly satisfied" with the critic's shouts of "Bravo!" After the second act the atmosphere had improved, after the third those involved felt confident of a "friendly success". Léon even went so far as to predict a run of forty to fifty performances.

Forty to fifty performances! (Lehár recalled years later what had gone through his head on the way home.)[1] He had hoped for more

---

[1] From written and oral accounts by Lehár, and from his article *Confessions*, written in 1946.

from *The Merry Widow*, despite Léon's brusque letter after he had played the score to him for the first time: "Shall I be quite frank? I miss any strong, original music, anything absolutely compelling. Don't fob me off with the orchestration, in this context it's unimportant. Your waltzes, for instance, are run-of-the-mill, and with waltzes particularly we need novelty of rhythm and new turns of melody. Otherwise better not have them."

"Léon is musical," Lehár continued his reflections as he walked along the *Getreidemarkt*. "He's a friend of mine, and a practical man of the theatre. He should be able to distinguish style from the lack of it, strong musical ideas from weak—even when it all sounds new, unusual and different to him. Doesn't he realize that I can only write like this and no other way? Doesn't he notice the novelty in my work? Can't he hear that I am trying to give a different melody for a different age? A few years ago when I plunged into Viennese operetta blind and unsuspecting, I fancied that my ignorance of the *métier* would be an advantage for me, would make me an experimenter: someone to blast a tunnel through the dark mountain to the light on the other side. I wanted new subjects, new people, new forms! Because I'm a man of the present, not an echo of the past. *The Merry Widow* is an experiment! If Léon is expecting an ordinary musical farce from me with dance numbers and drinking songs thrown in—he's making a mistake. I recognize that as a commodity the operetta must consider the demands of the masses to a certain extent. All the same, it has no obligation to be farce or comedy. I'm against operetta nonsense. I want to write music for and around human beings: their hearts and souls, their emotions and passions, their joy and sadness. If as they all say I haven't succeeded this time, then I'll reach my goal next time or the time after. I'll let any friend, especially my collaborators, guide, warn, advise and criticize me. But there's only one court I can bow to, my own conscience."

Lehár had reached the Mariahilferstrasse. He opened the door of Number 5 and went up to the third floor. It was not till he entered his flat that he realized how tired the rehearsal had made him. He flung himself down on the divan, and fell into a deep, peaceful sleep.

PART TWO

Full Splendour
1905-1924

VI
LIPS ARE SILENT, VIOLINS WHISPER

A Find at Lindau's

On free afternoons Leo Stein often visited his well-read and helpful friend, Carl Lindau, the librettist of *Die Landstreicher* (The Vagabonds) and *Frühlingsluft* (Spring Air), to have a browse round his extensive theatrical library. During one most fortunate visit he took down a small book from the shelves, No. 124 of the collection called *Viennese Theatre Repertoire*:

The Attaché
A Comedy in Three Acts
from the French by
Henri Meilhac

Stein knew the writer as co-author of the books for *Carmen*, *Manon* and all the big Offenbach operettas; and he knew the play from its production at the Burgtheater. But it was only now, skimming through the pages, that he thought of its eminent suitability as a libretto. It was the story of the immensely rich young widow Madeleine von Palmer, who was to marry the dashing young attaché, Count Prachs: a match made by the Ambassador, Baron Scharpf, so that her native country, a small duchy in Germany, should keep her fortune. Effective situations were garnished with witty dialogue, spoken by interesting characters; and the Paris success soon made its way all over Europe. In April 1863 the play reached Vienna and achieved 110 performances, the last taking place half a year before the first performance of *The Merry Widow*.

From the moment when Stein brought him *The Attaché*, Léon had no doubts: the idea was splendid operetta material. The authors set to work straight away and with great gusto.

For the sake of the musico-folkloristic colour, the German duchy was turned into a Balkan principality. Madeleine became Hanna Glawari, Prachs became Danilo Danilovich, and Meilhac's slightly old-fashioned conversation piece was transformed (by the addition of a brilliantly invented story of the earlier relations between the young lovers) into a modern libretto ripe for music.

Léon and Stein did not worry about Meilhac's copyright: the Viennese custom of using stories "from the French" was older than the operetta. Meilhac had died in 1897, and no heirs could be found. They turned up with their claims only after the world success of *The Merry Widow*. But the famous Parisian barrister Raymond Poincaré (his political career had been interrupted at the time) succeeded in bringing about a settlement: the Viennese undertook to pay a share of the royalties, the French acknowledged the artistic independence of the operetta book.

As for the choice of composer, Léon and Stein were agreed directly they sketched out the libretto: for its light tone and Parisian subject *The Merry Widow* could be set to music by only one man: Richard Heuberger.

The Obvious Choice

Heuberger was a gifted musician: conductor, composer, musicologist and critic.

After a few unremarkable operas and ballets he wrote his masterpiece: the operetta *Der Opernball*. For years he had been looking for librettos, when he had a brainwave: "The plan to base an opera or operetta on the comedy, *The Pink Dominos*,"[1] he recalled later, "came from me and Victor Léon simultaneously. I had asked him to meet me at a café to discuss a possibility of this kind, and had come with the intention of suggesting the French play to him. When Léon came, before he had even taken off his coat, he said on a hint from me, 'There's only one thing

[1] By Hennequin and Delacour (1876).

I've got in mind—*Pink Dominos.*' The matter was decided."

What Heuberger attempted was the creation of a new genre, the intimate operetta. He dispensed with elaborate costumes, grand choruses and high drama, continuing where Offenbach and Strauss (after *Parisian Life* and *Fledermaus*) had left off, and succeeded, according to the critic Eduard Hanslick, "in keeping pure the ideas and aesthetics of the Viennese operetta". His melodies have nobility and elegant catchiness; the score's jewel, "Come into the *chambre separée*", may be placed in the first class among all Viennese operetta songs.

Although he had established a direction, however, Heuberger did not succeed in ensuring continuity for the genre. None of his later operettas contained that one great enchanting and captivating tune one was always waiting for.

Nevertheless, Léon and Stein with their *Merry Widow* book set all their hopes on the repetition of an *Opernball*—miracle. They had conceived the libretto in the style of the new intimate operetta, and Heuberger—whether or not he was successful at the moment— was the master of the species: surely, therefore, he must be the right man for *The Merry Widow*. They presented him with the first act; and he started composing the music for it.

The Second Candidate

Between the prospective and the eventual composer of *The Merry Widow* there was an earlier connection, for which we must go back to the spring of 1901, when Lehár had said good-bye to military bands, and had not yet started as *Kapellmeister* at the Theater an der Wien. He heard there was a vacancy for a conductor of the special popular concerts given by the Wiener Konzertverein (Vienna Concert Society), applied for an audition and conducted a concert in the Volksgarten. On the judges' platform, full of dignity as befitted a man with a decisive vote, sat Vienna's musical pope, Professor Richard Heuberger, Like Herr Beckmesser in *The Mastersingers*, he marked

> every fault, both grave and slight,
> . . . on the board aright,

and in due course reached the verdict "outclassed and outsung". Heuberger's version of this was: "Lehár possesses a good knowledge of classical music, but fails when faced with the modern waltz."

Three years later, by an ironical coincidence, Karczag, Léon and Stein (with Louis Treumann tucked away in the next room) passed the same judgement word for word on Heuberger when he played over to them the first act of his *Merry Widow*. They were disappointed at the feeble, uninspired musical hotchpotch, and decided at once that they must take the book away from Heuberger. Yet they did not think at once of giving it to Lehár, although they had all had favourable experiences with him already.

Why was he not Léon's immediate choice? Perhaps his "deviation" to Julius Bauer (with *The Mock Marriage*) rankled; or perhaps, despite the discouraging outlook for Ascher's *God Bless You For It*, Léon wished to advance the cause of Lizzy's present favourite.

Lasting credit must go to the good Schlaraffian Emil Steininger for bringing Lehár into it and suggesting he should be asked to compose a specimen number. Perhaps Steininger's persuasiveness came at the right moment for Léon, who "let himself be dragged (as they say in Vienna) but was really quite pleased to go". The next morning Lehár received the text of the song "Silly, Silly Cavalier"; in the evening he played Léon his music for it, and from then on *The Merry Widow*'s road was clear.

As for Heuberger, he had never been quite happy about his work on the new libretto, and now abandoned the assignment without making difficulties. He made one further attempt at music for an operetta, but after it had proved a pathetic failure he gave up all aspirations in that direction.

In the summer Lehár retired to the Salzkammergut with Léon and Stein, and in September Karczag and Wallner heard the new music. There is an often-quoted story that Karczag's immediate reaction was to exclaim "That's not music at all"; but its authenticity may be doubted. He was excitable and very quick to come out with his views, but he had a reliable ear for a good tune. The fact that in later years he told the story himself is not very strong evidence: Karczag had a sense of humour, could enjoy a joke against himself, and was also vain enough not to leave the laughs to other raconteurs. Lehár denied having heard the famous exclamation, but admitted that he was on tenterhooks all the way through, that the reception of the music was "definitely not encouraging", and that afterwards, during the rehearsals, Karczag offered him a compensation of 5,000 crowns if he would withdraw the operetta.

The bitter words spoken in those days between Karczag, Wallner, Lehár and Léon should not be taken as a criterion of the prospects for *The Merry Widow*. It was common enough for the authors to demand a more lavish production, and natural enough for the managers to limit their generosity after the failure of the last two new pieces at this theatre. In fact, they felt obliged to rush on the première for the 30th December because the last one, Leo Fall's *The Rebel* had failed.

The disaster was caused solely by an execrable libretto (by Ernst Welisch and Rudolf Bernauer), full of idiotic situations and hackneyed jokes. Fall, however, had irradiated it to such an extent with the glow of his youthful inspiration that Karczag accepted it nevertheless, and gave the authors an advance of 12,000 crowns. The first night (on 25th November 1905) led to a riot, and the company was subjected to a chorus of hissing. The press agreed with the reactions of the audience, and *The Rebel* was taken off after five performances.

During its last night Victor Léon (rather like Julius Bauer at the première of *Viennese Women*) drew the house's attention to himself. He paced angrily up and down the stalls, and abused the audience loudly for their deafness to good music. "Bravo, Leo Fall, bravooo!" he shouted repeatedly—although he might have been the last person to regret the fiasco, since it cleared the way for his own *Merry Widow*. But where operetta and a bright new talent were concerned, Léon was like a man possessed; forgetting all about his own advantage, he fought for the cause.

Karczag fought, too, and not only to redeem his 12,000 crowns. He sent the authors back to Berlin, telling them to start at once on a thorough revision.

Meanwhile preparations for *The Merry Widow* were going ahead at a great pace. Unlike the management, no one in the company had any doubts about the coming triumph. They were all infected by the enthusiasm which Treumann and Mizzi Günther put into their work. Treumann had been a little jealous when he saw for the first time la Günther's sensational dresses (paid for out of her own pocket), since no suitable diplomatic uniform had yet been found for *him*. But then one day the well-known Viennese pianist Alfred Grünfeld showed his friend Léon a photograph sent to him in dedication by the Crown Prince of Montenegro, showing the Prince in full regalia. Both Léon and Treumann fell for the costume, and it became the gala dress worn from then on by every Danilo to strut through the second act.

As the Theater an der Wien was empty at the time, rehearsals often went on the whole day and until two or three in the morning. Léon ordered cartloads of sausages, beer and fresh rolls, arranged for coaches and cabs to take everyone home, and encouraged the whole company from his producer's table.

The first night achieved a sweeping success, according to the *Volksblatt*, "thanks to the magnificent music, based on an intelligent book, and to the excellent production". Other critical voices sounded less enthusiastic—but Treumann and Mizzi Günther took the audience by storm. Vienna's *arbiter elegantiarum*, Karl Kraus, hated the new production and considered it "the most distasteful I have ever seen in a theatre".

Scarely anyone at the first night guessed the unprecedented success which lay ahead for *The Merry Widow*, or the operetta's decisive significance.

Karczag felt he should cover his retreat, and at the beginning of January sent a telegram to the librettists of *The Rebel* in Berlin: "Expedite revision stop expect you soonest with book." A week later: "When can we expect you?" After another week: "Completion Rebel brooks no postponement".

Then early in February, when Fall, Bernauer and Welisch were about to leave Berlin with *Princess Caprice* (the new *Rebel*), a letter came from Vienna, telling them not to rush things: they should take their time over completing the work, and would shortly be hearing further. "We never did hear anything 'further'," Bernauer recalls in his memoirs.[1] "*The Merry Widow*, for which the takings had been very low until its twenty-fifth performance, suddenly soared, bringing nothing but sold-out houses every day for months—and years."

Desires, Impulses, Passions

Forty effervescent prestissimo bars, and the curtain rises on a ball in the Pontevedrin Embassy in Paris—only a slight change, of course, from Montenegrin. The French colony are celebrating the birthday of their Prince. Valencienne, the beautiful wife of Zeta, the elderly ambassador, is flirting vigorously with the young Camille de Rosillon, but her husband cannot at the moment be bothered with such trifles. His Highness has foisted on him the widowed Hanna Glawari, giving him the commission to marry off the young lady—so that his country shall keep her twenty-million fortune—to his attaché, Count Danilo. Danilo refuses. He is at home at "Maxim's", where there are "undoubtedly the most doubtful little ladies!"

Years ago he had loved Hanna, when she was the daughter of a small farmer and his aristocratic family would not consent to such a misalliance; then Prince Glawari, the richest man in Pontevedro, snapped her up under his nose. Now they meet each other again: free, but irresolute, hesitant, stubborn. Which of them was it in those days that let the other down? Zeta calls for a "lady's choice"; Danilo is at once surrounded by sirens of the ball, but pines for Hanna, who has fixed her gaze on him. The sound of a waltz is heard:

[1] Rudolf Bernauer: *Das Theater meines Lebens* (The Theatre of My Life), Berlin, 1955.

Violins and 'cellos, harps, *Glockenspiel*. The old feelings are still intact; she fights for a while, then flies into his arms and dances with him: "You horrible man! How beautifully you dance!" And he laughs back: "One does one's best."

Act II: At the Pontevedro festival in the gardens of the Palais Glawari in Paris, Hanna sings the song of the nymph Vilia:

She courts Danilo, but the "silly, silly cavalier" rides on. His basic principle is:

> Fall often in love, betroth yourself seldom,
> But at all costs never wed.

In an almost silent dramatic scene the great love tune sounds for the first time, and without words:

Camille and Valencienne come together for their romance: "See, there's a little arbour"—one of Lehár's richest inspirations.

To save her friend Valencienne from the Ambassador's jealousy, Hanna says that *she* had the rendezvous with Camille—and had become engaged to him. Danilo is furious. For the marriage ahead he tells the widow the story of the two prince's children:

ES WA-REN ZWEI KÖ-NIGS-KIN- DER, DIE HAT-TEN EIN-AN-DER SO LIEB- - - - -

He pretends not to be worried about her infidelity—"That's where you are wrong—ha, ha!" He makes an elegant bow, and goes off to where he is at home, to Maxim's. Hanna is jubilant: he has fallen into her trap—he loves her!

The third act takes place again in the Palais Glawari. Hanna has rearranged the great hall to be like Maxim's, and invited the "little ladies", Lolo, Dodo, Jou-jou, Clo-Clo, Margot and Frou-Frou, to perform their famous can-can. The old Ambassador is in despair over the alleged engagement between Hanna and Camille, which will mean bankruptcy for the Pontevedrin economy. Danilo is sent off to appeal to Hanna's patriotism. She explains to him what really happened in the little arbour. Then she tells him she has lost her whole fortune. Danilo interrupts her: "What, Hanna, you have no money?" He falls at her feet: "I love you!" Hanna goes on: ". . . lost by Glawari's will, lost—to my new husband!" The country is saved. Danilo has to accept his destiny—"but," he insists, "I'd have married you if you'd had forty million!"

The complete novelty of *The Merry Widow* lies in the frankly erotic nature of its subject, and in the ingenious boldness with which the vibrant sensuality of the story is musically interpreted. From the moment right at the beginning when Valencienne, the "respectable wife", dupes her lover by informing him bluntly that she takes her marriage seriously and would on no account risk "adventures of this sort", to Danilo's last waltz phrase, 'Lips are silent, violins whisper: love me, do!' the hundred melodies in the score sing of nothing but desires, impulses, passions, embraces and kisses.

The gay "top hat, white tie and tails" canzonetta about Maxim's, the transition in Hanna's entrance song from the Slavonic mazurka to the Parisian *valse lente* (with the shimmering A of the flutes over the melody of the violins), the jubilant five upbeats of the "Sirens of the Ball" waltz, the elemental vigour of the "Women!" march, the daring temptation in Camille's $\frac{6}{8}$ aria, the coquettishness of "Silly, silly Cavalier"—they form a single intoxicating flow of musical ideas of sublimest stamp. It is controversial whether the operetta's most popular number, "Vilia, o Vilia", represents its high point or its low. The first four notes are the same very characteristic ones with which the great waltz starts, only here the inspiration is more primitive, and certainly not at all in keeping with the folkloristic colour of the Slavonic rest of the score. The statement may sound surprising only if we forget that this "most Slavonic" Lehár melody was conceived as a duet for the *Göttergatte*, the least folkloristic of all his works. It was cut before the dress rehearsal, dug out by Léon at the time of the *Widow*—and had therefore by no means gained its timbre through its origins. For the most part the folkloristic quality arose from the composer's deep-rooted Slavonic feeling and style of musical thinking; from the general "Pontevedrin atmosphere" on the stage; and above all from the striking individuality of Lehár's orchestral treatment.

In the score of *The Merry Widow* he tried all possible tonal devices, however bold and hazardous. Orchestral colouring, as used up till now only by Richard Strauss, Mahler or Debussy, suddenly became part of the operetta palette. The violins, divided three- and fourfold, sang at heights never reached before in this type of music—or kept up there their alluring harmonies; most surprising was the use of the clarinets' lower register; the flutes scurried across the pages of the score, joining up with the glissando of the harp; and the harp—released from the Oompapa of ordinary hack treatment—illuminated the orchestral scene. The oboe piped the tune enticingly, the bassoon was given special comedy counterpoints, guitars and tambourines thrummed, and the brass, instead of blaring, was arranged for soft velvety sounds. All these effects gave the music its surprisingly different style, and played their part in lifting the genre operetta from the *gemütliche* old Viennese into the universal and international sphere.

In Vienna, Lehár has often been criticized for following his own artistic voice, and not remaining attached to the Viennese soil—even though his music displays (in the words of one critic) "a truly Viennese ecstasy of colour to be heard in his glorious, variegated, delicate waltzes". Is *The Merry Widow* less Viennese because of its geographical setting than *Vienna Blood* and *Viennese Women*, or than the *Gypsy Baron*, set in Hungary, *The Beggar Student* in Poland, and *Boccaccio* in Italy? Is being "Viennese born and bred" an absolutely essential part, in fact, of the Viennese operetta, so that Italians like Suppé, Magyars like Kálmán and Czechs like Ralph Bentatzky could not contribute their delightful powers to it? Was it not finally time, after the dull and brainless operettas of the nadir, to lead the gay genre to the spirit of the new music, the new century?

Old Girardi referred to the new operettas contemptuously, with an understandable resentment, as "Ibsen dramas with a hop, skip and jump". The young, on the other hand, despised the operetta of the past as (in the words of Ernst Decsey) a "refuge of stupidity". "Its tonic-dominant barrel organ-grinding was merely pitiful. Now it had class. The new harmonic consciousness sounded through the simplest cadenzas. The unpalatable became highly enjoyable, the unattractive delightful: *The Merry Widow* meant a new turn in the history of the operetta."

"Why did no one get bored now?" asks the historian H. E. Jacob.[1] "It was real people who sang; it was a matter of gay, contemporary *joie de vivre*. The music had lightness and clarity, and it also administered a series of bewildering small electric shocks. It was healthy and charmingly over-perfumed. *Fledermaus* 1906!"

The Road to Success

The final curtain on the first night came down at a quarter past ten. Lehár was duly applauded, but admitted having "by no means the impression of a big success". He waited till Mizzi Günther had

---

1 Heinrich Eduard Jacob: *Johann Strauss, Vater und Sohn* (Johann Strauss, Father and Son), Hamburg, 1953.

changed, then they went off together to the near-by Café Museum. There Oscar Straus came to meet them. He had been at the premiére, and congratulated his friends. Lehár considered this more as professional politeness than artistic conviction. But Straus meant it. Without envy and with firm confidence he predicted a world success.

That *The Merry Widow* survived the first precarious weeks of its existence was again thanks to the pertinacity and assiduity of Emil Steininger. Undeterred by empty houses and warnings from expert café regulars, he distributed complimentary tickets, until the charms of the operetta began to be talked about all over Vienna. But that still did not mean a rush on the box office. From the middle of March onwards there was a threat of withdrawal. It did not seem worthwhile, however, with the end of the season in April, to rehearse a new piece; this was the only reason why the *Widow* celebrated its hundredth performance on 7th April, its 119th on the night before Lehár's thirty-sixth birthday. From the day after that the Raimundtheater in the suburb of Mariahilf happened to be free, and Karczag transferred the operetta there.[1] In the middle of September it "came home again" with fresh suburban laurels.

As with *The Tinker*, garden, park and café concerts had made the music popular. The nightly takings soared from 1,600 to 5,000 kronen, and the "sold out" notice hung on the window of the closed box office almost every evening. Now Karczag finally decided to give the operetta a worthier presentation: he had new décor painted, provided new tail-coats and evening dresses for the ballroom scene, new *frou-frous* for the ladies from Maxim's. The only thing he stipulated was that the old paper lanterns stayed: out of superstition, he said.

The Merry Widow remained now in the repertoire until the end of the 1907 season. On 24th April that year it had its 400th performance. The road to further success was well marked out.

Already during the 1906/7 season there was scarcely a provincial theatre in Austria which did not perform it. Now Germany

---

[1] Two years later he took over with Wallner the management of the Raimundtheater.

followed. Ludwig Karpath was in at the beginning here, too: immediately after the dress rehearsal he telegraphed to his friend Arthur Nikisch, the famous conductor then Director of the Leipzig Municipal Theatre, calling his attention to the operetta. It also came out in Hamburg and soon after in Berlin.[1] "Anyone who said that operetta was dead", wrote the Berlin *Börsen-Courier*, "will have corrected his mistaken view yesterday: it is alive, and will go on living."

In 1907 the *Lustige Witwe* conquered London, New York, Stockholm; in 1908 Copenhagen, Moscow, Milan, in 1909 Madrid and Paris; in 1910 Brussels: by twenty-five names, as *Merry Widow, Viuda Alegre, Den Glade Enke, Vessela Vdova, Veuve Joyeuse, Vedova Allegra, A vig Özvegy*, etc., it travelled and still travels all over the world. London may claim the credit of having given the Vienna and Berlin success a start on its international career.

After the glories of the Gilbert and Sullivan comic operas, Britain's light-music theatre was now taken over by a new, realistic and no less typically British kind of operetta, the musical comedy. Its pacemaker was George Edwardes, a tall, handsome Irishman, universally known as "The Guv'nor". He had served his apprenticeship in the Gilbert, Sullivan and D'Oyly Carte organization, and now went to work with immense vigour to help the new fashion become established in his own Gaiety Theatre. As theatre manager he was an impulsive gambler; he knew little of music or drama, but with his almost infallible flair for contemporary taste he managed to put the stamp of his mighty personality on everything: the piece itself, the music, acting, chorus, décor and costumes. The chief principle of his theatrical productions was: the public is always right.

His shows had unprecedented runs, and he boasted of having made four million pounds with Sidney Jones's *The Geisha* and *San Toy*. He succeeded in attracting a circle of brilliantly gifted composers, who left Offenbach, Strauss and Sullivan with their laurels and struck a bold new note. Edwardes's success is explicable first and foremost by the popularity of his Gaiety shows, Gaiety stars and the charms of the chorus girls, but secondly by the habit of

[1] On 1st May 1906.

regular theatre-going which was then just starting: parties of six, eight and a dozen people would quite often go to the theatre together, to enjoy birthdays, anniversaries or other family celebrations by "seeing a show". Evening after evening presents and prizes were distributed by Edwardes to enthusiasts who could prove they were seeing a particular musical comedy for the hundredth or hundred and fiftieth time.

At the end of 1905, when the magic of his repertoire was gradually beginning to wear thin, he directed his gaze on Vienna. In February 1906 he went there; but the operetta *Krieg im Frieden* (War in Peace), which he wanted to buy, had disappeared from the programme. A theatrical agent talked to him about a new composer, Leo Fall, who was working on an operetta that seemed just made for England: *Die Dollarprinzessin* (The Dollar Princess). Fall played over the score, Edwardes was duly impressed, signed a contract, paid an advance—only to be informed shortly afterwards that the operetta could hardly be ready for production within a year. How was he to meet his repertoire needs till then?

Fall suggested having a look at the operetta by his friend Franz Lehár, then running at the Theater an der Wien—*The Merry Widow*.

Delirium in London

The Merry Widow is not set, as *Die lustige Wittwe* was, in Pontevedro, but in Marsovia. The title role was not called Hanna but Sonia, Valencienne became Natalie, Camille Jolidon, Zeta Popoff. Vilia remained Vilia, Maxim's and Danilo also kept their original names. Danilo was not played by the typical young matinée idol, but by Joseph Coyne, a rather mournful-looking, chubby-cheeked American comedian of forty. Although in his way he possessed great charm, Coyne was not at all Danilo-esque, and originally refused the part. Edwardes had to work on him for weeks before he decided to take it on.

The Guv'nor didn't worry unduly. He was used to treating his theatre as an asylum, his actors as lunatics, and Coyne—with his phobia of starvation, his mania for ice-cream and his extreme stinginess—as their leader. Anyhow Coyne remained convinced right up to the end that, despite his world success in the part, he was miscast. Years later, when he took off his Danilo costume for the last time, he breathed a sigh of relief. "No tears from me," he told a friend.

While the English Danilo was completely different from the Viennese, the Widow, Sonia, except for a rather smaller waist, was like a twin of the Widow, Hanna, in Vienna. Lily Elsie came from the Midlands. She was twenty-one and had been on the stage for ten years, a beauty of the English Rose type. Edwardes sent her to Vienna to see the operetta; she came home firmly resolved on withdrawal: she was as scared of her part as Coyne was of his. So the Guv'nor had to redouble his persuasive arts.

With George Graves, where he might have expected to need them, they proved unnecessary. Edwardes realized from the start that if *The Merry Widow* was to have a chance of success in London it would require something almost entirely lacking in its Viennese form: a strong dose of robust humour. Graves had served his theatrical apprenticeship in pantomime, and was considered a specialist in the broad comedy which lies on the borders between wisdom and nonsense. After reading the thinnish part of the Ambassador, he made only one condition, that he should be allowed to adapt it to his own personality and expand it. This was exactly what the Guv'nor wanted, and Graves set to work: by alone, for he knew his trade and refused to try out his jokes on fellow members of the cast. He did not let himself go till the first night, when in three or four solo scenes, quite unrelated to story and characterization, he had the house roaring with irrepressible laughter. His Popoff—with red nose and snuff-box, his legs astride and his right hand on his cheek supported by his left elbow resting on his stomach—became a larger-than-life Falstaffian type.

He played the part for forty-two years, and whatever else he occasionally played in between, he was ever and again the Marsovian Ambassador. He played it before three generations, four English kings, nine British Prime Ministers and four Archbishops of Canterbury. He played it in eleven London and 250 provincial theatres, with thirty Sonias and thirty-five Danilos—and throughout the Second World War.

Shortly before his death he was asked by a journalist how often he had played Popoff. "Can't say exactly," Graves answered. "After the three thousandth time I stopped counting."

Lehár did not like him when he saw him for the first time. For one thing he considered the laughter of the audience chiefly as an unpleasant interruption of the musical or dramatic proceedings; for another, he did not understand a single word of what Mr Graves said. Altogether, since arriving in London and conducting the first rehearsal, he had been in a cantankerous mood, quite unlike him. Nothing suited him: the orchestra was too small, Miss Elsie too young, Mr Coyne's voice too weak, and so on.

Then came the delirium of the first night, the enthusiastic press next morning (8th June 1907)—and the rush on the box office. Lehár regained his old obligingness and affability. Before he returned to Vienna, Mr Edwardes informed him that advance sales had begun for performances over Christmas 1908—eighteen months ahead!

Like in Fairyland

Mama Lehár, who died[1] before the London triumph, still had great enjoyment in the last six months of her life from the Viennese one.

The story of her pride and delight is contained in her letters to Lehár's brother Anton. As early as the summer of 1905 she was telling the young officer—"since I am sure you will not let it go any further"—the story of the operetta. "The libretto is already finished, so that Franz can work in peace." "Don't reveal anything," she admonished, "be careful. I'm saying that to Franz, too, for in this respect he's terribly trusting." On the 18th March 1906 she wrote: "No one can blame me for feeling infinitely grateful to Franz. He has made such great sacrifices for me. May God repay them all to him many times over. That is my daily prayer. I couldn't go to the 75th *Merry Widow*. I prayed for Franz at home. I am often feverish. I can't get warm. It's only on sunny days that I feel a little easier. Oh well, as God wills."

[1] On 6th August 1906.

In May, when Lehár took her over his new flat, she commented: "Wherever you look, you find flowers, whole trees, lilacs, roses. When I entered the drawing-room, the view overcame me. The lighting was like in fairyland. Everything so nice and warm . . . we went from one room to another. Franz showed me everything. With his inimitable heart-warming kindness. My child seemed to me like a king—I could willingly have knelt down to thank God for so much happiness."

Her health grew worse; she was taken to Ischl. "I'm better, thank heavens," she reported. "I have hours without pain, and then I'm already content. Dear Toni, think often how fortunate you all are when you get up in the morning and nothing hurts! Take everything else in life as it comes. I always wanted to be an example to you, my children, of how to live frugally and within my means. But I shall always be grateful to Franz for taking away all the great worries from me. May God reward him! Good-bye. Can't go on. My hand's shaking too much."

Early in August the old Emperor came to the Ischl theatre to see the famous *Merry Widow*. Treumann and Mizzi Günther were in the company, Lehár conducted. That night he told his dying mother about it. "She couldn't speak any more," Anton recalls, "but she held my brother's hand and slowly, quite slowly, fell asleep."

Uniquer and Uniquer

"Curiouser and curiouser!" says Alice on looking round Wonderland. The story of *The Merry Widow* became uniquer and uniquer, the further it progressed in its starry orbit. The raptures of London were multiplied in New York, and a rampant Merry Widow craze developed throughout the United States. Cartwheel hats à la Merry Widow were all the fashion, Merry Widow shoes appeared, Merry Widow cigars, chocolates, corsets and perfumes; Merry Widow dogs were taken out on a lead. Merry Widow express trains whizzed through the country. Merry Widow escalopes were eaten and Merry Widow liqueurs drunk in Merry Widow restaurants to the accompaniment of a Merry Widow tambourine orchestra; and people went in for dance competitions where the best Danilo-Sonia couple were awarded prizes.

A model of the good-looking young composer with his intelligent light-blue eyes and boldly twirled moustache was to be found in every waxworks in the world; and in Vienna there was even a comedy put on, *Der grosse Name* (The Great Name), whose leading character was Lehár. Its authors: Leo Feld and his brother—Victor Léon.

The Montenegrin Embassy in Vienna protested against the undignified use of the word *njegus*, surname of the hereditary ruling family; while the Montenegrin Crown Prince Danilo stated with some amusement in a Paris interview that he did not intend to raise any objections against his alleged stage portrayal: it was, he said, by no means so inaccurate! In Cetinje (capital of Montenegro), Trieste and Constantinople there were actually political, anti-Austrian, anti-Merry Widow demonstrations. And we might note, while talking of politics, that Adolf Hitler saw his favourite operetta for the first time from the gallery standing-room at the Theater an der Wien in October 1907, at the time when he was trying in vain to get into the Viennese Academy of Art.

Among *The Merry Widow* conductors three names are worth mentioning: young Wilhelm Furtwängler in Zürich, young Erich Kleiber in Frankfurt and young Richard Tauber in Chemnitz. The actresses playing the title role included Marie Jeritza and Kirsten Flagstad, the Danilos Jan Kiepura and the great Swedish actor Gösta Ekman, who started his career in the chorus of Stockholm's first production. One of his young Scandinavian compatriots, the drama student Asta Nielsen, was so angry at the long-running *Merry Widow* which robbed her of all chances as a serious actress that she forsook the theatre and looked for new opportunities in the up-and-coming cinema.

During the rehearsals for the English operetta *The Maid of the Mountains* the producer asked the composer to produce a new waltz, "a bit like the one in *The Merry Widow*". "A bit like?" said Mr Harold Fraser-Simpson. "I'll simply write it once more—no, twice more!" He repeated each of the first four notes of "Lips are

WHEN THE TOWN GOES CRAZY

By T. E. Powers Copyright. 1908 by American-Journal-Examiner

The "*Merry Widow*" in New York. Cartoon from
The Evening American,
1909

Lehár at the time of
the Ninety-three days,
1910

Sophie Lehár
1920

Sigm. v. Skwirczynski: Die Fixsterne der Wiener Operette, umgeben von ihren Crabanten, im Café Museum.

"*The Stars of the Viennese Operetta, Surrounded by their Satellites*". Cartoon by Sigmund von Skwirczynski, 1912: Straus, Stein, Jacobson, Simon, Englander, Karczag, Reinhardt, Wallner, Willner, Herzmansky, Lehár, Berté, Lindau, Léon, Steininger, Bodanzky, Fall, Kálmán, Eysler, Schmiedell, Korngold, Bahr, Nedbal, Pallenberg.

Mizzi Günther and
Louise Kartousch, in
Eva, 1911

The "*Floh*" caricature. Fall,
Eysler, Straus, Lehár,
1914

The mountain scene from *Alone at Last*. Mizzi Günther—Hubert Marischka, 1914

SÜDDEUTSCHER VERLAG, MUNICH

Richard Strauss,
1909

ULLSTEIN GmbH, BERLIN

SUDDEUTSCHER VERLAG, MUNICH

Giacomo Puccini,
1920

Richard Tauber, 1923

Lehár in Ischl,
1922

PHOTO HOFER, BAD ISCHL

Lehár, Tauber, Jenbach, 1924

silent", and as "Whate'er Befall, I'll still Recall", the tune became
world-famous for the second time.

It is impossible to give an exact figure for *Merry Widow* performances. If we take 15,000 as maximum and 1,000 as minimum,
making an average number of 8,000 a year, we get a total of about
half a million performances within sixty years. One Saturday in
1907 in Buenos Aires *The Merry Widow* was put on in five theatres
in five different languages, ten times counting the afternoon and
evening performances.

The sale of piano scores, sheet music, and arrangements for
small and large orchestras, runs to between twenty-five and thirty
million, the sale of gramophone records between forty and fifty
million. The work in its entirety has also been selected twenty-
five times in seven languages for long-playing records. "I
don't let a month pass," confessed Alan Jay Lerner, librettist of
My Fair Lady, "without playing over *The Merry Widow* to
myself."

The first *Merry Widow* film was shot in 1907: in Sweden by
the Nordisk Company. It ran for fourteen minutes. In 1908 the
Pathé film, *La valse de la Veuve Joyeuse* (six minutes), followed, and
Edison's *The Merry Widow Waltz Craze*. In 1925 Erich von
Stroheim brought out the spectacular *Merry Widow* silent film
(John Gilbert as Danilo, Mae Murray as Sonia); in 1934 Ernst
Lubitsch shot his *Merry Widow* with Maurice Chevalier and
Jeanette Macdonald, in 1952 Curtis Berhardt directed his with
Lana Turner and Fernando Lamas.

The Merry Widow is the only musical stage work which had an
overture written thirty-five years after its first stage production:
for a concert by the Vienna Philharmonic Orchestra in celebration
of Lehár's seventieth birthday. (We remember the composer's
overture-phobia since *Viennese Women*.) It was a symphonic, contrapuntal arrangement of all the melodies of the operetta: effective
as a concert piece, though unsuitable for theatrical use because of its
length and the vast orchestra needed.

In the city council of Plauen in Saxony, a certain Dr Petzoldt
in 1907 made explicit reference to the indecency of the Lehár
operetta: "It is so shocking it does not belong on any decent

stage!" The citizens of Plauen responded by storming the municipal theatre's box office. "A mockery of municipal authority!" thundered the Doctor, and demanded that "similar productions" should henceforth be banned.

A manual for essays at American private schools for girls (published in 1910) contains under the heading "Love" three subjects (with musical illustrations from *The Merry Widow*):
A) "Love as pastime" ("I go off to Maxim's");
B) "Love as Adventure" ("See, there's a little arbour there"); and
C) "Love as Destiny" ("Lips are silent, violins whisper").

Among many strange productions of *The Merry Widow* some are indeed passing strange: in Chicago, for instance, the operetta was danced silently as a ballet; in an American student revue the words, including the lyrics of the songs, were recited without musical accompaniment; in Philadelphia a local society lady, with the musical assistance of her husband at the piano, performed it quite alone in a concert hall from first to last word, with all the props, like Danilo's evening cape, Popoff's snuff-box and Natalie's fan; in Tokyo the *Yokina Mibodshin* was played for the first time throughout a season in the traditional way, then a second year by an all-male company, a third one by an all-female, and the fourth time by a mixed cast, with the gentlemen taking the female parts and the ladies the male.

Finally, in 1929, there was a spectacular presentation at the Grosses Schauspielhaus in Berlin: it had a South American instead of a Slavonic setting; Hanna was not a farmer's daughter but a music-hall singer, and the antecedents of the story were not narrated but acted, showing the courting by Prince Glawari, Danilo's fury and Hanna's betrayal. And the wedding of Danilo and the Widow took place in a lavishly costumed epilogue, just in case anyone in the audience should still cherish any doubts as to the couple's final reunion.

VII
THE NEW OPERETTA

For Good or Ill

The operetta has been called "the most nonsensical thing in the world". With Lehár, the nonsense made sense again, though it was a special kind of sense: no longer the mere interplay of wit, grace and good humour. As in the new naturalistic drama and veristic opera, fancy made way for reality. The woman Hanna Glawari lived in a different world from Lady Rosalinda in *Fledermaus*, the man Danilo in a different world from Eisenstein the bon-vivant. There was psychological depth instead of simplicity, sexual passion instead of innocent amorousness. Discussions whether all this had an effect on the genre for good or ill, whether Lehár went too far, are attractive—and unprofitable.

The operetta lived again, the public took it enthusiastically to its heart. Three extremely talented composers bore with Lehár the chief burden of satisfying the sudden immense demand. His success helped to establish them, and with their varied abilities they were destined to enrich the genre with over a hundred new works. Different as Eysler, Fall and Oscar Straus might be in their attitude to the operetta, they were alike in their wealth of melodic invention, their facility in composing, and also their frequent carelessness over choice of libretto.

Like Lehár, they had a longing to write grand opera, but unlike him they possessed little of the "will to achieve work of outstanding value".[1] Eysler and Fall, each in his way, found a warm and

1 Karl Westermeyer: *Die Operette im Wandel des Zeitgeistes* (The Operetta in the Changing Spirit of the Age), Berlin, 1931.

"folksy" operetta tone, ideally suited to their special melodic sense. Fall and Straus were masters of the refined technique of chamber-music delicacy and, for all their sweetness, of parodistic undertones. Straus and Eysler shared a Viennese exuberance of feeling, which found its clear and authentic expression in lyrical, dreamy waltz tunes.

Eysler

Edmund Eysler was born in the Viennese suburb of Ottakring on 12th March 1874. His father, who came from southern Moravia, was a well-off conventional businessman, whose main interest was the Stock Exchange; his mother a Hungarian, cheerful and light-hearted, with a feeling for beauty and artistic sensitivity. When he was only seven the family's carefree middle-class world collapsed with his father's bankruptcy; and the ups and downs began of "Mundi's" seventy-five-year journey through life: triumphs, failures, prosperity, poverty, blessing and bane. The most precious thing Mama saved out of the financial disaster was an upright piano, which they dragged with them on the moves from one home to another. It soon became the boy's whole object in life. He wrote chamber music, piano pieces, an opera and a ballet. In 1902 he auditioned before Ignatz Schnitzer, the *Gypsy Baron* librettist, who offered him an opera book to set to music, but the hopes remained unfulfilled: one theatre after another rejected *Der Hexenspiegel*, till Josef Weinberger had the idea of using the best numbers from it for an operetta score.

Bruder Straubinger—as the new operetta was called—was first performed in the Theater an der Wien[1] two months after *The Tinker*, and turned Eysler overnight into the "second new man in the season whose operetta fortunes seem to be thriving". Girardi played the young journeyman Straubinger, whose identity documents have been stolen; he possesses nothing except the baptism certificate and army papers of his great-grandfather, and lets himself be displayed at the fair in costume and mask as a veteran of 114 years. The pearl of the score, "To kiss is no sin", in Girardi's

[1] On 20th February 1903.

compulsive interpretation, became a folk song. One hundred and eighty-seven *reprises* followed: Mundi's career had started with a triumph such as none of his predecessors had yet experienced with a first work.

After Girardi's departure from the Theater an der Wien came *Die Schützenliesl* (The Gunner Girl) at the Carltheater. Eysler's music again showed his "suitability for the wheedling triviality of popular tunes easily thought up and easily forgotten", and Girardi gave the warmth of genuine feeling to a nostalgic "Mother" song. In the title role the effervescent Mizzi Zwerenz[1] was discovered, "the most perfect type of the smart Viennese girl". With her the new Viennese operetta found its great dynamic, tragi-comic soubrette personality.

In the next Eysler piece, *Künstlerblut* (Artists' Blood), public and press again enjoyed the appealing freshness of the music, and benevolently overlooked the obvious technical failings of construction. The first triumphs won so easily turned Eysler the cheerful melodist into a writer of potboilers, the lovable trifler into a notorious spendthrift. All Vienna knew the genial gnome-like figure with his prematurely grey hair and beard; everyone greeted him as an old friend, often as one of the city's "easy touches". His princely extravagance—on women, horses, cards—swallowed up sums which could only be earned by a constant stream of advances, on more operettas put together in the greatest haste. Time and again, usually after a series of failures, one of these operettas would turn out to be a masterly achievement: that he could manage it despite the self-inflicted handicaps shows the full strength of Eysler's talent.

Fall

The Regimental Bandmaster Moritz Fall looked like a cross between Offenbach and Franz Joseph. On the morning of 2nd February 1873 he was just rehearsing with his band, when an orderly informed him of the birth of his first son. He beamed all over his face; the band congratulated him, and were promised an extra barrel of Pilsen beer. Then the rehearsal continued, and Leo

[1] 1876-1947.

Fall set out on his path through life, which took him from the elementary school at Olmütz and the grammar school at Lvov to the Vienna Academy of Music, and by way of Lehár Senior's regimental band to Berlin, Hamburg and Cologne as conductor. His first *chansons* spread from the Berlin cabaret *Böse Buben* (Naughty Boys) over the whole of Germany, and made the author-producer Rudolf Bernauer look round for a suitable operetta book for him. He found it among the drafts of his author-friend Ernst Welisch.

The failure of the resulting operetta, the ill-fated *Rebel*, did not deter the ubiquitous Victor Léon from offering his play *Die lieben Kinder* (The Dear Children) to Leo Fall to set to music. The managers of the Vienna theatres turned the work down because of its peasant setting and excessive sentimentality, but Léon decided to risk part of his *Merry Widow* royalties on a hazardous experiment. He rented the Court Theatre in Mannheim for the summer season, and organized an operetta festival which had as its highlight the première of *Der fidele Bauer* (The Merry Peasant).[1]

In Fall's score a new note sounded. This was unaffected music as far removed from the modes and manners of opera as from cheap Viennese tavern songs; it gave the audience simple tunes, yet managed great polyphonic ensemble effects; and it created its best effects out of real characters and situations. The first-night success was overwhelming, and resulted in twenty-seven sold-out houses. Now Karczag secured the production for the Theater an der Wien, and a well-known Berlin music publisher bought the world copyright. When Fall was handed his cheque for thirty-thousand marks advance, he stammered ". . . but there just isn't that much money!" and promptly fainted.

His appearance did not give any idea of a musician, let alone a composer of such graceful music: his stocky figure, massive, close-shaven head, voluminous paunch and inevitable monocle would have rather suggested a banker or industrialist. It was not till he fired off his volleys of wit, and by his own laughter lifted everybody's spirits, that you felt the triumphant charm of an outstanding personality.

[1] On 27th July 1907.

Six months after its first night *The Merry Peasant* was in the repertoire of every German theatre, Leo a rich and famous composer. "I feel," he wrote to his father, "as if we'd settled down in a pot of gold. Now I must keep together my little bit of money and economize, until I have my first million."

He had it earlier than he dared hope, for it was only three and a half months after Mannheim that he could register a second success, this time an international one, *The Dollar Princess*. The most delicate magic radiated from each of his fragrant, inspired numbers; he felt equally at home in the peasant huts of Upper Austria and in the palaces of American millionaires; and one newspaper called him "so expert that he was inspired even when he hadn't any inspiration".

Oscar Straus

The Straus family (with one S at the end) were not related to the Strauss family (with two). Oscar's father had been sent by his parents in Mannheim to Vienna, to learn banking there. Soon after his arrival he fell in love with his boss's daughter, married her and settled in No. 27 Lower Danube Street, where on Sunday, 6th March 1870, a son was born to him, the future composer.

Oscar Straus studied music, and at twenty had the chance to play his youthful compositions to Johann Strauss. "In your place I would forget all dreams of great music," the Waltz King advised. "I would write waltzes and collect material for an operetta! But first I would look round for a post as conductor in the provinces. There's no better place to learn your theatrical trade than the conductor's desk".

So Oscar went to Brno, Mainz and finally as Gustav Mahler's assistant to Hamburg. The summer months when he had no engagement he spent in Berlin, amidst a Bohemian set which included Leo Fall, Arnold Schoenberg, Rudolf Bernauer and the young lawyer Dr Fritz Oliven,[1] who wrote his pungent satirical verse under the pseudonym of *Rideamus*. One day the splendid wild-bearded Baron Ernst von Wolzogen happened to drop in at

[1] 1874–1956.

their regular café. He planned in the coming season to open a
cabaret, the *Überbrettl*; would any of the young musicians present
be willing to serve as resident composer and pianist?

Oscar expressed his willingness, and half a year later every
barrel organ in Berlin was grinding out his *Hazelnut*, every pair
of lovers hummed his *Merry Husband*, every grocer's boy hummed
The Band Comes.

As with Lehár in Vienna at about the same time, he importuned
everybody in Berlin for a libretto; till Rideamus lent a willing ear.
Like Straus himself, Dr Oliven was an enthusiastic Offenbachian,
and what was more obvious than to transfer the technique of
Offenbach's Homeric parodies into the world of the Nibelungs, to
set the Berlin of William II laughing as Jacques had set the Paris of
Napoleon III? Yet *Die lustigen Nibelungen* (The Merry Nibelungs)
did not at their first night, on 12th November 1904, at the Carltheater in Vienna find the right atmosphere for a success. The
audience laughed, hummed one or two of the tunes in the interval,
but felt they were watching some undergraduate revue rather than
an operetta.

Fourteen months later the second Straus-Rideamus opus did
not go much better: *Hugdietrichs Brautfahrt* (Hugdietrich's Bridal
Journey) was praised to the skies, but the company played to
empty houses. Rideamus had written two delightful and original
books, and Straus adorned them with two really humorous scores;
yet the collaborators could not help admitting a failure to attract
the masses; what they had offered audiences was caviar to the
general. So they drew the obvious and sad conclusion, parted from
each other, and turned to new goals.

"When I set about writing *Ein Walzertraum* (A Waltz Dream)
after seeing *The Merry Widow*," Straus once confessed, "I acted
with the direct, conscious, openly admitted intention of reaching
and if possible beating Lehár's world record." In *A Waltz Dream*
the old Austria shone forth once more before it faded: the world of
Masters of Ceremonies and the Prater, the pale young Archduch-
esses and sweet girls of Viennese suburbs, the dashing lieutenants
and the silly court flunkeys—the bland and glittering façade behind
which decay lurked.

A Waltz Dream was first performed on 2nd March 1907. In the view of the critics Straus's music was an "apotheosis of the Viennese spirit": "waltzes of quite delightful softness and sweetness" streamed from a score which "repeatedly soared to the highest level" and was "studded with humour and parody"; yet everything remained "elegant, despite occasional sentimentality, clear and, for all its lyricism, free from mawkishness". Oscar's daring hope of beating *The Merry Widow* record was soon to become reality: in the following years Vienna celebrated the 500th, 700th and finally the 1,000th performance. Straus became a European celebrity: his lean figure with lanky legs and arms, lofty brow and big nose, were soon as popular in Paris, Berlin and Monte Carlo as the free-flowing, seductive forty bars of the chief waltz from the operetta, "Softly, so softly", of which Hermann Bahr said: "You hear it, and you love Vienna more than ever before."

At the age of eighty-three, in the last summer of his life, Straus was taking a stroll in the fields near Ischl, when a peasant, with his small boy, came towards him. The man took off his hat, said his "*Grüss Gott*", and Oscar rewarded him with a smile. "Look, my lad," he heard the father say behind him: "Take a look at him—there he goes, the Waltz Dream."

As Lehár aspired to the operetta of human character, Fall to the contemporary and Eysler to the folk operetta, Straus's aspirations were to the intelligent operetta. In Bernard Shaw's comedy *Arms and the Man* he seemed after the *Waltz Dream* to have found the basis for it. But G. B. S., as was to be expected, refused to give his consent. Straus's friends intervened in London, and eventually Shaw yielded on two conditions. First, he refused to take a single penny out of the profits of the operetta; and secondly, he declared that not a word of the original dialogue might be used, and all programmes, libretti and scores must bear the words "Unauthorized parody of Mr Bernard Shaw's play *Arms and the Man*". He lived to regret his decision.

The Chocolate Soldier contained such a remarkable abundance of melodic ideas and musical brainwaves that its score may justly be called one of Straus's best. Of the great E-flat major theme "My hero" Franz Lehár said: "More than a hundred other melodies, it has helped to bring about the situation in which operetta as a genre is now taken seriously." Bernard Shaw's cynicism, however, proved all wrong for the Vienna of 1908. A second *Waltz Dream* had been expected, and *The Chocolate Soldier* was anything but that: daring, clever, surprising. It was taken off after sixty-two performances; but like the *Widow* it started from London to conquer England and America, where it remains triumphant time and again in new productions.

Voices from Berlin

The man who gave the German capital its melody in the time of William II was Paul Lincke. His operettas *Lysistrata, Venus auf Erden* (Venus on Earth) or *Frau Luna* belong to the pre-Lehár school, and each of them contains an abundance of robust and catchy melodies: none more so than the "Glow-worm Idyll".

In the days when he turned his eyes to revue and the *Metropoltheater*, two operettas by an unknown thirty-year-old composer both of which had been refused shortly before by every theatre in Berlin, were put on within a month at Cottbus[1] and at Magdeburg.[2] Before a year had passed, *Die keusche Susanne* (English title Girl in the Taxi) and *Polnische Wirtschaft* (English title Topsy-Turvydom) were successes running in Berlin, Vienna, Paris, London, New York; and the composer, Jean Gilbert, was world-famous. The crude heartiness of his music had an electrifying effect. The harmonic primitiveness with which in almost every number he landed in the sixteenth bar at the dominant was rather unseemly, but it was part of the melodic structure, and the public cared little for musical forms and aesthetics. It seized on the tunes and made immediate hits of them.

Gilbert was a lovable friendly mixture of Bohemian and big businessman. Ebullient, sociable, a born grandee, he bought a house on the Kurfürstendamm, several motor cars, and a castle on a lake near Berlin with park and motor boat. He travelled in sleeping cars from first night to first night, and found time

[1] 31st January 1910.   [2] 26th February 1910.

enough to finish ten operettas in four years, all heartily welcomed by audiences, and highly paid by theatre managers and music publishers. His detractors he answered proudly by saying: "My songs are songs for backyards and cheap taverns." Although this is only partly true, it may be said more justifiably of Walter Kollo that he wrote songs for the parlour. He conquered Berlin 1910 with the musical farce *Grosse Rosinen* (High Ideas), which he followed up till 1914 with nine others.

What gave the Gilbert and Kollo musicals their immense attraction was their verve and *élan*, their robustness and cheerfulness. The press raged against the "dirt of these so-called folk songs" and their "impurity of taste", called them "stupid and indecent", prophesied that the magic would vanish as fast as it had come. But the melodies obstinately kept going. Their continued existence is assured by their pleasant unpretentiousness and their rousing catchiness. Lincke, Gilbert and Kollo were respectable craftsmen. They did not dream of aspiring to the opera crown, and like few other composers they understood how to give their ideas the barest and pithiest form.

Kálmán

The news of an extremely pretty operetta, *Tatargaras*, which had been running for a month to full houses at the Budapest Lustspiel-theater, was spreading in March 1908 round the operetta cafés of Vienna; Karczag and Wallner decided to go and see it. As musical adviser they took along Leo Fall. After the performance they met the composer, then twenty-six years old, at their hotel. "They wanted to buy the operetta at all costs," he recalled in later years. "They were very enthusiastic about the libretto, and Leo Fall praised the music in terms a composer doesn't generally use for a rival." On 22nd January 1909 *Herbstmanöver* (Autumn Manoeuvres) had its first performance at the Theater an der Wien—Fall had again prepared the way for a success—and Emmerich Kálmán emerged as a new and important power in the Viennese operetta.

He came originally from Siofolk on Lake Balaton,[1] and had

[1] Born 24th October 1882.

from childhood only one dream: to become a piano virtuoso. "Scales and exercises, Chopin, Beethoven, Schumann . . . I sat for hours at the piano . . . suddenly I felt a pain in my arm . . . I waited for a time, hoped in vain; it didn't get any better—that was the end of my piano activities—I had fallen from the clouds, a very serious and a very sad young man."

He remained that all his life: even at times of his greatest triumphs the stocky man with the friendly blue eyes generally looked very serious and very sad. Raptures and high spirits were as foreign to his nature as bad manners and uncouthness. The *Csárdás* cavalier was a sober and careful citizen who did his work, kept his finances in order and went quietly on his way.

After his arm trouble his father hoped he would give up music and train to become a lawyer. Instead, he began studying musical theory. This fidelity to his first love was quite largely due to the influence of two young composer friends of his, Bartók and Kodály. Lehár's artistic example and fairy-tale rise to success led Kálmán to light music: he wrote satirical and popular songs, until he submitted to Karl von Bakonyi his idea for the Manoeuvres operetta and so gained the leading Budapest librettist as collaborator.

The attraction and freshness of *Autumn Manoeuvres* came from an unusual authenticity of setting, and above all from the gay, lively music: a synthesis of Hungarian bravura, Viennese sentiment and international stylishness.

Judged by Kálmán's later triumphs, *Der Zigeunerprimas*, his next operetta, was doubtless not his most successful work; but it remained his noblest and most accomplished. To analyse its musical beauties would mean picking out its formal structure, its thematic richness—and listing *all* its sixteen musical numbers: especially the most infectious of all Kálmán waltzes, *Dorfkinder* (Village Children), with its grandiose, dynamically heightened repetition of the half-tone step in the first four bars.

"In my work on this operetta," Kálmán admitted, "I spent the happiest days of my life as a composer."

With *Zigeunerprimas*, after the new Viennese and new Berlin operetta, the new Hungarian operetta was created.

Ascher, Jarno, Nedbal

There were, of course, other operetta composers working in
Vienna in the days before the First World War alongside the "big
five". Among these others the most promising were Ascher, Jarno
and Nedbal.

Ascher, after *God Bless You for It*, had fallen into libretto
difficulties, from which he did not emerge until he met two young
Bohemians: Julius Brammer, an actor who played small parts at
the Theater an der Wien, and Alfred Grünwald, barely twenty,
who worked for a theatrical agency. They told Ascher their idea
for a musical comedy of Old Vienna, *Vindobona, du herrliche Stadt*
(Vindobona, you wonderful Town), from which in 1912 grew the
composer's greatest success, *Hoheit tanzt Walzer* (Her Highness
Dances): a love story full of atmosphere from the Biedermeier
times, in which, neatly adapted, the *Waltz Dream* situation re-
appears. And if *Her Highness Dances* lacks the dash of *A Waltz
Dream*, it has enough charm to be counted among the great
Viennese operetta successes of the time.

Georg Jarno,[1] the son of a Budapest horse-dealer, was a well-
reputed and often-performed opera-composer, till he wrote his
first operetta, *Die Försterchristel*[2] (The Forester's Daughter) for
Hansi Niese, wife of his brother Josef, the Viennese theatre
manager. Its immense success is due to a healthy unaffected popular style in both book and music and the reappearance of the good
Emperor Joseph II, one of the best-loved figures in the suburban
comedies of Old Vienna. Jarno had transferred Wagner's *Meister-
singer* situation, the last flare of love in an ageing man, to the
operetta field, thereby developing for the genre one more formula
for success.

It proved its worth again three years later (1910) in *Das
Musikantenmädel* (The Musician's Girl). The heroine this time was
called Rosie, the hero was the composer Haydn, who fell in love
with her, only to find out at the end that she was the child of a
boyhood love, his own daughter.

[1] 1868–1920.
[2] First performed on 17th December 1907 at the Theater in der Josefstadt.

Jarno died at the age of fifty-two. The artistic merits of his operettas may be doubted; the fact remains that some of their elements had a lasting effect on the development of the genre. The occasional Hungarian tone led to Kálmán's wild rhythms, the tears in the third act to Lehár's tragic endings; the presence on the character list of a famous person from real life to the biographical operetta.

Few operettas of the time possessed the sparkle and glitter of Nedbal's *Polenblut* (Polish Blood). Oskar Nedbal[1] was very much the archetypal Bohemian musician, appealing, stirring, brimming with melodies. He studied with Dvořák in Prague, became co-founder of the celebrated Czech String Quartet, then conductor of the Prague Philharmonic Orchestra and the Viennese *Tonkünstlerorchester*. His first excursion into operetta did not quite come off, but brought him to Leo Stein and so to his second, *Polish Blood*,[2] which became one of the most enjoyable products of Viennese operetta; this was due to its abundance of humour, and the lack of any shallow pathos. The music was at once romantic and gay; playful, witty and full of feeling. The choruses roared, the orchestra played triumphantly, and soon every bar in *Polish Blood* was known to thousands. Nedbal, the genial Czech Falstaff, with his booming laugh and huge appetite, had reached the climax of his life.

Musical Theatre in the United States

The American operetta started long before Lehár as *extravaganza*, a lavish spectacle full of melodramatic incident, spiced with songs, choruses, ballets and pageantry. *The Black Crook*,[3] a classic product of the genre, was performed 474 times, and revived and imitated dozens of times up till the First World War.

Twenty-seven years[4] later ordinary American life was realistically portrayed on the musical stage for the first time: *A Trip to*

---

[1] 1874–1930.

[2] First performed on 25th October 1913 at the Carltheater.

[3] First performed on 12th September 1866 in Niblo's Garden, New York.

[4] On 7th August 1893, at the Madison Square Theatre, New York.

Chinatown was set in San Francisco, and showed two married couples strolling through the Chinese Quarter trying not to meet each other. In the robust, farcical book, suffragettes, watch-committee snoopers and local small-town politicans are held up to ridicule, and the waltz "After The Ball"[1] (five million copies sold), although only added afterwards to the thinnish score, started from here on its conquest of the world.

Meanwhile Gilbert and Sullivan had become quite at home on the New York stage, likewise Offenbach and Strauss. The beginning of the century brought into the limelight the amazing George M. Cohan,[2] whose vitality, energy, style and determination were symbolic of the new era. The child of Irish vaudeville artists, he had been on the stage since he was eight, wrote plays, lyrics and songs, played leadings parts, presented and produced his own musical comedies, and at twenty-six had become the city's major showman: "Mr Broadway".

His five hundred songs enchanted millions; his 80 plays were often turgid, vulgar and unbalanced, but always up to date and amusing. "What do the critics want of me?" he said when attacked in the press. "I can write better plays than any living song-and-dance man, and I'm a better song-and-dance man than any living playwright."

In the twenties little was heard of "Mr Broadway", but before his death he enjoyed one last satisfaction: Hollywood filmed his life story under the title of *Yankee Doodle Dandy*. George heard the ever-fresh old songs blossom to new life, and saw himself, played by James Cagney, conquering Broadway once more.

The triumphal progress of *The Merry Widow*, together with *A Waltz Dream* and *The Dollar Princess* exercised a decisive influence on the American musical theatre. Victor Herbert,[3] intermediary of this influence and also the first American operetta composer of international importance, was at this time already at the zenith of his creative activity. He was born in Dublin, played the 'cello under Eduard Strauss in the Strauss Orchestra in Vienna, got to know the famous personalities in the classic Viennese operetta and acquired that appealing Viennese flow of melodies so

[1] By Charles K. Harris.   [2] 1878–1942.   [3] 1859–1924.

characteristic of his style of composition. The charm of his musical ideas overcame the rather conventional libretti; and numbers like "Ah, sweet mystery of life", "Kiss me again" and "A kiss in the dark" have after two generations lost nothing of their originality. No one has given a better verdict on their magic than Andrew Carnegie, the multi-millionaire. "How do you imagine heaven?" an interviewer once asked him, when he was eighty. "Sit quiet," he answered, "do nothing—and listen to Victor Herbert's music all day."

The composers who with and after Herbert perfected the American Viennese operetta, and laid the foundations for its transformation into the "musical", all had their origins in the German or Austro-Hungarian Empires. None was older than twenty-three when he arrived in America, and each of them had established himself ten years later: Gustav Kerker with *The Belle of New York*, Ludwig Englander with *The Strollers* and Gustav Luders with *The Prince of Pilsen*.

Rudolf Friml,[1] son of a Prague baker, beat them all. He also had been a pupil of Dvořáks', and arrived in the United States as accompanist to the great Czech violinist Jan Kubelik. With *The Firefly* (1912) he came into his own as a composer for the stage.

During the next twenty-two years he composed twenty-two operettas, and there were often three of them running on Broadway at the same time. "I want to write music that's alive," he declared. "Flaring love-songs, blaring choruses. And for that I need hotblooded passionate books." He was soon to have them, one after the other.

[1] Born in 1879.

VIII
IN HIS PRIME

The Headquarters

"One went there," declared the genial Austrian Count Wicken-burg,[1] "and because 'one' went there, that's where one went."

"There" was Ischl, and the famous resort in the middle of the Salzkammergut now emerges as one of the capitals of Lehár's world. The Emperor Franz Joseph I spent eighty-three out of the eighty-six summers of his life in Ischl, and with the court came the aristocracy on their holidays, financiers, too, and prosperous middle-class citizens, scientists, artists, newspaper people, and those who have to be everywhere. "It was a nice intimate spot," recalled Alexander Girardi, who at the age of nineteen was acting at the Kurtheater.

It was more than that. Brahms, Strauss, Billroth the surgeon, Bösendorfer the piano-maker, and scores of other major and minor Viennese spirits would collect at Ischl every summer, to leave off for two months their town clothes and town habits.

Their day was well filled. In the morning you strolled along the promenade, and sipped a glass of wine, to recover from a short mountain tour or your medicinal bath. After lunch you rested; went to the famous patisserie for *Jause* (afternoon coffee). Cards for the gentlemen, gossip for the ladies, a visit to the obliging Herr Wiesinger's bookshop, spa concert, dinner, an operetta or a French comedy at the Kurtheater—and by eleven the town had retired to bed.

In 1906, when the composer of *The Merry Widow* turned up in

[1] E. G. Wickenburg: *Barock und Kaiserschmarrn*, Munich, 1961.

Ischl for the first time, it was already recognized as the official headquarters of the Viennese operetta. The authors and composers sat at work, the theatre managers decided production dates, the publishers paid advances, and the stars made their dispositions for the coming season.

Lehár took lodgings at the Wagner Mill in Salzburg Street: two clean, quiet rooms with respectable, old-fashioned furniture, a little way out of town. The following year, to be nearer things, he moved to the classic Ischl musician's apartment: the Rosenvilla. Set back behind the house Esplanade No. 6, it had formerly been the home of Meyerbeer, Joachim and Theodor Leschetitzky, the great piano-teacher. After Lehár, Kálmán moved in, then Bela Jenbach, the librettist of both of them, and finally the opera composer Julius Bittner. "My recollection of three lovely summers amidst the roses," wrote Kálmán, "remains associated with the grateful memory of my friend Franz Lehár, who revealed to me this wonderfully idyllic spot." It was a happy place, in which much famous music was created from Meyerbeer's *Dinorah* to *The Count of Luxembourg* and *Die Csardasfürstin*. Lehár did not leave it till 1910, when he acquired the fine three-storey house opposite the Hotel Elizabeth on the *Traunquai*: his home, the "Lehár-Villa".

The ground floor there had the dining-room on the right of the hall, a garden drawing-room on the left with a veranda; above, on the first floor, were the music-room, the great reception-room, bedroom and bathroom. The top floor contained a Biedermeier drawing-room, and the study. It was there, at the splendid *bureauplat* presented to him by George Edwardes, that Lehár wrote all his works for the stage from *Eva* to *Giuditta*.

In his spare time he cycled enthusiastically in the neighbourhood, or worked in the garden charmingly laid out round the house. Guests came from all over the world to inspect the Master's residence: many he got rid of politely and quickly, others were invited to stay for coffee or a meal.

At night he composed; the world left him in peace then. His method of work was like himself, down to earth, calm, regular, without ecstasies, fury or despair. When everyone was asleep he would step out of his study on to the balcony, right up under the gable, and listen to the murmur of the moonlit blue-green river beneath; then the inspiration came.

The Woman and the Women

It was from the window of the Wagner Mill that Lehár caught sight for the first time of Sophie Meth in the house opposite: Sophie, who for forty-one years, until her death, remained *the* woman in his life. She was then twenty-eight,[1] of Titianesque beauty and charm, intelligent, gay, tender and extremely attractive. The daughter of Siegmund Paschkis, a Viennese carpet dealer, her great aim as a girl was to escape from her *petit-bourgeois* environment. She let herself be talked into a marriage which could never satisfy her, and from which she tried to obtain release immediately it had been solemnized.

She found it flattering that the much-wooed composer should be infatuated with her; and it confirmed her in her decision. Lehár was thirty-six, a man of poise and appeal, smart and slightly military-looking; in Ischl he wore grey knickerbockers during the day, and in the evening the fashionable black jacket edged with braid, high turn-down collar, and fashionable tie.

Anyone who appeared in his company was, like him, the centre of attention; and even before Sophie really knew it herself, all Ischl, all Vienna, knew that she and Lehár belonged together. She entered the glittering scene of his world-repute in its early days, and became his sweetheart, companion, helper, mother and confessor. She refused all her life to assert special rights over him; if she was possessive (as many supposed), she did not show it. It always seemed the natural thing to her to share him with others: those who were vital to his creative activity, and those who played a peripheral part in it. She may not often have given him an incentive in his work; but she never inhibited it. She provided him with the background he needed: comfort, peace, a well-run home—and even acquiesced in his strange demand for completely separate sleeping accommodation. At Vienna she lived near Theobaldgasse, in Paulanergasse; at Ischl, in the "small house" of

[1] Born on 7th December 1878.

the Villa. At the Schikaneder-Schlössl in Nussdorf, Lehár went so far with his *idée fixe* that he had the doors leading from his rooms to hers walled up. The house had a double staircase, and if either of them wanted to reach the other, the only way was to go down one staircase and up the other.

It was fifteen years before Lehár legalized the partnership: the main reasons for this astonishing delay lie in his own character. It was neither lack of love nor the difference of religion; not his brother Anton's steady dislike for Sophie nor Herr Meth's insistance that he would release his wife only under certain conditions; least of all a marriage (as was suggested in gossipy Vienna) which the *Marinekapellmeister* was alleged to have contracted in Pola. No: it was rather Lehár's extreme caution before doing anything irrevocable; the composer's shyness of having somebody "listening to him" during the creative process; the old bachelor's fear of losing his freedom—all these made their effect together. Sophie's middle-class standards were no doubt diametrically opposed to the situation: she bore it because she never questioned the sincerity of his words: "No one understands me as you do."

In autumn 1921 he came into her flat one morning: "Get your mink coat—we're going to be married!" She had won her victory.

Beside Cosima Wagner, Adele or Pauline Strauss, Sophie Lehár for all her charms was rather a pale figure. As the guardian of a successful, contented, productive artist's home, however, her equal can scarcely be found.

To see in Lehár a model husband is as far from the truth as to try to make him out a romantic rake. In his work he gave theatrical life to three groups of female characters: the great ladies, Danilo's Hanna, Luxemburg's Angèle and Paganini's Anna Elisa; the children of nature, Eva, Margit, Friederike; and the 'ladies of easy virtue', Cloclo, Frasquita, Giuditta. He could not have created them, and their less sharply drawn sisters, musically had he not loved them at all times. If they entered his life as reality, overrunning him and making demands on him, he was delighted—until he discovered that his melodies had given them a promise of erotic sensations which he could never fulfil. So he became afraid of each in turn, and wearied of her—until the next one presented herself. Their names are little to the point, their methods and achievements still less.

On the crossing from Calais to Dover for the London *Luxembourg* première, he noticed a smart young lady, obviously in English high society. Before their arrival at Dover she had confessed to him that she was a mannequin from Grosvenor Street, and had recognized him as the *Merry Widow* composer. They arranged a rendezvous in a private room at Romano's, met—and drank a great deal of champagne. The following evening George Edwardes took Lehár to a party at the house of Sir Algernon V.; Lady V. turned out to be the mannequin. (For years afterwards Lehár tried in vain to persuade his librettists how effective his Channel crossing experience would be for the background for an operetta book.)

One day an attractive girl of about twenty-two appeared from a German provincial town; she had come all the way to Vienna to pay homage to her favourite composer. She paid it, and he received it. The next morning she was there again—with two wardrobe trunks. She said she was married to a schoolmaster, but divorces weren't so difficult these days, and if only lovers were willing . . . Lehár was not willing. He found out his adorer's home address. "The husband arrived within forty-eight hours. I had sent him a telegram saying she had travelled to Vienna in a slightly confused state. A somewhat distressed, very sensible schoolmaster found her in the next house, with a respectable elderly lady of my acquaintance. They held out their arms to each other, and after that she looked at me again with a friendly, harmless look."

In Ischl once, while he was sitting at the piano with a librettist, a young Budapest singer was announced. She came in, handed him a letter of introduction, and then, without more ado, an envelope containing photographs. Lehár opened it; the librettist, full of curiosity, had a look, too: there were twelve huge portraits showing the lady as Nature had created her. Slight blushes all round, then the librettist coughed and withdrew.

Ernst Decsey has examined how Lehár's sensual impulses swell into his waltzes—these "waltzes of one who is lonely and sick with longing: Danilo dances alone round the beautiful Glawari, until she succumbs and dances with him. The situation is common to all Lehár waltzes. They yearn, and win by humble wooing . . . the inhibitions are overcome, the melody hypnotizes through submissive tenderness: I am your slave. That is very Slavonic: a masochistic element always preceding the Corybantic fulfilment."

Lehár needed women: at forty to prove himself to himself, at sixty to give him a delusion of youthful strength. He felt no temptation or willingness to give them up. His eagerness to possess them, and the fear of not escaping from them, may explain his much-criticized preference for unhappy endings. It is a significant reflection on Sophie's mentality that she who intervened so rarely in his artistic problems, and even then with the most extreme delicacy, often called in question just these unhappy endings. The ideal wife knew of her "bachelor husband's" escapades, and she had to choose: to be the *maestro's* jealous wife, like Elvira Puccini, making life a hell for herself and for him; or to ignore the amorous adventures and see them for what they were: superfluous necessities.

The New Fame

Mascagni complained all his life that he was crowned at twenty-six before he had even become king. Lehár was thirty-six when he became king of the Viennese operetta, and two years older when he saw himself crowned by the world. The new fame scarcely changed his character: he remained friendly without condescension, self-assured without arrogance, and modest without hypocrisy— the personification of Austrian amiability. If at times he appeared oversensitive or insincere, and gave vent to scathing remarks, it was more to protect himself from getting hurt than to hurt others. Enlightened hedonism, the doctrine of happiness as the highest objective of all moral activity, was the clear if unarticulated philosophy of his life. A naïve Catholic faith, without any trace of bigotry or asceticism, was deep-rooted in his heart: he prayed till his last hour, as his mother had taught him in Komorn, and as his sense of piety dictated to him. To all appearances completely uncomplicated, cool and dispassionate, he "went wild (like Richard Strauss) on the music-paper". His world fame, of which he remained aware, sometimes pleased or irritated him; in general he took it elegantly for granted.

His character enabled him to turn his fortunate good health into work, work into possessions, possessions into enjoyment of life. The world was fair for him (as he sang), life was worth living. He had no hobbies, and could only smile at Richard Strauss's passion for cards or Puccini's for hunting. His day and a large part of his night were filled with music: music as art, work, craft, profession and vocation. He followed with critical interest all the musical developments of the period, Debussy, Schoenberg, jazz; and examined every new harmonic or orchestral device for its possible utility.

Lehár regarded it as the great tragedy of his artistic existence that Fate never granted him a "Hofmannsthal": the partner, intellectually his superior, who could have guided him.

Like Puccini, he felt empty and lost when he was *inoperaio*, without a new libretto on his desk. The times when he had to hunt for books were now replaced by the times when books hunted him: "on an average ten a week", and mostly hackneyed, bad, unserviceable. "If I send one back," he complained, "unread to the author, he's cross; if I send it back read, then he's cross at *that*; if I leave it around a few months and then send it back he's equally cross, of course; and if I set it to music, and it falls through, then he's crossest of all!"

He described other dilemmas he was faced with: "If I write serious music, it's too operatic; if I write cheerful music, it's too trivial; if I write a hit, people say, 'He's writing for the gallery!'; if I don't write a hit, they say, 'He didn't have any inspiration.' If I ask a lot of the singer, people say: 'Well, they aren't opera-singers, after all.' If I ask little of the singer, they say: 'In the old days composers used to write for real voices.' If I give the chorus a lot to do, they say: 'Superfluous stuff!' If I give it nothing, they say: 'How magnificent the old choruses were!' If I bring out a work a year, they say: 'A hack.' If I don't, they say: 'He hasn't any more ideas.' I have thought over all that for nights on end—and I am still baffled."

He was never really baffled: either in artistic or in financial matters. *The Merry Widow* had made him a rich man; from the proceeds of it he first fulfilled every Austrian's dream: even before he bought the Ischl villa, he became a "four-storey Viennese landlord". His property in Vienna, No. 16 Theobaldgasse, was an imposing block of the highest value, with shops and flats, bringing in the best rents. He occupied a roomy apartment on the first floor, and furnished it in the practical, comfortable and slightly over-crowded style of the time.

His often-derided carefulness in money matters, in which Mama's "little bags" and Grandmother Neubrandt's "will to possess" lived again—was dictated by prudence. Like Puccini and Richard Strauss, he saw others reaping fortunes out of the fruits of his talent and work. He didn't begrudge it them, but made no secret of the fact that he himself—again like Puccini and Strauss—wanted to be the first beneficiary of the yield. For twenty-five years he had aspired to financial security: now he had achieved it, should he not hold on to it, the basis of his simple, exemplary musician's existence?

The reverence he felt for Puccini and Strauss was reciprocated by Puccini with friendship and admiration, by Strauss with malice and hatred. The composer of *Salome* (accordingto WalterThomas,[1] his biographer) had "scarcely given any attention to the early successes of the Hungarian military bandmaster". But since the world success of *The Merry Widow* Lehár had become a target for Strauss's sarcasm and abuse, especially when this successful operetta even found an entry into the repertoire of the great opera-houses.

When Hofmannsthal intended to introduce into *Arabella* a "gipsy violinist", he was warned by the master that such a character smelt "strongly of Lehár". Strauss claimed there was "more music" in a few bars of any of his operas "than in a whole Lehár operetta". Only Hofmannsthal drew the conclusion from this that rather less music, subordinating the orchestra to the vocal line, was the way to "steal from the operetta its magic ring with which it holds so

[1] Walter Thomas: *Richard Strauss und seine Zeitgenossen* (Richard Strauss and his Contemporaries), Munich, 1964.

completely in thrall the souls of audiences". It is doubtful whether the poet really made the statement attributed to him by Alma Mahler (the composer's wife): "If Lehár had set the *Rosenkavalier* to music, what a masterpiece it would have been!" The fact remains, however, that Hofmannsthal had an open and grateful ear for the melodic charm of his collaborator's *bête noire*; whereas Strauss could still say in 1940:[1] "The danger threatening our whole cultural level through Lehár and his accomplices, to which it has already mostly succumbed, can no longer be overcome simply by ignoring it."

When Lehár spoke of Strauss, on the other hand, "you felt (according to Thomas) how very much this dream-manufacturer, so well loved in all corners of the world, has suffered all his life at the contempt of the *Rosenkavalier* composer. It may not be true, as Lehár claimed, that Strauss never took the trouble to listen to one of his works; at any rate Strauss found it extremely unpleasant that Lehár should describe him as 'the model' for his own creative activity."

The model—after Puccini. Since the turn of the century the Italian master had come to Vienna often and with pleasure. In October 1913, while he was rehearsing his *Girl from the Golden West*, he heard *The Count of Luxembourg* and *Eva* for the first time. In a newspaper interview he expressed his delight with both works, and also the wish to have a try at operetta himself. The managers of the Carltheater took him at his word, and offered him between 200,000 and 400,000 crowns[2] (according to different sources), should he be willing to write a dozen musical numbers for a libretto to be supplied by them. The contract was signed, and the sad flight of *La Rondine* (The Swallow) began.

It was only seven years later, on the occasion of Puccini's first postwar visit to Vienna, that a personal encounter took place between himself and Lehár. He had seen *Wo die Lerche singt* (Where the Lark Sings) at the Theater an der Wien, and Lehár was just studying the score of Puccini's *Rondine*. So they talked of their joint "bird works", and the scene has been described by Anton Lehár:

[1] Letter to Clemens Krauss.   [2] 10,000–20,000 U.S. dollars.

"From his period of service at Pola, Franz spoke pretty good Italian. I spoke a little of it, too, Puccini hardly any German. But there was no problem of communication, for already during the meal the two masters were conversing almost exclusively by quoting alternately from their works. Singing softly, they indicated the melodies. Then they both sat at the piano and played: Puccini with the right hand, Lehár with the left. The most wonderful harmonies sounded forth, Puccinisms and Lehárisms, one surpassing another in sound effects and original turns of phrase. Lehár took the opportunity to tell Puccini about his own ambition to write a tragic opera. The *maëstro* shook his head. He referred to his own rather disappointing operetta experiences, and said: '*Chi vol fare l'altrui mestiere, fa la zuppa nel paniere!*'[1] Returning to his "quiet little nest" at Torre del Lago, he thanked Lehár for the time in "enchanting Vienna, the town where the music vibrates in everyone's soul, and even lifeless things seem to have a rhythmical life". He continued:[2] "I can't tell you how happy I was to get to know you at close quarters, and to have the chance to admire your kindness as a man and the melodies of your world-conquering music. Thank you for all the hospitality you have shown me.' The two composers were united by a bond of deepest friendship, a friendship (Lehár declared) "based on the complete harmony of our musical feeling, on mutual understanding of all that each of us wanted to express—and had to express!—in music".

The musical bond between them went hand in hand with an "almost tender affection" for each other. It might be "based, for all the difference in the intellectual levels of the two composers, on an undeniable similarity of character in the melancholy, sensual aroma of their melodies, the erotic sweetness of their seductive, mondain and slightly wanton music; and it was to be felt in an almost touching way when the two most successful stage composers of our age were together. Two sovereigns who revered each other in noble modesty."[3]

[1] In free translation: Cobbler, stick to your last.
[2] Letter of 11th February 1920.
[3] Richard Specht: *Giacomo Puccini*, Berlin, 1931.

Trifles

Lehár has often recalled how after *The Merry Widow* he felt like the legendary man riding across Lake Constance: he had charged unsuspecting over the snowy plain on to the frozen waters of operetta. But when he reached the other side, and realized the dangers he had escaped, he did not fall off his horse dead from shock (as in the legend), but stayed in the saddle, not knowing where to go. Others were now galloping the way he had shown, using opportunities he had created. It was the only time in his life that fear of a new venture blocked the road to renewed achievement, and made him unproductive. The years 1906, 1907 and 1908 brought three trifles: a children's play, a farce, and a little one-acter.

The idea for the first, *Peter und Paul im Schlaraffenland*, had been born at the Schlaraffia; and when you listen to it closely you discover the customs and idioms of the brotherhood. The two boys of the title travel into fairyland, meet the good fairy Industry and the wicked spirit Sloth, Schlampamprias king of the realm with his ministers Pimpfl and Pampfl, moonflowers, honeynymphs, soldiers—and country-folk who dance *ländlers* as if they were Friederike Brion's neighbours from Alsace.

Lehár's librettists were two very young Viennese writers, Robert Bodanzky and Fritz Grünbaum, both newcomers to the trade, both destined for considerable careers.

Peter und Paul anticipated much of the atmosphere of later Disney films, and after the première at the Theater an der Wien[1] became a Christmas play often produced on German and Austrian stages. Well before the first night the new trio were at work for the second time—this time with a little burlesque one-act musical for the "*Hölle*" (the miniature cabaret stage opened in the building of the Theater an der Wien): a self-parody, called *Mitislaw der Moderne* (Fashionable Mitislaw). Lolo, Dodo and the rest of the ladies from Maxim's appeared, Treumann parodied his Danilo, and the whole thing was cheerful, free-and-easy, unpretentious stuff.

[1] 1st December 1906.

Lehár's next opus, *Der Mann mit den drei Frauen* (The Man with the Three Wives) was anything but that. Again Julius Bauer had delivered a book quite as silly and clumsy as *The Mock Marriage*. The story centred on a Viennese tourist guide, who was always on the move, and to be sure of a comfortable home everywhere, kept a "wife" in Vienna, Paris and London. The Viennese wife found him out, allied herself with the other two, provided them with other husbands and married him properly.

After the first night at the Theater an der Wien[1] one critic fancied he could feel "Lehár literally struggling with himself, apparently recognizing his mistakes, and trying to overcome them with honourable, almost self-tormenting zeal and a sternness which sometimes appears quite puritanical."[2]

None of all that was anywhere near the truth. If Lehár struggled with himself, it was to squeeze a drop of music out of the cardboard characters, and if his self-tormenting zeal produced a few pleasant tunes, it was not due to Bauer's efforts but in spite of them.

Der Mann mit den drei Frauen—Lehár's first full-length operetta since *The Merry Widow*—was a regrettable anticlimax on his road: all the more regrettable because it followed the masterpiece.

The Ninety-three Days

In the ninety-three days between 7th October 1909 and 8th January 1910 Franz Lehár came into the limelight with three operettas, *Das Fürstenkind* (The Prince's Child), *Der Graf von Luxemburg* (The Count of Luxembourg) and *Zigeunerliebe* (Gipsy Love), which are among the best not only of his own works but of all operettas.

That he worked for scarcely a year on all three is already remarkable on the purely physical level, since they comprise fifty-eight separate musical numbers with six elaborate finales, about 450 pages of vocal and about 3,000 of orchestral score. That they contain ten of his best marches, twelve of his loveliest lyrical melodies and twenty-two of his most famous waltzes, shows an inspiration which seems to verge on the miraculous. With the three works, Vienna's three best musical theatres remained booked

[1] 21st January 1908.   [2] *Neue Freie Presse* for 22nd January 1908.

up for months; and other new operettas had to be content with second-class stages. Over 200 provincial theatres had to decide willy-nilly on taking all three Lehárs. The result: 8,000 performances.

The book for *Das Fürstenkind* came from Victor Léon. Here again (as in *The Tinker* and *The Merry Widow*) he offered the composer local colour at two levels: the Greek-Macedonian and the modern American. The setting was taken from a story by Edmond About, a Lorraine novelist and journalist.

Hadji Stavros, the Prince of Parmes—so the story of *The Prince's Child* relates—is secretly the chief of a band of brigands who carry out their nefarious work in the woods round Athens. (Treumann played the part at the first performance at the Johann Strauss-Theater[1] with an uncanny skill in characterization.) His daughter Photini—the Prince's child of the title—knows nothing of Papa's dark activities. She has fallen in love with Bill Harris, an American naval officer, while the ageing Stavros loves the beautiful banker's daughter Mary Ann, who has been captured by his henchmen. Despite all obstacles Photini and Bill come together, whereas Mary Ann must remain for the Prince a dream which vanished.

From *Rodrigo* Lehár had a predilection for brigand stories, from *Viennese Women* for a final renunciation scene. Here he found both united. From Stavros's "Robber Song" the operetta leads by way of Balkan national music to Brahms-Goldmark harmonies ("Be silent, my heart"), framed in Lehár's triplets, to a lively medley of waltzes; and to

Valse lento

as crown of the score.

In the middle of the *Fürstenkind* composition Karczag appeared at the Rosenvilla: holding the *Luxemburg* libretto in his hands and indicating the penalty clause in their old contract—surely Lehár could "sandwich" the operetta into his schedule and write it in

[1] 7th October 1909.

three or four weeks, before he started on *Gipsy Love*. Lehár read the manuscript, and agreed. "It was the only time in my life where I worked sloppily," he used to declare in later years, although even the most thorough examination of the score fails to reveal any trace of sloppiness.

The history of *The Count of Luxembourg*, first performed[1] at the Theater an der Wien thirty-six days after the *Fürstenkind* première, begins twelve years earlier. In a weak moment Johann Strauss ("when there's a game of cards in view, I praise librettists—just to get rid of them") had promised Dr A. M. Willner[2] to set to music his book *Die Göttin der Vernunft* (The Goddess of Reason); and when he regretted his decision was forced to compose by the threat of a lawsuit.

He had by that time reached the age of seventy-two, went to work with little enthusiasm, and did not even attend the first night. After a four weeks' run the operetta disappeared for ever; the disaster anticipated had promptly taken place. Willner thought he would never live it down.

He was a quiet, cultivated, elegant man, originally a philosopher, musicologist and composer, Operetta seemed to have better prospects, so he turned to that, and for a generation brought very respectable powers to it. His well-known remark: "Nothing's easier than making an operetta—you just borrow a story and go to a café!"—was something he least of all took seriously. In meticulous work over months he planned scene after scene, until a book took on the desired final form; and more than any of his colleagues he was a composer's ideal librettist. Fall's *Dollar Princess* (with Fritz Grünbaum) placed him in the front rank of operetta librettists. He had a bond of eleven years of partnership with Lehár, wrote *Das Dreimäderlhaus* (Lilac Time) and almost three dozen useful books for Fall, Oscar Straus, Kálmán, Eysler, Nedbal, Granichstädten, Stolz, Reinhardt—all the composers of his time.

The idea never left him that the story of *The Goddess of Reason* contained more than old Strauss had been able to give it; so a request by the Strauss family in 1909, that the Waltz King's music

---

[1] On 12th November 1909.   [2] 1858–1929.

should be released, came as a godsend. He discussed the situation with Karczag, then set to work with Bodanzky, Lehár's new favourite, on rewriting the libretto. René, the pleasure-loving Count of Luxembourg, is broke, having "flung his money far and wide"; so at the suggestion of the wealthy Prince Basil Basilovich he accepts a fee of a half a million francs, and marries the singer Angèle, who needs his count's title. The ceremony takes place with a screen between bride and groom; "She goes left, he goes right!" and in the second act they fall in love, without knowing they are married to each other; in the third act the formal marriage becomes a real one.

All this was a magnificent variation on *The Merry Widow* "arrangements", with Hanna as Angèle, Danilo as René and Zeta as Basil. A new Lehár sounded forth in the score, transfigured and refined, and yet with the old luxuriance of melody so basic to him and so characteristic. Here was the fragrance of the *trèfle incarnat*, there they "danced cheek to cheek, lip to lip", "sauntered through life, aimless and free"; and from everywhere the waltz rang out: "Tell me, can this be love!"

The audience raised *Luxemburg* on to *The Merry Widow*'s pedestal. They took little notice of the critics, who heard in the music nothing but "waltzes which travel up and down the scale on a few notes, and are long familiar to the practised operetta-goer", and "the noisy hotch-potch of Bohemian polkas, Parisian can-cans and cabaret *chansons*, English grotesque dances and Austrian military marches".

In the *Luxemburg* presentation at the Theater an der Wien[1] the sensation of the evening was Max Pallenberg as Basil. "A powerful bit of vulgarity," Alfred Kerr had called him, Drews "an inspired genius", and Polger "a living pamphlet against pomposity". Human absurdity was the theme of his comedy; he displayed it in

[1] Première on 12th November 1909.

unending variations, and seldom more penetratingly, insistently and definitively than in *Luxemburg*.

After a year, and three hundred consecutive performances in Vienna, Lehár's new operetta, like *The Merry Widow*, had conquered the world; also like *The Merry Widow*, London was the starting-point for its world conquest. George Edwardes welcomed the composer in London as an old friend, Lily Elsie played Angèle, the dashing Bertram Wallis was René. King George V and Queen Mary came to the first night,[1] and Lehár received Their Majesties' congratulations at the end of the performance. (In his excitement at being presented, he could not find his silk hat, and as he felt it would be *lèse-majesté* to appear in the royal box without a hat, he picked up one in the wings belonging to a member of the chorus.)

Thirteen months later, *The Count of Luxembourg* was superseded in London by the third of the "ninety-three-days" operettas.[2] This time, because of the exotic setting, Edwardes and his associates had not reckoned with the Lehár triumph now traditional in London; so they were pleasantly surprised when *Gipsy Love* nevertheless achieved a run of 299 performances. Lily Elsie was no longer in the company: she had married and said good-bye to the stage—and Edwardes had to look round for a replacement. He found one in the smart Budapest soubrette Sari Petras, and provided her with a first-class partner in Robert Michaelis, Coyne's understudy as Danilo. Lehár conducted; it was to be nineteen years before he saw London again.

Zigeunerliebe (Gipsy Love) had originally been produced on 8th January 1910 (the ninety-third day) at Vienna's Carltheater. Willner and Bodanzky had again given the composer a book with inner music, but, unlike the laughing *Luxemburg*, full of deep, romantic melancholy. Zorika, daughter of the rich Dragotin, is to marry the Roumanian noble Jonel, but her longing is for a fiddler, the gipsy Jozsi. On a moonlit night she drinks a beaker from the magic stream, the Czerna, which flows past her house. Water-nymphs sing her to sleep, and she dreams of a life with Jozsi, a life full of privations, bitterness and jealousy. Then her dream is over,

---

[1] On 20th May 1911.   [2] On 1st June 1912.

she clasps her Jonel in her arms, and the fiddler goes back to his
wild life. The *Gipsy Love* melodies do not make it easy for the
listener: they are more dramatic than lyrical, but avoid any cheap
effects. That like

and

they nevertheless became known all over the world, and remained
so, is evidence of their magnificent authenticity. The critics ignored
them, accusing Lehár of having written "the noisiest operetta
music one has ever heard", and with three operettas in one season
"having presumed too much on his rich talent".

None of this was true. In the ninety-three days he had achieved
an unparalleled feat. With the *Fürstenkind* he had given his best
in Balkan fieriness, with *Luxemburg* in international elegance. With
Gipsy Love he brought out the full Magyar side of his musical
nature: his melodies sounded like old folk-songs, and breathed like
sad, beautiful fairy-tales the great melancholy of the Hungarian
countryside.

The Summit Marked Genius

The inspiration which filled Lehár for the ninety-three days seemed
still to be good for a further operetta. Once the working- and
success-formula had been found for the new style, only a well-
made story and a well-organized score were needed to turn it into
theatrical reality.

Only? Quite apart from their great creative talents, Lehár,
Willner and Bodanzky were such superb masters of their craft
that even the possibility of a second-class job was excluded. For

Eva they brought into action, besides their experience and ability, a healthy contemporary awareness.

The idea of the "social" operetta was in the air. When the first press announcements came out, they produced a sensation: Lehár was going to handle the subject of rich and poor in waltz rhythm! Karczag saw himself becoming involved in political arguments, which might endanger the season's box-office takings. "I keep reading," he declared in an interview, "that Franz Lehár in his operetta *Eva* was trying to solve social problems. Now, where is there a single word about them in this musical work? The workers want nothing else than to protect their Eva—against the young boss who wants to seduce her. That is, after all, a matter which has nothing to do with politics."

The story about the workers who wanted to protect their Eva against the boss came from a play first produced in Berlin in 1890 called *Die Haubenlerche* (The Crested Lark), by Ernst von Wildenbruch. Wildenbruch was not concerned with socialism: his dramatic conflict (like Bernard Shaw's twenty years later in *Pygmalion*) was the transplanting of a girl of the people into a higher social sphere.

Willner and Bodanzky set themselves between *Die Haubenlerche* and *Pygmalion*, of which of course they had no inlking then (it came out in 1912). Their Eva was a strong, resolute operetta character, with a great longing for happiness in her heart:

WÄR' ES AUCH NICHTS ALS EIN. TRAUM VOM GLÜCK

Lehár has strewn her story with passionate and sometimes also with merry music. From the broad Eva motif, which introduces the prelude, to the "Pavements of Paris" march (with a reminiscence of the "Sirens of the Ball' in its five up-beat quavers) and the *Valse moderato* "My sweet Cinderella", he has produced inspiration as fine as any in the "ninety-three days". So for once we may agree with the press notices after the first night,[1] which praised

[1] On 24th November 1911.

"the Master's rich measure of serious artistic work", and the "rich, dazzling and fascinating sound of his orchestra".

For the sake of completeness, and only in passing, mention should be made here of two Lehár trifles which were again written for *Die Hölle*. One, whose book was by Julius Bauer, and which was first performed a year before *Eva*, bore the title *Rosenstock und Edelweiss*; the other, *The Musical Box*, was conceived by Lehár's friend Theo Zasche, the cartoonist.

Like the father who loves his weaker children more fondly than his stronger, Lehár always had a deeper bond with his failures than with his triumphs. Of the latter he was duly proud; the former were close to his heart. He believed in them, and did everything to make others believe in them. The rule was not kept strictly: it often happened that he revised works which were generally acclaimed, like *Gipsy Love*, and did not trouble any more with fiascos like *The Mock Marriage*. But his own firm conviction of a work's merit or demerit was decisive, and remained so against all the whisperings of theatre managers, librettists and actors.

"The master wants to see his mastery confirmed before his own judgement," says Decsey. "When he detects a weakness in an older work, his peace is lost. An inner urge drives him on, he suffers from an almost physical pressure until he has quietened his conscience by revision. The revision is no sport for him, but a necessity."

No skill in revision could save *Der Göttergatte*, *Endlich allein* (Alone at Last), *Kukuschka* or *Der Sterngucker* (The Star-Gazer). Julius Brammer and Alfred Grünwald appeared at Lehár's house early in 1913 and pointed out to him the eminent suitability of their *Ideale Gattin* (Ideal Wife) story for his *Göttergatte* score. They told him of the Count of Cavaletti: how he neglects his delightful wife Elvira, how Elvira pretends to go away and returns as her own sister, the lively Carola—and brings the rascal back to herself. A simple farce, not new but attractively constructed, with witty dialogue and nice lyrics. For Lehár a chance to "go Spanish". He did not really exploit it to the full, relying more on the old well-tried melodies. "What I dreamed of long ago" became "A thousand red roses", and the newly added numbers included

WENN MEI-NE GAT-TIN SO KÜS- SEN KÖNNT', WIE

DU, MEIN SCHÄTZ-CHEN, WIE DU - - - - - -

one of Lehár's best-constructed and rhythmically most original waltzes.

The temporary success of *The Ideal Wife* was quite largely due to the brilliant acting of Hubert Marischka as the husband. He revealed himself from the first night[1] as the coming leading man of the Theater an der Wien, with which he remained connected all his life, which he served as nobody else had done since Girardi.

Lehár had an excellent understanding with Brammer and Grünwald during the work, yet *The Ideal Wife* remained their only collaboration.

The reason was that Lehár, soon after the Berlin première of *The Ideal Wife*, found himself involved in a protracted and unpleasant lawsuit: the writer Ludwig Fulda was laying charges of the infringement of his copyright. He established similarities between *The Ideal Wife* and his own play *Die Zwillingsschwester* (The Twin Sister), published in 1901. Brammer and Grünwald produced dozens of old Spanish, French and English comedies handling the same theme, which they, like Fulda himself, had used as source. In the end everything was amicably settled, but Lehár decided in future to have nothing more to do with the gifted but not too scrupulous young authors.

In his next work, *Endlich allein* (Alone at Last), he did something which no composer for the stage, and certainly no operetta composer, had ventured on before: for a whole act two young people alone on a mountain-top sang of their love:

SCHÖN IST DIE WELT - - WENN EIN SCHIM-MER VON GLÜCK SIE ER HELLT - -

Upwards and ever upwards soared the hymn, uniting with all the

[1] 11th October 1913.

other music of the rich score in a glorious Alpine symphony. But for all the abundance of musical ideas *Endlich allein* was an enterprise as hazardous as it was hopeless—a summit climbed in bold ambition, the crown of an estimable artistic aspiration, yet in the end nothing but a tragi-comic travesty. People mockingly called the work Lehár's *Tristan*, found fault with its high-flown manner, described it as a return to operetta cliché over boulders of pretentiousness. He clung tightly to the *Urlaut* which he heard through the Alpine scenery of *Alone at Last*, and always regarded the great second-act duet as a peak in his whole creative *oeuvre*. Whenever the thought of an adaptation came up, and it was in the air for sixteen years, it was invariably Lehár's first condition that no alteration should be made in the structure of the central scene.

As Willner and Bodanzky after *Eva* brushed aside the unlucky Calais–Dover idea which Lehár had wished to carry out, they suggested stories to him of all kinds and origins.

Meanwhile it was already summer, and the three really had to settle down to work in Ischl, since the Theater an der Wien had fixed the première of "the new Lehár" for the end of January. "It was then," Willner recalled in bitter-sweet recollection, "that I felt the Chief's hard hand." Lehár summoned him to the Café Esplanade, took him "to the table where once Brahms and Goldmark, meeting as fellow musicians, used to make bad jokes about some other member of their guild. A sultry day in July, almost suffocating. Consequently Lehár was wearing his thickest suit and woollen stockings. He had lost his famous smile; his eyes narrowed, and had a green glitter like a cat's: 'I must have a libretto at once, by tomorrow morning, or I'm off to Léon at Unterach' (a Salzkammergut village near Ischl). In my mind's eye the ghost of a second *Merry Widow* appeared. 'You shall have a new book,' I announced. 'Tomorrow morning—by St. Karczag!' "

On a walk through the small town that night, as he looked at the mountains all round, Willner got the idea for a story: two young people, up in the magic world of the Alps, alone at last. "And there, too, I already had the title: *Enfin seuls, Finalmente soli, Alone at Last* . . ."

He began to write the second act. "At half-past eight it was finished. Better than nothing, I said to myself, and rushed over to Lehár. I could see at a distance that he had found his smile again."

Lehár was aware of the riskiness of *Alone at Last*, but was not risk for him (as a music critic once remarked) "always the mother of invention"? With assistance from Bodanzky they agreed on the action before and after the second act: it was one of the weaknesses in their plans that they considered this of little importance. The impoverished, rather stupid Count X is to marry the rich young American Miss Y; she longs for adventure, and for the men who will go through it with her. The mountain guide Z takes her on the great tour. He is, of course, a baron in disguise, who has long loved her, etc. etc. etc.

The "heaviness" of the music was to be enlivened by a few comedy numbers. But their lightness made the conception of the great love scene seem all the more out of place.

La Günther and Marischka[1] sang the two leads. Their performance, like Lehár's music, was duly admired, though considered rather bombastic.

Nevertheless, a caricature published around then by the Viennese satirical magazine *Der Floh* (The Flea) reflected the current assessment of Lehár, and also cast a significant critical side-glance at the situation of Viennese operetta just before the First World War. It showed the steep rocky summit of theatrical achievement, with the abyss of failure yawning below, and round the ridge four well-loved figures in mountaineering kit: on a small protruding plateau marked "Success" the gnome-like Eysler has settled down contentedly, unpacked his fried chicken, and is enjoying his little glass of wine. Above him Fall and Straus are struggling up the mountain "Talent". The corpulent Leo clings desperately to the rocks, Oscar with his long legs is already at the top. But on the summit marked "Genius", which he has apparently climbed without special exertion, smiling affably, waving his hat—sits Franz Lehár: alone at last.

Alone at Last ran for 115 performances. The next operetta novelty at the Theater an der Wien was called *Gold gab ich für Eisen*—"I gave up my gold for iron".

[1] The first night was on 30th January 1914.

IX
ON THE PRECIPICE OF CHAOS

June–July '14

The fierce summer sun blazed down on Ischl, enveloping the valley all round in a quivering blue haze that warned of thunder. It was Sunday, June 28th 1914, and the Lehárs sat in their garden after lunch, drinking black coffee with three guests. Sophie recounted how on the previous afternoon amidst a crowd of tourists, "locals" and schoolchildren she had watched the arrival of the Emperor. The old gentleman of eighty-four looked very spry, in his light military tunic and black trousers, though leaner than ever. The usual reception committee stood stiffly on the platform, hats off; the ladies made deep curtsies. His Majesty gave a friendly salute, walked briskly over the carpeted steps to the exit, and climbed into the royal coach drawn by two white horses. A pretty and attractive scene, remarked Sophie, which was repeated every year, and which people in Ischl were so proud of because there was nothing at all of the ceremonial reception . . .

She could not finish her sentence, for suddenly spa manager Berkovits had burst into their hall showing all the signs of extreme agitation. When he was facing Lehár, he stopped and brought out a few incoherent words: "Franz Ferdinand . . . the heir apparent, and Sophie . . . Sarajevo . . . assassinated . . . both of them . . ."

The little party sprang to their feet, and set off for the centre of town to learn more details. The streets were full of people, with special editions being sold; and a journalist friend who had just talked on the telephone to his Viennese paper confirmed the first news.

The Emperor received the news at twelve o'clock. "Despite my anxiety," his daughter, the Archduchess Marie Valerie, noted in her diary, "at how Papa would bear the calamity, I realized that it was only a shock for him, not a grief": an observation which characterizes the mood of both the Emperor and his Empire.

Franz Ferdinand and Sophie enjoyed no special sympathies among the population. Now they were dead, and the first excitement had abated, so the normal Sunday pleasures could go on in all the Austrian amusement places. Music poured out everywhere, the dance-halls and the summer-season theatres were crammed full.

The victims' bodies arrived in Vienna at 10 p.m. on Thursday, 2nd July. The Imperial Court Chamberlain, Prince Montenuovo, even after the tragedy an irreconcilable enemy of Franz Ferdinand, had according to Karl Kraus[1] ordered a "third-class funeral": no foreign monarchs, no bell-ringing, no torch-bearers. And none of the twenty-five conspirators proved to have been involved in the assassination was condemned to death. Their leader, the student Gavrilo Princip, declared during the trial: "I am not a criminal, I have destroyed a pest."

It was left to Karl Kraus, the great Austrian poet and publicist, to write Franz Ferdinand's epitaph: "He was the hope of this state for all who believed that, on the precipice of chaos, an ordered State life could still prevail. No Hamlet he who, had he come to power, would have surely proved most regal; but a Fortinbras. Yet when Fortinbras himself falls, there must be 'something rotten' outside the State as well."

For forty-three years, longer than ever before, Europe—except for "war and battle-sound on distant Turkish ground"[2]—had enjoyed the blessings of continuous peace. Now that Austria and its Foreign Minister, Count Berchtold, had received William II's agreement of "support in case of a European complication" events followed hard on each other:

On 27th July the British Foreign Minister, Sir Edward Grey,

[1] *Die letzten Tage der Menschheit* (The Last Days of Mankind), Prologue, Scene 3.
[2] *Faust*, I, 861.

suggested mediation in the dispute. The German Chancellor Bethman-Hollweg answered: "Impossible".

Austro-Hungary declared war on Serbia, Russia and Germany mobilized, Germany declared war on Russia and France and invaded Belgium; whereupon Britain declared war on Germany, and Austria on Russia.

On 29th July Franz Joseph issued from Ischl the high-sounding nobly written manifesto "To my peoples" starting with the words: "It was my dearest wish to devote to works of peace the years still allotted to me by God's grace, and to protect my people from the heavy sacrifices and burdens of war. In the wisdom of providence it was decided otherwise."[1] Next day the old emperor boarded the train which was to take him to Vienna. It was the last time that he saw his beloved Ischl, saw the people who stood mute and bareheaded round the station square and felt that an era had come to an end.

"The beauty of summer all round sank into nothingness", wrote Felix Salten,[2] "amidst the shock of Fate's sudden intervention. Terrified and utterly stunned by the war, we hurried off, without turning round even once to look at the valleys and mountains which lay smiling in the bright July sun, under a radiant blue sky . . . breathing their fragrance, untouched by our troubles."

. . . and Hold His Peace

The shutters of the villa on the Traunquai were nailed up, the doors bolted, and the Lehárs travelled home to Vienna. Time-tables were cancelled, crammed local trains crept from station to station, past whizzing troop transports. The soldiers, with posies in their caps, laughed, winked and sang the old soldiers' songs.

[1] As a small gloss on world history, it may be noted here that the famous document was drawn up by Maurus Bloch, a Jewish editor on the Prague paper *Union*. Old Bloch was considered the official Austrian "ghost-writer" for speeches and texts by exalted personages: among others Franz Ferdinand had already ordered from him the proclamation to be delivered on his (Franz III's) accession to the throne.

[2] Austrian author (1869–1945).

Vienna was in a tumult. The reservists thronged from the outer suburbs to the centre of the city, collecting on the square outside the Hofburg. In front of recruiting offices the volunteers of all Austrian nations, classes and ages, stood in queues; and for a brief moment of world history it seemed as if the monarchy had once more recognized its mission under the old symbol of Franz Joseph.

Soon the first Austrian offensive against Serbia started; in the West the Germans threatened Paris; Japan came into the war on the Allies' side, Turkey on the side of the Central Powers; the Russians broke through in northern Galicia, entered Lvov and reached the Carpathians; and in the battle at Tannenberg Hindenburg took 150,000 prisoners. On the German and Austrian side all hopes were on the quick ending of hostilities and "Christmas at home". But slowly, as the war of movement turned into trench warfare, the wave of patriotic exaltation died.

On 19th November Karl Kraus delivered his "Day of Judgment" speech against the war and the warmongers: "In this great age," he thundered, "which I knew when it was so small, which will become as small again if the war lasts long enough . . ." And he finished: "Anyone who exhorts to deeds violates word and deed, and is twice contemptible. Those who have nothing to say now because deeds speak, they are the truly eloquent ones. Anyone with anything to say, let him come forward—and hold his peace."

Franz Lehár held his peace. The voice of the ex-soldier, soldier's son and Pan-Austrian remained silent. War meant complications, uncertainty, interruption of his work, the negation of his firm belief that the Monarchy had nothing to gain by it and everything to lose.

Managers, publishers and agents besieged him to take advantage of the unexpected theatrical boom. He refused, and regarded the scene, sick at heart. His brother Anton was fighting in Galicia, the only sons of his friends Wilhelm Karczag and Josef Weinberger died in battle. He went to military hospitals, conducted for war casualties, saw a great deal of distress and little to change his mood.

He did not always manage to hold his peace, to extricate himself from the demands made on him for patriotic music. But the meagreness and second-rate quality of his productions in those days ("Watch on the Carpathians", a Militia March, a March of the Piave Fighters, and a March of the Bukovina Heroes) is eloquent enough from the man who not so long before had presented the world with three masterly scores in three months.

In the middle of September the four verses of the Song of the Austrian Cavalryman by Hugo Zuckermann came into his hands. He knew that the poet, a young lawyer from the province of Bohemia, had died a hero's death and that his wife had killed herself at his grave from grief. As if by itself the simple melody formed in Lehár's mind, which became the soldier's lament of the time:

In November the news reached him that Anton was seriously wounded. The courageous general staff officer's life could be saved only by a swift amputation of the left leg. Lehár hurried off to see him, brought the best specialists from Vienna, and "with the whole weight of his admirable acceptance of life" (Anton related when the amputation had been avoided, and all was happily in the past) "set about saving me. Day and night he was at my sickbed, took my temperature, made me eat every hour, was continually spurring me and those round me to a new will to live. I should and must live on."

The artistic product of the experience is to be found in a ballad-like aria, "Fever", which Lehár set to music and called (perhaps somewhat pretentiously) "Tone Poem". It was none the less an honest piece of music and deserved a better fate than to come out in an album to which a mood-exploiting publisher, despite Lehár's indignant protest, gave the questionable title: *Aus ernster Zeit* (In Grave Times).

Ersatz World

The grave times: 1915, 1916, 1917. Subordination of every view-point to that of the military, "total war". Italy's entry into the conflict, the first tanks, the first gas, the unlimited U-boat war, American troops in the West, the hunger blockade, ersatz fabrics, ersatz food, ersatz medicines, ersatz everything: soup-kitchens, communal meals, queues outside the stores, ration cards, black market, turnips, turnip dishes, turnip soups, turnip hash, turnip dumplings, turnip salad, turnip paste, turnip jam—and no end in sight.

On 21st November 1916 Franz Joseph I died after a reign of sixty-eight years and his twenty-nine-year-old grand-nephew Karl ascended the throne. He was distinguished in character by his piety and integrity; he was handicapped in his high office by an indecision bordering on weak-mindedness. His Empress, the former Princess Zita of Bourbon-Parma—brought up as a Francophile and against the Hohenzollerns—was the stronger personality: energetic, ambitious, resolute and courageous. The confessed objective of both was to bring the war to a quick end and save the monarchy from ruin.

"Let the Whole World Fall to Pieces!"

Like the first enthusiasm of war, the patriotic mood on the Viennese and Berlin operetta stages had ebbed away. The flight into Fairyland started, and age-old characters like Cinderella, the Sleeping Beauty or the Ugly Duckling entered the musical theatre under the strangest disguises. The prelude to the great boom was supplied by Oscar Straus with *Rund um die Liebe* (Love's Rounda-bout), then came the splendid young Bruno Granichstädten with the Maria Theresa operetta, *Auf Befehl der Kaiserin* (By Order of the Empress), and finally, on 13th November 1915, Kálmán's *Csárdásfürstin* (Gipsy Princess). Out in the world, in the Ardennes, in Russia, Poland, and on the Piave, the war raged; yet at the box office of the Johann Strauss-Theater people thronged to get in and hear the *Leitmotiv* of those "last days of mankind", the jubilant love-song: "Let the whole world fall to pieces; I've got *you*"—and all the other glorious melodies of the rich score. However, the bonanza of *Gipsy Princess* proved fatal to the thirty-three-year-old composer. A haunting fear seized him that he would never be able to repeat his achievement, that he might even lose what he had already achieved; and this turned him into a constant self-copier.

Two months after *Gipsy Princess* came *Das Dreimäderlhaus* (Lilac Time), after *The Merry Widow* the most often produced Viennese operetta in the world. The argument that it did great harm to Schubert is as irrelevant as the counter-argument that it helped to make Schubert really popular for the first time. Franz Schubert's work and character remained untouched by *Lilac Time*. The operetta was translated into twenty-two languages, produced in sixty countries. In its first run it achieved six hundred performances each in Vienna, Berlin, London, Paris, and New York, has been restaged repeatedly ever since, and continued in second and third instalments. From now on Offenbach, Strauss, Schumann, Mendelssohn, Chopin, Tchaikovsky, Liszt and Smetana were all treated in a similar manner, without the original success ever being repeated.

Leo Fall's creative activity had in 1908 reached a magical peak in *Die geschiedene Frau* (The Girl in the Train); now he gained fresh powers of inspiration through the youthful verve of his collaborators, Brammer and Grünwald. Their first product, *Die Kaiserin* (The Empress), was strikingly under the influence of *Der Rosenkavalier*; the second, *Die Rose von Stambul* (The Rose of Stamboul), achieved more performances at the Theater an der Wien than any other operetta, apart from *The Merry Widow*.[1] For the first time the composer tried himself out in a tonality unfamiliar to him, the Oriental, and caught the colour from the first bars of the introduction, without giving up the rousing originality of his waltzes. All the more unexpected was the effect of the success on

[1] Here are the official figures, quoted from Anton Bauer's *150 Jahre Theater an der Wien* (150 Years of the Theater an der Wien): *The Merry Widow*, 483 performances; *The Rose of Stamboul*, 480; *The Gipsy Baron*, 477; *Der Orlow* by Granichstädten, 428; *Where the Lark Sings*, 416; *Die Fledermaus*, 411; *Maritza*, 396.

Fall himself: sated with applause and approval, and tired of light music, he turned his back on operetta—and took up grand opera.

One of his most gifted disciples was Ralph Benatzky, who as author and composer brought to the medium the powers of a remarkable intellect. He wrote operettas, musical comedies, vaudevilles, farces, revues; music for radio, films, plays, an opera; and 2,000 *chansons*. In the musical comedy *Liebe im Schnee* (Love in the Snow)—1916—he retold the old story of the Princess who tries to escape from court life, and falls in love with an opera singer: choosing the simple tale to demonstrate through it the delicacy, gaiety and vigour of his melodic inspiration.

Of the three big successes of the time in Berlin, one came from Leo Ascher, *Der Soldat der Marie* (Marie's Soldier); one from Walter Kollo, *Drei alte Schachteln* (Three Old Spinsters); and one from Leon Jessel, *Schwarzwaldmädel* (Girl from the Black Forest).

The most enduring of all soldier songs of the First World War was British—"It's a long way to Tipperary". It had been written two years before the outbreak of hostilities, and was never intended as a marching song. The author of the words, a cripple called Harry Williams, lived in his father's public house, the Plough Inn at Temple Balsall in Warwickshire. He died before his song had achieved its world fame. (Today its first line adorns his gravestone.) The tune comes from a music-hall comedian, Jack Judge of Oldbury near Birmingham, who had sold it as an additional number for a New York operetta, *Chin Chin*. From New York, too, came the stirring song "Over There" by George M. Cohan, and a recruit's lament, "How I hate to get up in the morning" by young Irving Berlin.

During the war London saw two musical shows with exceptionally long runs: the Oriental spectacular *Chu Chin Chow* (music by Frederic Norton) achieved 2,238 performances; *The Maid of the Mountains* (with the "doubled" *Merry Widow* waltz) 1,352.

Small Tears–and Big Ones

Lehár, asked in later years why he had been silent so long during the war, never managed to produce a convincing reason. He simply couldn't write, was all the answer one got. His friend Fall admonished him not to fritter away his best creative period, to return to his desk, to look for a libretto; and with continued urging finally persuaded him.

Yet what Lehár found in the autumn of 1915 set him back two more years.

Fritz Löhner,[1] from the northern part of Bohemia, was a powerful and striking personality: razor-sharp in intellect, athletic in appearance, lawyer, classical scholar and officer; highly musical, bold and aggressive; an attacker of anything fake, an admirer of anything new and unconventional, a dauntless fighter when justice and fairness were at stake. All Vienna knew him and called him Doctor Beda, since the time when he had composed lyric poetry and satirical verse of compelling brilliance under the pseudonym of Beda.[2] From cabaret he tried to find a way into the theatre proper (he wrote an excellent Oscar Wilde drama *Der König des Lebens*) and from there to the operetta.

The libretto for *Der Sterngucker* (The Stargazer), which he now offered Lehár, had been written entirely by him, story, dialogue and lyrics. Perhaps the composer was so dazzled by the young author's personality that he failed to give the necessary attention to his work; perhaps Lehár was weary of long inactivity and wanted to show the successful composers of the day that he still could if he would. At any rate he opted for a book that lacked all the qualities which distinguished its author: originality, musical sense, wit, youthful power.

First performed at the Theater in der Josefstadt,[3] *The Stargazer* was greeted with a quiet but decided rejection by the public. Nobody bothered, not even Lehár himself, about a few bars hidden somewhere in the score:

Only Beda kept it in mind for future reference.

[1] 1883–1942.   [2] Beda is the Czech equivalent of Fred or Fritz.
[3] On 14th January 1916.

After the war the Milanese author and theatre manager Carlo Lombardo came to Vienna in search of new material. He liked the music of *The Stargazer*, and Lehár promised to polish it up with a few modern numbers. The new version was moderately successful in Italy as *La Danza delle Libellule*, in England as *The Three Graces*, and finally in Vienna as *Libellentanz*. Not that the libretto, the story of the young Duke of Nancy and his flirtations with the ladies Hélène, Toutou and Charlotte, was much improved; but the score had been given a very catchy new tune, which swept like lightning all over Europe, called "Gigolette":

And Beda? At the beginning of the twenties he became the most productive exponent of 'hit songs". Besides turning out witty or sentimental lyrics, he wrote one or two small operettas with Ascher, Eysler and Stolz. Ten years went by before he again approached Lehár: with *Frederica*.

The Stargazer disappointment left scars which did not heal quickly. Nevertheless, Lehár worked with Victor Léon for some time on a new idea, with a Chinese background, only to put it aside because story and setting were too remote from the war and wartime existence. Now and then Willner turned up, bringing along Heinz Reichert, his *Lilac Time* partner, and suggested possibilities. There was nothing in them to supply Lehár with his *Urlaut*.

In June 1917 Dr Franz Martos, a friend from the Budapest "Otthon Club" days, wrote to the composer, suggesting it was time for him musically to remember his Hungarian origins, and asking if he would be interested in a homely Magyar story— synopsis enclosed. Lehár read the few pages, they appealed to him, and he showed them to Willner and Reichert. The two experts recognized on the spot that Martos had taken the idea from an old German melodrama, *Dorf und Stadt* (Village and Town), and transplanted it from the Black Forest to the Puszta. But Lehár liked— and accepted it.

His primary inspiration for the new work, *Wo die Lerche singt* (Where the Lark Sings), came from its two main characters, the venerable old grandfather Török Pal

Allegretto Moderato

WAS GEH'N MICH AN DIE LEU - TE IN WEI -TER WELT? MEI-NE WELT DAS SIND NUR ZWEI, AND'RES IST MIR EI- NER LEI! EI- NER LEI!

and his grandaughter Margit, the Lark. She leaves the village, follows the call of the artist Sandor, which draws her to Budapest, and breaks the old man's heart. In the big city she inspires her beloved to paint the picture which makes him famous. He knows that he has her to thank for everything, but also that he is fated to give her up for a sophisticated city lady. (Just like the artist Cornelius Schutt in the opera by Smareglia, Lehár's friend from Pola days.) So Margit goes home, and has to forget her disappointment and find happiness with some village lad.

The soubrette Louise Kartousch, with long golden hair and childlike eyes suggesting all the joy and sadness in the world, took the part of the village girl; the comedian Ernst Tautenhayn, heartwarming and endearing with undertones of Girardi, played the grandfather. At this time all Vienna was in suspense about the great Girardi's life. In mid-April 1918 he suffered a slight injury to his left foot; because of his diabetes it swelled up immediately, and on the 19th led to the amputation of his left leg. An embolism of the lung which set in twenty-four hours later gave him a peaceful and painless death. The Viennese poet Fontana expressed what millions felt: "With him died Austria."

But Austria had another six months to live: six months of privations, war-weariness and strikes. *Where the Lark Sings* survived them all, as it survived the *débâcle*, the end of Tsarist Russia, the flight of the Kaiser to Holland, and Karl's banishment from Austria: the last Imperial and Royal Austro-Hungarian operetta. Undeterred by the lack of public transport and the fact that evening performances now started in the afternoon, audiences thronged to the

Theater an der Wien, clapped, laughed and shed a few small tears —as if there were not enough big ones to shed.

The critics found the music soft, lovely and skilfully orchestrated, but could not refrain from declaring, in the half-contemptuous, half-indulgent tone which they habitually adopted towards Lehár, that it was "only in the common *Csárdás* idiom" and possessed "no striking new waltz line". Time has proved the opposite. The folkloristic part of the music is anything but stereotyped; the waltzes, fifteen in number, are without exception of striking originality. Where the Hungarian element in *Gipsy Love* was all fire and passion, in *The Lark* it became idyllic and tender. The score shows, too, a clear step towards the great transformation: Lehár's change from the dizzy heights of *Alone at Last*, with its unclimbed summit, to the bucolic landscape of his late works: the definite recognition of an aim which carries with it the promise of magnificent fulfilment.

X
THE SHEAF-BINDER

New Delight in Creation

Lehár was nearing the end of his forties. The sadness around his world in those days was different from the one four years before. It was challenging, surmountable, no longer hopeless. World peace, though for the moment uneasy, swept away his despondency: he learned with satisfaction that his music had not been boycotted abroad, that the Viennese operetta was not, as he put it, "on the casualty list of the world war". The success of *The Lark* gave him a new delight in creation. With the emergence of the Parisian revue and American jazz two important modern elements penetrated into the field of the light musical theatre: it was advisable to come to terms with them. Both interested Lehár, he found them attractive, and in the end he decided to use them in his work, but only on certain conditions, in certain dramatic circumstances. If the operetta needed technical regeneration, he argued, it was in the raising of the style of libretto, not in tricks of production, however ingenious. Revue effects were to find an occasional place in future Lehár operettas for the sake of smartness and originality, and where they were a logical motif serving the situations of the story.

And jazz? Lehár studied the music from gramophone records which old friends in America sent him. He was impressed by the New Orleans master Jelly Roll Morton, by the Chicago jazz king Joe "King" Oliver, by W. C. Handy, the Alabaman blues composer; still he did not feel inclined to water down his own rhythms and melodic cadenzas, and thereby his own individuality. But

Music, he knew, was an ever-flowing, constantly self-renewing
power, and no honest musician had the right to close his ears to a
new wave: so Lehár's comedy numbers would from now on
contain rhythmical flourishes and syncopated piquancies which
clearly originated in the world of jazz. Yet the true musical development of the operetta, his operetta, had to come from his own
heart, not from outside.

The melodic resources that he had shown in *Luxembourg, Alone
at Last* and *The Lark* were far from being exhausted, Lehár saw his
future artistic progress simply in them and their further steady
development. At the end of 1919 Leo Stein came to him with his
friend, the librettist Bela Jenbach, and they agreed to celebrate
Lehár's fiftieth birthday with a new Lehár operetta: one with a
Polish setting which was to start where most others end: with the
wedding of the lovers. *Die blaue Mazur* (The Blue Mazurka),
Jenbach's first and Stein's last collaboration with Lehár, may have
attracted the composer more for its musical content than for the
story. It told of the gay Count Julian Olinski, who is today
abandoning his wild bachelor life in order to marry the beautiful
Blanka von Lossin. They had fallen in love with each other a few
weeks before at a ball, during the blue mazurka, the last dance,
just before dawn:

Now one of Julian's former mistresses, the dancer Gretl, turns
up at the wedding. The innocent Blanka's dream world collapses,
and she runs away, finding shelter with a boyhood friend of her

dead mother's. Julian searches for and at last discovers her, but she refuses to return to him—until the good-hearted Gretl brings them together again. Day has come outside: "Let in the sun," cries Julian. "May it shine on the blue mazurka which has given me my wife for the second time!"

The *Mazur* score, very much underrated, is one of Lehár's freshest and most inventive. Its full-blooded *Krakovjak* and *Polonaise* rhythms are interspersed with songs, marches and waltzes; what all of these have in common is a rare melodic grace and an inspired delicacy.

The first night of the "birthday operetta" took place four weeks after the actual birthday,[1] but the late date did not impair the festive rejoicings. Never before at the Theater an der Wien had the customary mass of bouquets, garlands and laurel wreaths reached such immense proportions. The Government, press and musical well-wishers tumbled over each other in proclaiming their loyalty to the "most famous Austrian in the world". From his circle of friends Victor Léon referred to the benefits of collaboration with the Master "granted him by a merciful providence"; Karczag saw in his mind's eye the Lehár statues which would one day stand everywhere in honour of the composer who has "created enduring music and sung it from his heart to all hearts"; and the faithful Mizzi Günther recalled how often she had played each part—Alkmene 50 times, Elvira-Carola 100, Dolly 100, Photini 100, Eva 200, Suza 250, Hanna Glawari 700—how she had appeared, in fact, as the star of Lehár operettas over 1,500 times.

The Blue Mazurka ran without a break up to the composer's fifty-first birthday. Then it sank, undeservedly, into oblivion: Lehár never ceased to believe in its inner merits. Out of respect for his dead friend Leo Stein[2] he refused to make any attempt at a revision.

With Daring Folly

Brother Anton came home from the war as Major-General Anton Freiherr (Baron) von Lehár, Knight of the Order of Maria

[1] On 28th May 1920.   [2] He died on 29th July 1921.

Theresa. After his first serious injury he had received bullet wounds a second and third time, but had returned to the front with the command of a newly formed infantry regiment. The mention in dispatches referred to his valiant conduct on the Piave front, the young Emperor summoned him to his headquarters and decorated him with the Officer's Gold Medal for Bravery.

Three years later the General intervened in world history with daring folly on behalf of Karl I. The ex-Emperor had moved with his steadily growing family into the Villa Prangins near Nyon on Lake Geneva. From there he carried out in Easter week 1921 the first of his two abortive attempts to regain his throne. He appeared in the Budapest Hofburg, and demanded that the Regent, Nikolaus von Horthy, should hand over power. Horthy rejected his sovereign's call despite the assurances of loyalty he had often given, and Karl turned back, feeling betrayed and discouraged. When he reached the Swiss frontier, he was informed by the authorities that he would from now on be under strict control and that they hoped he would not remain in Switzerland much longer.

He remained for six months and two weeks. Karl had not learnt his lesson from the fiasco: in October he set out for the second time to reconquer his throne. The operation this time was planned and prepared for by one of his boldest and most loyal officers: General Lehár. Horthy guessed at something of the kind and warned the General; but Lehár believed that a sudden resolute stroke would come off, and succeeded in persuading his Emperor.

On 20th October, their tenth wedding anniversary, Karl and Zita flew in a charter plane to Sopron, and were there hailed as King and Queen. At Buda-Oers a confrontation with Horthy's troops took place. Lehár attacked with a few loyalists; they were defeated and had to ask for a truce.

On 1st November the royal couple were driven to Budapest and put on a British gunboat. It took them down the Danube to Galatz in Rumania, from where they travelled in the cruiser *Cardiff* to Gibraltar, and to exile at Funchal (Madeira). The children left Switzerland three months later to join their parents. Karl had grown old, grey and emaciated. The damp, cold climate of the island led to pains in the chest and severe influenza. On 1st April he

died, aged thirty-five, and was buried in the Church of Nossa
Senjora do Monte. Soon afterwards his family moved to Lequeitio,
a Basque fishing village on the Bay of Biscay.

Baron von Lehár had taken leave of his sovereign at Buda-
Oers, and disappeared the same night. For a week he wandered
round in disguise near Lake Neusiedel, then he managed to get
across the Czech border near Komorn. In Prague he found his old
friend Max Pallenberg, who provided him with money and papers,
and arranged transport home. Early in November he arrived at
his brother's house in Theobaldgasse.

On the Grey Danube

"What shall we Austrian artists do now?" Hugo von Hofmannsthal
was asked in those days of general disintegration. "Die!" he
answered.

Vienna was just entering a new time of horror. The American
dollar, which before the war had been worth five Austrian crowns,
now stood at over five thousand; the inflation began, and with it
economic chaos, a whirl of pleasure-seeking, and the great sell-out.
Furniture, pictures, carpets and jewellery found their way from
solid citizens' houses to the newly acquired palaces of the *parvenus*;
bars, gambling and night-clubs opened on every corner; the
impoverishment of the middle class led to the moral degeneration
of its members, the dismalness of its streets. The Danube, which
had once been beautiful and blue, the symbol of sublime gaiety
and good humour, flowed dull and turbid. "With a seedy-coloured
Straussian melody" (in Decsey's phrase) Lehár sang for it the
waltz lament "On the Grey Danube":

At the same time he set to music for the "*Hölle*" a delicate, old-
world one-act operetta called *Frühling* (Springtime),[1] with a
book by Rudolf Eger. Lehár had agreed to compose the music in
order to escape from a dilemma. He had received offers, both

[1] First performed on 20th January 1922.

novel and bold, from two opposing parties, both important to him. Bela Jenbach's idea was to draw him away from his growing tendency towards opera, and lead him to gay operetta: Jenbach thought in terms of a Parisian vaudeville in a modernized Lecocq or Hervé style. The scheme had much to recommend it; but there, on the other hand, was Victor Léon, claiming his old rights, suggesting that drama with magnificent Chinese colouring.

Lehár hesitated between, and while he hesitated Willner and Reichert came up with yet another project, for which he at once decided.

The Melody that Seduces

Puccini had unwittingly provided the *Urlaut* for the new work. After *Madame Butterfly* (1904) he had considered half a dozen stories for composition—and rejected them. One was from a rather obscene novel by Pierre Louÿs, *La Femme et le Pantin* (The Woman and the Puppet).

Lehár received it fifteen years later from Willner, who together with Reichert had toned it down slightly. The wanton female lead, and Puccini's abortive attempt, far from acting as a warning, stimulated him. While still working on *Frühling*, he began the the composition of *Frasquita*.

There had not been a Spanish operetta since *The Ideal Wife*, nor a Spanish opera since Manuel de Falla's *Vida breve* (A Short Life). Determined to avoid all superficial stereotypes of Spanish melody, Lehár plunged into the study of great Spanish music, de Falla leading him to Albeniz, Granados, Ravel—and to Ruperto Chapi's charming *zarzuelas*. The result of his efforts is revealed unmistakably in the mood and attitude of the *Frasquita* score. It stands between the works of his middle and those of his late years, breathing the light melodious magic of the former, foreshadowing the exuberance and purity of the latter. Its vigorous invention is equalled by its admirable taste and technical perfection.

The character of the heroine Frasquita grows out of a Lehár triplet theme ("*Fragst mich, was Liebe ist?*"—You ask me what love is?), which in its complex variations reflects the complexity of her character: her brutality, courage, attractiveness, defiance, sadism. Armand, her lover, is like no hero of a Lehár operetta before him, garlanded with amorous melodies (here the way points clearly to *Paganini*, *Tsarevich*, *Frederica* and *Land of Smiles*), among them the most *galant* and enchanting of all Lehár's love songs:

The sauntering moderato-sweep and the constant up-and-down, up-and-down of the tonal line have made the Frasquita serenade the "melody that seduces" for lovers all over the world. Although every tenor and baritone, every crooner and pop-singer, lends it the sweetness of his voice; every violinist, 'cellist, trumpet-player and saxophonist the tenderness of his tone; although it is in the repertoire of every band, on the programme of every radio company, in the catalogue of every record firm—it is still one of those rare musical inspirations which in almost fifty years has remained evergreen.

In the musico-dramatic structure of *Frasquita* a special place was reserved for the dance: the dance not as a comedy relief or an adornment to the staging, but as a factor of definite significance to the story. Lehár had often before used the technique of expressing action through choreography: in Danilo's wooing of the Widow, the finale waltzes in *Eva* and the *Lark*, Olinski's mazurka. Frasquita dances from instinct: she dances hate and devotion, rage, ardour, grief, hope, jubilation—she dances the *Jacara*, the *Tirana*, the *Fandango* and *Zapateado*, the bacchanalian Spanish and the gentle Parisian waltzes: and while she dances you begin to understand her, and she becomes human and appealing.

Her story has altogether lost the crudity and unsavouriness given it by Pierre Louÿs: the gipsy Frasquita, who lures the good Armand into the labyrinth of her love, is no longer shocking; the happy end which Willner and Reichert provided for her both makes her "respectable" and stops her lover appearing a mere dupe. It may indeed be hard to imagine the two of them enjoying serene conjugal bliss for the rest of their lives; but the magic of Lehár's music almost enables one to believe even in that.

Leap Across the Years

Die Gelbe Jacke (The Yellow Jacket) goes back to 1916, and a summer Sunday afternoon which Lehár spent at Léon's villa in Hietzing. Lizzy had come with her young husband Hubert Marischka, they were chatting about pre-war Vienna and the people they knew who were now all scattered to the winds. The conversation turned to the attractive young attaché at the Imperial Chinese Legation, who in those days had been such a regular and welcome visitor to Wattmanngasse. He talked so charmingly about his native land, and often escorted Léon's womenfolk to the opera or took them on an outing to the Prater. It was never quite clear which he was actually courting, mother or daughter: both were well content, and Mama called him her "Toy Prince". Even before the overthrow of the Manchu dynasty, Monsieur Sou Chong had been summoned home; in the chaos of the great Chinese revolution he had disappeared without trace.

Lizzy wondered if there wasn't somewhere in this a theme for an operetta—and a part for her Hubert? Lehár went to the piano, and—as if he had heard the *Urlaut*—played a few sequences in fourths and fifths, Chinese style:

With his celebrated sweep of the hand, Léon brought the silk handkerchief from his breast pocket, and invited his daughter to have a try herself as librettist, perhaps write a brief synopsis: East-West, the Viennese *salon*, the pagodas of Peking, the girl—the man . . .

In the next two years they often spoke of the project: the war always made it seem inopportune; all the same, Lehár put down one or two numbers for it in his notebook. In the middle of October 1918 Léon and his daughter came to Theobaldgasse. "You at the piano," the librettist wrote to Lehár later, "Lizzy to the left of you, I on your right. Our six eyes skimmed over a notebook with pencil scribblings—*sanctissima scriptura*. You played *The Yellow Jacket* to us. Lizzy gave us the idea for it, and now you had immersed it in your glorious sea of sounds. From you she bore away the joy of hearing her ideas caught up in the mighty flood of enchanting melodies. It was her last visit to your house, an unwitting good-bye to the loveliness of your magic. She had been the first to appreciate this years before, and appreciated it more deeply than almost anyone except your mother. *Les derniers adieux sans le savoir*."

A fortnight later Lizzy was dead; and all who knew her felt "shattered by a grief which would not and should not abate".

Four years afterwards, when Lehár and Léon finally joined up to work on *The Yellow Jacket*, they did not guess that the work was still five years ahead of Lehár's own evolution: that he had anticipated the time of his important late development, had leapt across the years, bringing an aural image to premature sound. Examination of the score shows that it represents the end, not the beginning, of the *Paganini*, *Tsarevich* and *Frederica* line. Two years before Lehár started composing the works of his older years, he had already written the finest of them, save for slight changes, cuts and technical details. That is why *The Yellow Jacket* should not be classed here as the original, and *The Land of Smiles* as its revision. It was not a repetition of the rewriting process such as created *The Ideal Husband* out of *Der Göttergatte*, *The Three Graces* out of *The Stargazer*. *The Land of Smiles* must be considered the definitive version, the last form, of a work conceived—and tried out—as *The Yellow Jacket*. The try-out failed.

Although for brilliance of décor and taste of costume the production[1] surpassed anything the Theater an der Wien had offered in the 122 years of its existence, this did not prevent a failure. The failure can be attributed to several possible causes.

[1] Première on 9th February 1923.

Léon's complex of dramatic problems was unusual for an operetta. The spectacular scenes in silk brocade made a glaring contrast with the poverty in the streets outside. Audiences were bewildered by the musical drama offered them, and the press belittled everything with superior irony. Finally Lehár himself can be faulted for refusing during the preparations to recognize and remove mistakes in the work. Whatever the causes, when it was all over he dismissed the whole matter with a typically Lehárian comment. "It's a temporary disappointment," he declared, "which doesn't mean anything; time is on my side."

Near to *Opéra Comique*

The time on his side was the time of the inflation nightmare, when a United States dollar in Austria was worth 70,000 crowns; in Germany hundreds of thousands, soon millions, and finally billions wastepaper marks; when salaries lost half their purchasing power between morning and evening, when a continual rise in prices made any speculation risk-free, when every debtor found himself cleared of debt, and when a thin upper crust of nabobs were faced by a mass of paupers.

It was the time when Mussolini carried out his grotesque march on Rome, bankers and industrialists like Stinnes and Castiglioni collected their economic and financial empires; when the number of unemployed climbed in Germany from forty thousand to five hundred thousand; when a hundred private armies kept 150,000 men under arms; and when out of 376 political assassinations 304 went unpunished. "One does not like reporting these things", writes Golo Mann in his *German History 1919–45*[1]. "The historian has to understand, and by understanding help to reconcile, rather than revive old quarrels. But one must report them even so, because they were the harbinger of later and still worse things."

While Lehár waited, his three friendly rivals gathered renewed and decisive triumphs. Oscar Straus regained his position as an operetta composer of great stature with *Der letzte Walzer* (The Last Waltz); Leo Fall had achieved only meagre success at the

[1] Frankfurt, 1958.

Dresden *Hofoper* after four years' work with his opera *Der goldene Vogel* (The Golden Bird); but with *Madame Pompadour* now his genius for operetta rose to its highest peak; and Kálmán returned with *Gräfin Mariza* (Maritza) to his well-tried gipsies, Hungarian girls and night-club clients.

Soon after the unfortunate fate of *The Yellow Jacket* was decided, Bela Jenbach felt the time was ripe for approaching Lehár again with his idea of writing a deliberately un-Lehárian, un-lyrical vaudeville. In a pseudo-French Viennese farce, he believed he had found a story basis for Lehár's stylistic volte-face.

The work progressed easily. Jenbach was a cheerful partner, who always gave the impression that he was practising his craft for his personal amusement, that writing was the source of his inexhaustible good humour. Much of this good humour can be heard in the score of *Cloclo*.

A cheeky *vivace*, not unlike the introductory bars of *The Merry Widow*, announces the revue *vedette* Cloclo and her bodyguard of admirers:

Then a leisurely fox-trot bids her "sugar-daddy" Severin, Mayor of Perpignan: "Go home to your wife!" Severin's respectable wife Melousine, finding in his coat pocket a *billet doux* from Paris, "Darling Papa, send me money immediately", suspects him of having an illegitimate daughter, and—overcome with mother-love—wants to bring the lost girl home. Cloclo, about to be sentenced to prison for insulting a policeman, and preferring Perpignan to jail, accepts the invitation.

The three of them settle down "in the parents' house"—until the idyll turns to tumult and scandal. First, Cloclo's sweetheart, Maxime, arrives and tries to lure her back to her old milieu; then all Perpignan comes out to congratulate the Mayor on his sixtieth birthday. The Minister of State appears, decorates him with an order on behalf of the Government, and proves not insensitive to the charms of the chaste little daughter of the house; finally the police enter and arrest the long-sought offender. The farce ends in the cell, which Cloclo's admirers have transformed into a luxurious apartment. The young lady places herself under the Minister's protection—though without giving up her Maxime; and Severin has to "go home" to his Melousine.

Cloclo is a *capriccio* tumbling from situation to situation, allowing no tears or melancholy to arise. After his fall from the Chinese clouds, Lehár wanted to face new challenges, struggle with new problems and their solution. Jenbach's attempt to lead him to musical comedy might well have succeeded, if it had taken place on a higher artistic level. The composer was looking for a change; but the librettist was on the wrong track when he hoped to bring it through a simple vaudeville, even if the vaudeville had been a great deal better than *Cloclo*. Lehár's nature, approach, temperament and ambition drove him towards opera, and would not let him be diverted from it. One of the ironies of his career is that he never came nearer to it—the *opéra comique* type of opera, not the lyric-dramatic—than in the almost Maupassantian theme of the Paris *cocotte* who finds herself transplanted into a narrow provincial family.

The critics misunderstood Lehár as usual, and pounced on "the product of degeneration". Having faulted him for twenty years for sentimentality and false pathos, they now attacked him for frivolity and heartlessness. "He indulges in an almost trifling artificiality", they said, and "audiences liked the earlier Lehár a great deal better".

Without causing much stir, *Cloclo* made the round of provincial theatres now almost automatically guaranteed to a Lehár operetta (though *The Yellow Jacket* was denied even this). There were attempts to adapt it for an English and a French production: both miscarried.

The Birthday Present

At Ischl, Lehár's stock had reached its lowest point; in the Viennese operetta cafés he was considered written out. Since *Mazur*,

Frasquita, Yellow Jacket and *Cloclo*, the critics gave him to understand, he had been living "in a world of sound which increasingly eludes the sympathies of the audience". Was this really so? Had he "passed the peak of his graph of success", so that there was now "nothing more of importance to be expected of him"?

He smiled at these comments: never at any time did he have any fear of drying up. Once, seeing him in front of his scores, displayed in cabinets, Decsey had a vision of a sheaf-binder in the Hungarian cornfields, where under a radiant August sky everything is overflowing with fertility. No thought of withering, crumbling, declining. True, Lehár had aged with the years, his hair was greyer; but his eyes flashed as ever and looked out on to the world with confidence. He had retained his military walk, erect posture, magnetic temperament, man-of-the-world charm. He had retained also his ambition and drive to work. Every morning at nine he would sit at his desk or piano: working calmly, coolly, forming musical phrases, looking for new harmonies, orchestrating—until everything was as he had heard it with his inner ear.

In the afternoon—without the aid of typewriter or secretary— he would deal with his world-wide correspondence in his clear meticulous hand, and leave the copies neatly filed in a long series of copy-books. His letters are impersonal, sober, lucid, mostly concerned with the business side of his activities. It is very rare to find a witticism in them, or an attack against a contemporary. His character was peaceable, cautious, conciliatory—unwilling to be involved in arguments.

Fame and prosperity, together with his own inner nature, imposed on him obligations to prudence. He knew that he was a world celebrity, and a very rich man. The consciousness of this never made him presumptuous and overbearing, condescending or insolent. Friends and women made claims on him at all times of the day. Everyone knew him, or wanted to know him, and with characteristic affability he had time for them all. He was ready to receive those with letters of introduction and those who wanted them; he would see not only would-be advisers and gossips but artful dodgers, cranks, wolves in sheeps' clothing, and sheep in wolves'. He had time, as a matter of course, for theatre people of every age, sphere and sex, novices and veterans, the gifted and the bunglers—and for all the great stars of the profession.

In the late afternoon of 29th April 1924 Lehár lay in bed with a slight cold, and looked without special interest through a bundle of manuscripts and libretti that were always coming to him. One title-page caught his attention. It read:

PAGANINI
Operetta in Three Acts

That was all. No author, no publisher, no covering letter. Lehár remembered that a few weeks earlier an old friend, the music-arranger Victor Wögerer, had brought it to him, saying he would not disclose who had written it until and unless the composer showed an interest. "In that case I'm afraid I shall never find out," Lehár reflected with a smile.

Now he turned the pages of the book. Nicolo Paganini, he read in the list of characters; Anna Elisa—Napoleon's sister; Prince Bacchiocchi, her husband; Bella, prima donna of the Prince's Opera Company . . . All that did not sound too bad . . . Lucca, at the beginning of the nineteenth century, a smuggler's inn . . . "The first scene with the fascinating violin play in the distance already had me sitting up. I read on—and music, music streamed towards me from every character, every situation . . ."

Suddenly he is at the piano. The left hand strikes a low D in octaves, the right a soft C major chord—and the melody builds up higher, ever higher, until it abruptly flows into a wild violin cadenza. While he makes notes in his little book, his thoughts hurry on: to the entrance of the young Princess, to the *tarantella* of the devil's fiddler, to the first love duet, to the finale with its intense G major melodies.

Lehár worked for five hours. The first act was finished, and he looked at the clock on the wall: midnight, the 30th of April. He was exhausted. Filled with the deep, naïve religious feeling which had inspired Haydn and Bruckner before him, he wrote beneath the final chord: "My birthday present from dear God."

INTERLUDE

The Dearest, Grandest Fellow
Saturday, 16th August 1924

Bel Canto

So long as Enrico Caruso's sun blazed in the firmament of the opera world[1] the tenors of the age had to move in his shadow. Only his death opened the way for a new generation of tenors, who were trained on him and his gramophone records, and who aspired eagerly towards his perfection. This generation included the Italians Gigli, Martinelli, Schipa and Lauri-Volpi, the Irishman MacCormack, the "Viennese" Englishman Piccaver, the Swede Björling, the Spaniard Fleta—but it was only in Richard Tauber that Caruso's musical culture and bravura seemed resurrected.

It was not the lyrical grandeur of Tauber's voice alone which established his fame: he handled his material in a new way, subtly refined, yet always artistically perfect. In concert, opera and operetta he found an individual correct style, and from the first note direct contact was always established between singer and audience.

When criticized for descending from his unique Tamino and Florestan to operetta, he answered almost defiantly, and without a trace of apology: "I'm not singing operetta, I'm singing Lehár." Lehár declared: "We are brothers, without the luxury of blood relationship. Musically, with his all-embracing abilities, he stands far above his craft; as a heaven-inspired singer he is master of the

---

[1] Caruso (1873–1921) became world-famous with the première of Giordano's *Fedora* on 17th November 1898 in Milan's Teatro Lirico. He remained so, right up to his last appearance, in Halévy's *La Juive* on 23rd December 1920 at the Metropolitan Opera, New York.

voice which I hear when I am composing; as a person he is the dearest grandest fellow!"

The great moment of every Lehár-Tauber evening occurred when in the middle of the second act the star remained alone on the stage. A vigorous orchestral introduction, then a short pause— and Tauber began. The spell-binding magic of the dark organ radiated through the hall, now strong and passionate, now soft and vibrant: noblest, purest *bel canto*. The applause burst out, prolonged, frenzied. Tauber looked triumphantly at his audience, bowed deeply three or four times. People shouted "Encore, encore!" A smile played round his lips, he glanced at the conductor—and started again. *Pianissimo* this time, almost a whisper. Again the hurricane of applause, and again an encore—another and another. Until he shook his head, waved at the audience, went off.

One evening at a Berlin performance of *Friederike*, after he had repeated "O maiden, my maiden" six times, the grand old lady of the German stage, Adele Sandrock, came into his dressing-room. "Magnificent, Riccardo!" she trumpeted. "Quite magnificent! I wish I were forty years younger—and your maiden!"

Somewhere in the Wings

Tauber's mother, Elizabeth Denemy,[1] was an operetta soubrette at the municipal theatre at Linz in Upper Austria. Slim and graceful, with a pretty, laughing face and strikingly good legs, she played the leads in contemporary operettas by Strauss, Millöcker and Suppé. When she gave birth to Richard at the Black Bear Inn, No. 9 Herrengasse,[2] she was forty-two and had passed her peak.

The boy was reared in his mother's Catholic faith, and grew up somewhere in the wings, in theatre dressing-rooms and rehearsal-rooms. His great pleasure was to attend a performance, hidden in the orchestra, peering into the instrumentalists' parts and sometimes up at the stage.

The splendour came to an end in the spring of 1899, when Mama went on a tour of the Balkan countries with a Viennese operetta company. Richard was taken away from school, and sent

[1] 1849–1940.   [2] On 16th May 1891.

to live with a peasant family. "At first I liked it immensely," he used to tell his wife Diana a generation later.[1] "The farm labourers sang lovely old songs while threshing the corn, and in the big kitchen there was always marvellous food: bread, sausages, butter and eggs as much as you could stuff into yourself. My stomach was happy. But at night I often wept, longed for Mama, her soft arms, her dear voice, her dressing-room. Of the dreadful weariness which came over her after each performance, the wrinkles and folds which were beginning to show in her face, I had never noticed anything. For me she was the loveliest and gayest being in the world."

In February 1938, just before the *Anschluss*, Tauber saw her for the last time, when she was almost ninety. He had installed her in a comfortable little flat in Salzburg. ("My oasis into which I flee from the great world.") There she sat in an old-fashioned rocking-chair, surrounded by pictures showing her famous son as "beau": Almaviva, des Grieux, Cavaradossi. Despite her deafness she listened for hours to the gramophone, playing Tauber records incessantly at full volume.

The Balkan tour collapsed, and Mama came back to Linz in debt, not having saved a single florin. The former star had to accept a return to the municipal theatre at a reduced salary, and could no longer afford the money to feed and clothe the fast-growing boy. So she reluctantly applied for help to her son's father.

Papa

Richard Denemy was a plumpish nine-year-old with a squint and an untidy mop of hair when he met his father, the provincial *bon-vivant*, Richard Anton Tauber, for the first time. Tall and slim, the stranger in elegant fur coat and top-hat smiled at him, and presented him with half a dozen cardboard boxes, containing all that pertained to a toy railway: engines, coaches, rails, switches. The boy's disappointment was obvious; it did not subside until the conversation turned to the theatre.

[1] Diana Napier Tauber: *My Heart and I*, London, 1959.

The elder Tauber[1] was of Viennese-Jewish origin; while a guest star at Linz, he fell in love with Liesl Denemy, of the operetta company; then moved on to Berlin, Vienna, Prague, America. Sometimes she heard from him—a picture postcard, a good notice, or a little money. "But my parents never married," said Tauber.

When Mama's letter reached the father, he had just settled at Wiesbaden as producer and leading actor at the court theatre there. On the way to a summer holiday in the Tyrol he stopped at Linz. He liked the theatre-mad boy immediately and: "Thus began my new life."

The father wanted to make his son a doctor, but the son was dead set on the theatre. After some hesitation, old Richard took young Richard with him to Wiesbaden, and put him in the grammar school.

Richard Junior reports: "I didn't want to learn, was disobedient and lazy, and to my great joy had to be taken away from school. I rather liked the private tutor I was given: he went for long walks with me in the Taunus forests, told me about the stars, flowers, countries overseas, and of the great men in literature and art. My supreme idol at this time was the Wagnerian tenor Heinrich Hensel. I ran behind him like a little dog, carried his music case, went scarlet when he spoke to me, copied him in clothes and mannerisms. Papa laughed—but he had recognized that it was futile to struggle against my enthusiasm for music and the theatre. An expert should decide whether my talent was sufficient for a stage career, and I must hand it to Papa, he chose the best: Carl Beines."

Professor Beines, a huge, bald, dictatorial Swabian with protruding ears and thick glasses, lived at Freiburg, and was considered Germany's leading singing teacher. When Tauber, aged seventeen, began singing the Grail Narration from *Lohengrin* to him, he interrupted the boy after eight bars: "Don't yell, man— sing! Not Wagner—I'd rather you sang some folk-songs, if you please."

After eighteen months of the strictest schooling, daily lessons

[1] 1852–1941.

and unflagging practice, Beines could with a clear conscience recommend young Tauber to start his career at the Mannheim theatre. His father had a better idea: why not Wiesbaden? Richard auditioned, and: "What then happened surpassed my highest expectations. I was offered a two-year contract for secondary parts —and with a pretty decent salary. But Papa hesitated. The career of a singer was not secure enough for him. I had already thought of becoming a conductor, he said. Why not, besides my work in Wiesbaden, study musical theory? It was only an hour to Frankfurt, and the *Hoch'sche Conservatorium* was an excellent music college. The management made no difficulties, and I was in the seventh heaven: conductor trainee and member of the Wiesbaden *Hoftheater*!"

In Case Anything Should Go Wrong

The steersman in *The Flying Dutchman*, the shepherd in *Tristan and Isolde*, the smuggler Dancairo in *Carmen*: these were the first roles Richard Denemy sang at Wiesbaden; he also travelled to Frankfurt four times a week, and learned the craft of a *Kapellmeister*. Even before Papa's appointment as general manager of the municipal theatre at Chemnitz, the head of the Dresden *Hofoper*, Count Seebach, came to Wiesbaden with his musical director, Ernst von Schuch, heard the young man he had been told so much about, and offered him a five-year contract with an annual salary of 2,000 marks. For a boy of twenty-one it was a decisive step forward. Yet Papa again had doubts: "Too early for Dresden! Shouldn't Richard get more experience first as singer, and also as conductor?" Chemnitz seemed the right place. The gentlemen at Dresden gave their consent; they only reserved the right to call their new member away when they saw fit.

They saw fit on 2nd March 1913, after Richard had sung Tamino for the first time in a performance of *The Magic Flute* at Chemnitz. Papa was radiant. He had announced the evening as a guest performance—in case anything should go wrong, and the young hopeful was not up to the requirements of the Chemnitz audience. On the following day he could inform them that the "guest" had been engaged immediately for Dresden. At the same time, he legalized Richard's status: to distinguish his son from himself, Richard A. Tauber, the son was from now on to bear the name Richard D. Tauber.[1] In the following five years Tauber's salary grew to five times the original amount, he acquired the first of his many motor cars, and became a man of the world.

His roles included the whole lyric repertoire. People talked of his amazing stage personality, his effect on audiences and his skill at taking over a part at short notice. They told the story of how he learned the leading role in d'Albert's *Die toten Augen* (The Dead Eyes) during a train journey to Budapest; how on a single day he sang Hans in *The Bartered Bride* in the afternoon at Dresden and the evening at Leipzig; how he was sitting in the stalls during a performance of *Bohème* at Prague when he was fetched on to the stage in the middle of the performance to deputize for a tenor who had fallen ill. In 1922 his first gramophone records came out, the following year he said good-bye to Dresden: with contracts for the State Opera Houses in Vienna and Berlin in his pocket.

Schnappula

"A child! A mighty, eternal child!" This is how Tauber was described by the soprano Vera Schwarz, his partner for many years. "He has only to see his favourite sweet, apricot dumplings, and at once the world is beautiful for him!"

"Once he has a telephone near him, his happiness is complete," Diana recalled. "It took me many months to get used to his constant phoning. Often in one day he called up Paris, Munich, Copenhagen—and Hollywood twice in succession. Then I suddenly discovered the reason—the child has to have an answer immediately to its questions!" Richard's "medalomania" was a special quirk: he may well have already had two dozen medals when the *Légion d'honneur* was awarded to him, and his pride was exceeded only when the Holy Father named him a Papal Chamberlain. If anyone smiled at his weakness, he would thunder: "What

[1] He soon discarded the D (for Denemy); his mother had meanwhile become Frau Ernst Seiffert and retired from the stage.

is there to laugh at? It's nice, after all, to know that I am honoured
—although I'm nothing but a stupid *Schnappula-tenor*!"

Schnappula was his favourite word, his own nonsense invention,
which he used on every occasion. A marvellous Schnappula was
an attractive girl, a horrid Schnappula a tiresome woman; a
Schnappula play or meal might mean praise or blame, a Schnappula salary or performance indicate either pleasure or anger,
depending in each case on the intonation.

In music he preferred the romantic-dramatic, in literature the
naïve-adventurous. Karl May[1] was his favourite author. Where-
ever he went, Tauber took with him the first edition of May's
work, and read the fifty-five volumes of the *Winetou* saga repeatedly. (When in 1940 it was burnt during an air raid on London, he
advertised for another copy of the whole set in the English papers
until a fan turned up and presented him with one.)

Money meant little to him. He knew from the age of twenty-
one that he could obtain it whenever he opened his mouth to sing.
Between 1923 and 1933 he probably earned about twelve million
marks in Germany, between 1935 and 1945 about half a million
pounds in England. It was only in his last months, when he could
no longer work, and the tax authorities were pressing him with
demands, that he contracted debts. They were completely redeemed two years after his death through the immense posthumous success of his gramophone records.

Women he took as an essential of his life, the incentive for his
art, the indispensable complement and confirmation of his own
personality. They were not to him as to Don Ottavio "the source
of eternal faith", but as to Don Giovanni "Chambermaidies, nice
young ladies, princesses, baronesses, young and old, fair or ugly to
behold". Yet he believed, like Pedro in d'Albert's *Tiefland* (The
Lowlands), the part he so much enjoyed singing, that one day from
across the water a woman would approach him, "before whom the
trees would bow, for whom the flowers would smell their sweetest,
and the birds would sing". All his life he retained this belief.

All his life, too, he retained the piety inherited from his mother.

---

[1] Karl May (1842-1912) wrote many thrilling and very popular adventure
stories for boys.

During the night of terror in Coventry,[1] after a performance of *The Land of Smiles*, he strolled serenely through the falling bombs, along the blazing streets, past crashing houses and crumbling walls. A policeman recognized and stopped him. "If I were you, Mr Tauber, I'd go back to your hotel. You are putting yourself in danger. This is a nasty night."

"A historic night, my friend," Tauber answered. "Your grandchildren will talk of it. But I am not in danger. You see: up there (he pointed heavenwards with his right forefinger) somebody watches over me!"

The Alliance

The Viennese took Tauber to their heart from his first appearance, but in Berlin he did not have quite such an easy success. "They'll just have to get used to him," said Erich Kleiber, who had called him to the State Opera House. They got used to him very quickly: a year after his arrival Tauber was an essential part of the Berlin scene, as if he had always belonged to it.

The crowds cheered him wherever he showed himself, especially when he appeared at the six-day bicycle race—a famous beauty on his arm, surrounded by his *entourage*, nodding amiably to all sides. The floodlights fell on him, and with complete silence all round (even the hum of the bicycles dying away) he began, champagne glass in hand, *pianissimo, sotto voce, solo* the Lehár-Tauber hit of the day.

The great alliance had begun in the summer of 1921. Tauber sang Jozsi in a lavish new production of *Gipsy Love* in Salzburg, and Lehár came over from Ischl. He was much delighted by the young star. At tea in the villa a day or two afterwards he played numbers from *Frasquita*, on which he was just working—and then it was Tauber's turn to be delighted.

The following spring, when *Frasquita* had its first night at the Theater an der Wien, Tauber was in a box with Sophie Lehár. After a few weeks he took over the leading part. At first he played to half-empty and, despite the July heat, icy houses. The

[1] 14th November 1940.

temperature climbed only after the Serenade. One evening—he had already done an afternoon performance and was feeling the strain—he made a gesture asking the conductor to muffle the orchestra: he wanted to sing the encore softly, not with full voice. That was the moment when the great *Frasquita* success was born, and with it Tauber's celebrated technique for encores.

In the meantime Wilhelm Karczag died, and Marischka, married since 1921 to Karczag's daughter Lilian, took over the theatre-management and publishing business. One of the first events of his regime was a brilliant revival of Strauss's *Nacht in Venedig* (Night in Venice) with Tauber as the Duke. The new style of production was (after *Mariza*) successfully continued with Granichstädten's *Orlow*, Kálmán's *Zirkusprinzessin* (Circus Princess), Straus's *Marietta* and Eysler's *Gold'ne Meisterin* (Golden Mistress).

Lehár was excluded from the traditional home of his success. With the aid of Tauber he hoped—inside or outside the Theater an der Wien—to continue the path once chosen. The singer was in 1924 under contract for the Salzburg festival, and they agreed to tackle the *Paganini* project together during the summer.

On Saturday, 16th August, about noon the Berlin theatre-manager Heinz Saltenburg, a stocky, energetic-looking gentleman with a bald pate and bull neck, entered the dining-room of the Hotel Post in Ischl. He had no inkling that his visit (like Monsieur Offenbach's to the "Golden Lamb" sixty-two years before) would have historic consequences: that he would be the chosen instrument to open the way for Lehár's second career, provide the practical basis for the Lehár-Tauber association, and bring the Viennese operetta to its final blossoming. He sat down at Tauber's table, and asked for the news in the operetta village. Tauber told him about *Paganini*, and Saltenburg said what a lucky chance this was, because he had come to look out for a new operetta to be presented at his Deutsche Künstlertheater.

A minute after they had entered Lehár's study Tauber sang "Girls are made to love and kiss", and directly he had finished Saltenburg offered to give the work its first production. But Lehár had to decline regretfully, saying (which was not quite according to the facts) that he had promised the first production to the Theater an der Wien for autumn 1925. The Berlin manager was undeterred: then he would just produce *Paganini* after the Theater an der Wien, in January 1926.

He pulled out his fountain pen, and there and then drew up a contract. The Deutsche Künstlertheater agreed to payment of the normal royalties to composer and author, to a fee for Tauber far above normal, and to a minimum of fifty performances. The contract was signed by all the parties concerned.

PART THREE

Late Harvest
1925-1948

XI
SENTENCED TO SUCCESS

"There Must be Some Mistake!"

At the age of fifty-four Lehár had reached the beginning of his third creative period. The first had comprised the years of self-assessment, the second those of development, and now the third was to lead him to the heights of perfection. Until *The Merry Widow* he was still testing his powers, until *Paganini* he was extending them organically; now he grew beyond them. From 1925 to 1934 he produced six works of lyrical character, bursting with the full richness of sound, yet far removed from the operetta ideal of *La Vie Parisienne* and *Die Fledermaus*. To adapt Richard Tauber's remark, Lehár no longer wrote operettas—but Lehár.

That he thereby moved further and further from the Offenbach or Strauss conception may be considered a fault in him or a merit; it remains a historical fact. If we accept Egon Friedell's remark that chaos is operetta's element, then Lehár's methodical sense brought order into the chaos. If, as another philosophical observer believes, operetta owes its continued existence to its capacity for revealing the plebeian hidden in every aristocrat, then Lehár's triumphs prove the reverse: that the better-class operetta reveals the aristocrat hidden in every plebeian.

Whatever operetta purists, enthusiasts for Offenbach, Sullivan and Johann Strauss may say, Lehár's last works, more than all his others, contributed to a definite rise in the level of the genre. For the Viennese operetta, perhaps, they represent a setting sun; for its rebirth, soon to start in America, they signify the basis for a future standard.

As regards the libretto, *Paganini* was a regression to Jarno's biographical operetta. Like the Emperor Joseph or Haydn in Jarno, it was the violinist Paganini here who went through the *chagrin d'amour* before finding his true vocation. What put Lehár's work far above his predecessor's was the intensity of the music: an intensity which held him in its grip from that inspired birthday eve for almost a year and a half.

Meanwhile the question of the book's anonymous author had been answered. In its original form it came from a Viennese book publisher and music-lover, Paul Knepler,[1] a late successor to the turn-of-the-century amateurs who hoped to draw the winning number in the operetta lottery. He had written an operetta in the Eysler-Reinhardt vein (and set it to music with the help of the experienced Viktor Wögerer), which had been quite well received. Encouraged by his beginner's luck, he now decided to try a more ambitious work.

The life story of Paganini gave him the inspiration: he roughed out a libretto, *Der Hexenmeister* (The Wizard), and set about elaborating it. His friend Wögerer recognized that Knepler's musical powers were inadequate for the subject, and that there was only one person who could write the music for it: Lehár. So, after simply changing the title-page, he brought the libretto to Theobaldgasse without mentioning the author's name.

In the first week of May, Lehár began making inquiries as to who had written the *Paganini* book. Wögerer confessed, and suggested inviting Knepler to tea. "There must be some mistake," declared the author in perplexity, when the famous composer revealed his plans. "I don't know how the book came into your hands, but anyhow I wrote it for myself, not for you, *maëstro ...*"

Greatly put out, Lehár protested that in unsuspecting enthusiasm he was already half-way through the score, that he felt he was giving of his best—and wouldn't think of abandoning his intentions.

Then he went to the piano, and began to play the first bars of his *Paganini* music. Knepler was too musical not to recognize at once the superiority of Lehár's compositions—too crafty not to see the advantages which would accrue to him from the new

[1] 1880–1968.

Tauber as Sou-Chong
in the *Land of Smiles*
film, 1931

PHOTO HOFER, BAD ISCHL

ULLSTEIN GmbH,BERLIN

Lehár,
1934

Lehár and Tauber rehearsing for their last concert, Zurich, 1947

Lehár and Tauber in Zurich, 1947

Sophie and Franz Lehár
in Zurich, 1946

Lehár at his writing desk
in Ischl, 1948

The Lehár-Villa at Ischl

Lehár and Mausi, 1947

Lehár's funeral, 30th October, 1948

Lehár's, Sophie's and
Mama's last resting
place in Ischl, 1948

Lehár monument in
Ischl,
1958

constellation. After brief hesitation he let himself be persuaded to release his book; and from then on became a much-sought-after and reliable librettist. Besides *Paganini* he wrote a series of useful operettas with Oscar Straus, Kálmán and Künnecke—and *Giuditta* with Lehár, who remained his close friend for life.

Vision and Reality

Despite his enthusiasm, Lehár soon saw that there were dramatic weaknesses in the *Paganini* book. To get rid of them, he called in Bela Jenbach, who accepted the assignment on the condition that he also wrote the lyrics. They are among the finest achievements of this ingenious librettist, and contain, besides many others conceived with the music in mind, the verses for Tauber's *"Gern hab' ich die Frau'n geküsst"* ("Girls are made to love and kiss").

The melody had come to Lehár in a summer night at Ischl—a week before Saltenburg heard it for the first time. "Lehár played it over to me at once next morning—and I was enchanted," Tauber recalled, "but he was very far from satisfied himself. Here a phrase was not smooth enough for him, there a harmony not precise enough. Again and again he asked me to sing one passage or another, trying to discover the best vocal line, a new emphasis, a different way of entry. We worked with an intensity as if the première had been taking place next day."

It did not take place for fourteen months, during which time Lehár thought, felt, planned and dreamed nothing but *Paganini*. He transformed his world into a world of Paganini's, surrounding himself with Paganini pictures, documents, memories. To refresh his violin technique he got his old instrument out of its case, and started practising again, after over twenty-five years.

Reality broke into his world only twice: with the death of his friends, Puccini and Fall.

In August 1921—Puccini was once again a guest at Theobaldgasse—Lehár brought the conversation round to the work on which, according to newspaper reports, the *maëstro* had started: *Turandot*. "It was a solemn moment," according to the Hungarian writer Geza Herczeg, who was an eyewitness. "With his long fine fingers Puccini picked out a chord, as if he wanted to test the piano. Only with the left hand, as though in fun. Then he put away his cigarette, covered his eyes with his hand—a suggestion that he must first think what he could play. He grew serious, became absorbed in his thoughts, and finally played only for himself, as it were, quite impersonally: it was the first closed rehearsal of *Turandot*."

It was also the two friends' farewell. They corresponded regularly until Puccini's illness. The last letter, which Lehár wrote to Brussels on learning that Puccini was to undergo an operation in a clinic there, had its answer not from the *maëstro* himself but from his son Tonio:[1] ". . . I am glad to inform you that Papa is getting better every day, and we hope soon to bring him home quite well again."

Even before Lehár received these lines, Puccini had passed into eternity. He was followed scarcely a year later by Leo Fall, who had been an intimate friend of Lehár's ever since their days together as violinists in Lehár senior's band. In the spring of 1925 he had gone as conductor on a tour of South America. The exertions and disappointments of the journey led to a gall-bladder complaint and complete physical collapse. He died on the morning of 16th September 1925, at the age of fifty-two.

A Defective Enterprise

The première of *Paganini* took place on 30th October 1925, in Vienna's Johann Strauss Theatre—and without Richard Tauber. Its story is like that of many other celebrated musical first-night fiascos, and Lehár may well have asked himself, like Verdi after the *Traviata* disaster in Venice: "Was it my fault or the singers'? Time alone will tell."

The trouble started by the failure of negotiations with the Theater an der Wien. Marischka had arranged to put *Orlow* into production after *Gräfin Mariza*, and Lehár was not willing to fill a gap between Kálmán and Granichstädten. Saltenburg, who was asked to advance the date of the Berlin première, regretted that he

[1] Dated 29th November 1924.

would not have the Künstlertheater free before the agreed date of January 1926. So Lehár saw no alternative but to transfer the operetta to the Johann-Strauss-Theater.

Tauber learnt in Berlin how unpromising things looked. Since his intentions of singing *Paganini* had been made public, he was under cross-fire from the papers. Did money really mean so much to him, they asked, that he would risk his reputation as one of the first tenors in the operatic theatre? Was he willing to jeopardize his voice by singing every day? Could he imagine his great model, Caruso, singing in operettas? He wavered, listened to these promptings, and eventually decided to accept an offer for a Scandinavian concert tour—withdrawing from his commitments to Lehár.

Directly after his decision became known, Vera Schwarz, too, who was to have sung Anna Elisa, made excuses. Lehár, trying as priority to solve the problem of Tauber's replacement, hit on Carl Clewing, that strange jack-of-all-trades on the German stage. Wagnerian tenor, tragedian, *Lieder*-singer, elocutionist, very tall and broad, fair-headed and virile, Clewing seemed the very last person to represent the gaunt, demonic violinist Paganini. For partner he was given Emma Kosáry, a graceful girl from Budapest, who as singer or actress was by no means up to the demands of the part.

The inadequacies of the two leads showed up all the other defects in the enterprise, including a producer with few ideas, an incompetent management, a thin orchestra and shabby *décor*.

Lehárians young and old collected for the première, determined to win the day for *Paganini*. Many of them were already familiar with parts of the score; they all knew of its exquisite quality. When the master appeared at the conductor's stand they gave him an ovation in which the whole house spontaneously joined: it remained the only one for the rest of the evening. The music faded away in the general apathy of the evening, and when at the end of the performance Lehár went from dressing-room to dressing-room, as was his custom, and thanked the whole company, he encountered only gloomy faces. As calmly as ever, he took note of the usual comments in the morning papers. The pitying tone of several of them annoyed him—annoyed him more than Decsey's assertion pleased him: "*Paganini* is the best thing Lehár has so far written: a peak in the development of operetta."

Four days later, in his Stockholm hotel, Tauber received a letter from Lehár: "Empty seats at the first night: just imagine, Richard. You *must* sing in Berlin, a second fiasco is unthinkable for me. I am suddenly afraid of everything to do with the theatre —I'm growing old!"

In the last week of *Paganini*'s short run in Vienna, Tauber saw the operetta. Fascinated by the work, and indignant at the unjust treatment it had suffered, he informed Lehár, Saltenburg and Vera Schwarz that he was determined to honour his obligations for Berlin.

The Enrichment

The short *Paganini* prelude—the birthday present from dear God —is in its lofty simplicity one of the most beautiful orchestral introductions in the musical theatre. From the magnificent sweep of the *crescendo* to its passionate climax the note of Lehár's new inspiration can be heard, sounding forth "all his thinking, all his feeling, highest joy and deepest pain". As motif for "voluptuous bliss and avid longing" the noble G-major melody, which Lehár always called his "musical confession of faith", accompanies the story of the dangerous love of Nicolo Paganini and Anna Elisa. Like her brother Napoleon I, the young Princess at her court enjoys "*bals parés* and parties, brilliant receptions—in a word, the grand sensation". In a village tavern she meets the devil's fiddler, and falls under his spell. The dream of love is followed by an abrupt awakening. The Emperor, to avoid a scandal, has given orders for Paganini's deportation; after a last painful reunion the lovers are parted and return to their own worlds.

With this straightforward plot, Jenbach and Knepler's book contains a depth of feeling the composer instinctively sensed and exploited. Very few operettas, apart from the following three Lehár works, contain more love music, and nowhere is the *psyche erotica* of its creator more clearly brought to light. Every melodic phrase seems steeped in it, and the variety of its expression surprises again and again. The romance "Girls are made to love and kiss",

the *valse lente* "Love, you heaven on earth", and the *cavatina*
"Your sweet rose-lips", are the more obvious pearls in a treasury
of melody which avoids any pandering to popular taste and yet
cannot help achieving great popularity.

The duet "No one loves you as I do" was written by Lehár four
days before the première: chiefly because another number designed
for the two leads exposed their weaknesses all too clearly. In the
delicate *continuo* of its alternating G and F

NIE-MAND LIEBT DICH SO   WIE   ICH.----   BIN AUF DER

WELT------ JA NUR FÜR   DICH------

the lovers' heart-beats can be heard; the ingenious raising of the
tenor voice over the soprano produces a vocal effect of unique
beauty. But the total effect of the *Paganini* music does not consist
only in its jewels: the solo- and ensemble-scenes, choruses and
finales show an enthralling dramatic spirit which is perfectly
reflected in the colouring of the truly inspired orchestration.

Paganini has been condescendingly called an "operetta tragedy",
a "small music-drama", and (which hurt Lehár more than anything) a "small opera". He wanted to see it as simply an operetta
—if you like, a "grand operetta". "Why," he complained,[1] "do
I have to read over and over again that I am 'flirting' with opera,
when I am only looking for human interest? Art cannot be pressed
into rigid formulas; forms and artistic methods are in a process of
continual development, subject to lasting changes. Others may, if
they wish, see the salvation of operetta in its simplification; I see
it in an enrichment, accessible to an operetta composer through
the technical progress of music in general and opera in particular."

Miracles and Magic

When Saltenburg in Berlin received a letter from Tauber saying

[1] In the *Berliner Tageblatt*, 5th February 1926.

that he was available, as agreed, for rehearsals of *Paganini* at the Deutsche Künstlertheater from the beginning of January, he could not believe his eyes. Months before, soon after the first news arrived of the difficulties in Vienna, he had already felt growing doubts as to the chances of the work's success in Berlin. The fiasco at the Johann-Strauss-Theatre confirmed his fears. He wrote to Tauber and Lehár, thanking them for their readiness to give their services, but regretting that the failure at Vienna left him with no alternative; he hoped subsequently, however, to find other possibilities for co-operation, etc., etc.

Saltenburg had not reckoned with Lehár's determination to clear out of his way any obstacle that might stop him reaching his objectives. Relying on the contract of 16th August 1924, he had the manager summoned before the arbitration committee of the Deutsche Bühnengenossenschaft (German "Equity"), whose judgement was binding on the whole theatrical profession. Saltenburg was alarmed, for he had been in a similar situation three months before: the arbitration committee had to sentence him to put on a comedy he had accepted but not produced, because on further examination, he explained, it did not seem to him sufficiently promising commercially. The matter would have been less embarrassing for him had the play, Carl Zuckmayer's *Der fröhliche Weinberg* (The Merry Vineyard), not proved one of the greatest triumphs of the German theatre, and Saltenburg's opinion a crass misjudgement.

The judges were amused when he stood before them again; on the other hand, they did not want to make him a public laughingstock. As Lehár and Tauber also proved ready to compromise, a settlement was reached whereby Lehár renounced his royalties and Tauber half his salary, and the performance guarantee was reduced from fifty to thirty evenings. The press reported this with big headlines,

IS SALTENBURG AGAIN SENTENCED TO SUCCESS?

all Berlin laughed, and the *Paganini* rehearsals started. The manager interrupted them constantly with sarcasms and abuse. "And what will you do," asked Tauber, "if it should be a success after all?"

"Success?" said Saltenburg. "I'll be glad if it doesn't lose me every *pfennig The Merry Vineyard* is bringing in. I don't believe in miracles and magic, you know."

Miracles and magic occurred in the Deutsche Künstlertheater on 30th January 1926: exactly seven years before that other 30th January which put an end to all Berlin's enjoyment of life and exuberance, Lehár's melodies and Tauber's voice immediately brought a cynical, arrogantly *blasé*, big-city audience back to romance, sentiment and emotion.

Terrific applause after the first act, two encores for "Love, you heaven on earth", three for "No one loves you as I do", five for "Girls were made to love and kiss". The audience shouted, cheered and yelled in a frenzy which embraced stalls and circles alike. Saltenburg had put Lehár in the back of a box, refusing to let him conduct, "to protect him from the possibilities of a theatrical scandal". Now a spotlight found him and brought him to the front of the box. Then he was dragged on to the stage.

Tears poured down his cheeks. "Thank you, Richard," he stammered again and again. "Thank you—today I have been born a second time." Tauber could have returned the compliment with the same sincerity. Gramophone and radio companies, theatrical and concert agencies competed with each other to gain him; and the "Sold Out" notice hung over the box office of the theatre for over three months. The aftermath of Zuckmayer's success, which the playwright describes in his memoirs,[1] was exactly repeated with *Paganini*: Saltenburg "stalked around like a cock which had not only covered the hen but also laid the egg and hatched it. He was now firmly convinced that he had 'always known it'."

Tauber insisted on "fining him" for his behaviour at rehearsals: exacting back payment of all that he and Lehár had renounced at the arbitration court. Saltenburg paid up with a groan. The only condition he made was that he might put on the next Lehár-Tauber product in his theatre very soon—of course, with increased royalties for the composer and increased salary for the star.

[1] *Als wär's ein Stück von mir* (as if it were a Piece of me), Frankfurt, 1967.

XII
CROWNING GLORIES

A Chivalrous Gesture

To understand the meagre prospects for *Paganini* in the smart Berlin of the second half of the twenties (and at least partly to excuse Saltenburg's attitude), one must remember the situation at the time of the light musical theatre in the German capital. The place so long occupied in the public's heart by the romantic Viennese operetta had been taken over by four or five other variations of the species: by Oscar Straus's wittily intelligent *parlando* operettas *à la Viennoise*, Jean Gilbert's and Walter Kollo's *vaudevilles*, and the *Singspiel* by Eduard Künnecke.[1] With *Der Vetter aus Dingsda* (The Cousin from Nowhere) he achieved a stylistically large-scale operetta in a "chamber operetta" frame: no chorus, no ballet, and yet a superb score, splendid parts, humour, emotion.

The great Berlin revue,[2] which had started at the beginning of the century at the Metropoltheater, was now presented by James Klein, Hermann Haller and Erik Charrell; the intimate one by Mischa Spoliansky and Friedrich Holländer. In Brecht's and Weill's *Dreigroschenoper* (Threepenny Opera) the entry of cabaret into the world of the legitimate musical theatre found its final justification and conclusive triumph (1928). Kurt Weill's idea of opera music as *Gebrauchsmusik* (music for everyday use), of the hit song as character aria, was admirably matched to the social criticism

---

[1] 1885–1953.

[2] The word revue was used for the first time as the name of a genre by the American manager George W. Lederer for his production *The Passing Show*. (1894).

of Bert Brecht's lyrics. Although *The Threepenny Opera* should not be measured by the standards of operetta, it was a unique phenomenon and one of the guiding and galvanizing influences on the Broadway musical of the forties and fifties.

Amidst all the varied developments, modern and super-modern, in the Berlin musical theatre, the Lehár operetta, which in the last resort stood on yesterday's ground, had again come into fashion. Lehár felt that the *Paganini* success was bound to be repeated, enhanced and multiplied in the German capital during the coming years; so he decided he must be near the scene of that success, and transferred the centre of his activities from Vienna to Berlin. The decision contained no *ressentiment* towards Vienna, as was assumed in the operetta cafés there: he bore no grudge against those who wanted to throw him on the scrap-heap, nor did he envy those whose works were breaking his own records there for length of run. Following where long-term self-interest led, he set out from the comfortable suite in the Hotel Eden—his Berlin base—in pursuit of new goals.

Meanwhile the première of his own operetta *Gigolette*, which was *The Stargazer* and *Danze della Libellule* with a revised libretto by Giovacchino Forzano,[1] took place in Milan on 30th December 1926.)

The Tsarevich had been occupying Lehár ever since 1917, when Sophie saw the play by the Polish writer Gabryele Zapolska[2] at the Deutsche Volkstheater and drew his attention to it. While still working on *Paganini* he talked about it to Jenbach, who soon afterwards began with the preliminaries, in partnership with Reichert.

He was very much surprised when the composer informed him some while later that he had decided on further consideration not to write the music for *The Tsarevich*. The reason Lehár gave was that he found the disguise of the heroine as a boy immoral, in fact indecent. It was in vain that the librettists pointed to *Rosenkavalier*, and stressed all the advantages of the project: Lehár, remembering the embarrassing experience of *The Mock Marriage*, remained adamant.

An adventurous idea then occurred to Jenbach: he would offer

1 Librettist of Puccini's *Suor Angelica* and *Gianni Schicchi*.   2 1860–1921.

The Tsarevich to the composer of *Cavalleria*. Mascagni after his first tumultuous success had experienced twelve operatic failures, was in financial difficulties, and agreed to take on the job—for an advance of 400,000 lire from the publishers. Two years passed without his writing a single bar; Jenbach lost patience, parted company with Mascagni, and offered his book—to Künnecke.

The composer of *The Cousin from Nowhere* approached with his usual care a subject which was not really congenial to him. He had finished composing the first act when he received a visit one day from Jenbach, who stammered in embarrassment that Lehár, for whom *The Tsarevich* had as a matter of fact been originally designed, had again changed his mind. He bitterly regretted having given up the libretto, and wanted now definitely (on Tauber's advice) to set about the composition. "So I'd be terribly grateful if you would understand my position and release *The Tsarevich*."

Künnecke showed every understanding. With a chivalrous gesture he handed the book over to Jenbach. "Give my regards to my friend Lehár," he said. "It is a great pleasure for me to help him towards the production of a new masterpiece."

Behold–a Tenor!

The time of working on *The Tsarevich* score was one of the happiest in Lehár's life. Bursting with health, he had triumphantly surmounted all setbacks and troubles over a long period, and had his private life admirably organized. Sophie continued to be his loving comrade, quietly guiding him; the world popularity of his music was still growing; and—of the utmost importance with his fear of being *inoperaio*—his next assignment, *Frederica*, was already fixed in its outlines.

In May he returned to Ischl, in July the piano score was finished, September and October saw the orchestral score written. Everything went without snags or stoppages, fuss or fury. At the beginning of 1927 the rehearsals began in the Deutsche Künstlertheater. Saltenburg the lion had turned into a lamb. Every wish of Lehár's was read in his eyes, the orchestra was expanded, the production given all glamour and spectacle. In the première on 21st February

Tauber sang the title role, Lehár conducted, and received ovations before which next morning even the most scornful critics had to capitulate. They released their sarcasm on the poor librettists. "My good Jenbach and Reichert," sneered the man from the *Morgenpost*, "I do not want to know at 7.20 how the thing ends at 10.55. If you are incapable of writing a book with a small amount of suspense . . . I shan't object if you go and get buried."

Far from responding to his advice, Jenbach and Reichert enjoyed for many years the fruits of their labour and the fame of having provided Lehár with one of his most effective libretti. The Zapolska drama was taken out of politics, humanized and cleared of all superfluous historical matter. The love story in its passionate eroticism was at the centre of proceedings—the writers deliberately dispensed with inorganic operetta humour. The composer (on the model of Puccini) exercised a decisive influence on the dramatic structure. He knew what he wanted and carried it through. More than in *Paganini* the unhappy ending was to be psychologically founded, and prepared for as the only possible solution of the conflict.

The hero, Crown Prince Alexei, is an unworldly youth. In his loneliness he fears "the great secret which surrounds all women". He wants to have a comrade, a friend and confidant. To prepare him for a coming marriage, the ballet girl Sonya, disguised as a Circassian, is smuggled into his rooms. The intrigue miscarries: the young people fall in love, and elope. In Naples the inevitable parting comes. Sonya must sacrifice herself, give him up, lead him to his mission, to duty and obedience.

In the *Tsarevich* music you can hear, as if in the far distance, the old *Kukushcka* colouring: a stealthy major-minor half-darkness, the soft elegiac melody of desire, fulfilment and parting. It sounds in the rich E major of Sonya's "One day someone will come", *con tenerezza* in Alexei's "Why is there only one May to every spring?" —in the discreet *valse lente* rhythms of the duet: "I have only you"; and plaintively, longingly, solemnly in the Volga Song

which Tauber himself discovered in a half-forgotten exercise book of Lehár's and which was one day to be the Master's death lament.

Schnappula had meanwhile married the elegant and much-courted Carlotta Vanconti, first met during the *Frasquita* days at the Theater an der Wien. Tauber Senior gave her the chance to perfect herself as actress and singer at his Chemnitz theatre; Richard intended to make her his permanent leading lady. Now he established his first household with her in a spacious villa in the Schöneberger Stadtpark, which he furnished with all luxury: here he entertained, and led a regular, well-ordered life, whether he liked it or not.

The Tsarevich was the operetta role he loved more than any other, perhaps because it corresponded to his own shy, innermost nature, because in it he could express his most secret wishes and fears. Whenever there was an opportunity to appear as Alexei, he seized it; and on reaching the age of fifty gave up the role only with extreme reluctance. Even after the Second World War he hoped to be able to sing it again. When a London costumier wanted to buy off him the magnificent Russian attire, which he had worn so proudly, he refused with indignation: "What? All the uniforms, helmets, swords, cloaks, boots? Don't people know that I may be needing them again tomorrow?" His superb art, the glittering force of his personality, the ecstasy of his soul, could not and would not be parted from the youth of the prince.

"The world was under his sway", wrote the Viennese poet Ludwig Ullmann; "listening enthralled and captivated. Comparisons were shaken, standards shattered, in the silvery wind of his *falsetto*. How he modelled, shaped and built the tone—great architect of the vocal line—building it up into a thrilled and thrilling glory: here was the gift of a careless perfection, laughing, radiant, dazzling and intoxicating. Behold—a tenor! He is born only once in decades."

The Great Controversy

Ten years after the *Stargazer* time Beda, still full of youthful enthusiasm, came to Lehár with the explosive idea of a Goethe musical. Explosive because it might be attacked on grounds of taste, aesthetics and possibly even politics. All the same, claimed Beda, it presented a unique artistic challenge. Lehár said he was not afraid of challenges, and was used to attacks. Löhner had drafted the *Friederike* book with his friend Ludwig Herzer, a Viennese gynaecologist who was also a talented playwright.[1] Now he told Lehár about the Whit Sunday of 1771 in the Alsatian village of Sesenheim, the magic of spring, splendour of blossom, and the young Goethe's love for the pastor's daughter, Friederike Brion:

"O Mädchen, Mädchen,
Wie lieb' ich dich!
Wie blickt dein Auge!
Wie liebst du mich!"

Then he described the lovers' last meeting—and the *Urlaut* was aroused.

Lehár's *naïveté* when it was a question of any new work he wanted to write excluded any doubts, scruples or objections. Friederike for him meant love, heart-break and renunciation; Goethe (like the Genoese fiddler or the Russian heir apparent) meant Tauber: not the poet, the ageless, all-embracing spirit who "created, bore and cherished a world in himself", but just Tauber. The great tenor himself hesitated at first, and invited opinions: "Have I the right to sing Goethe? Am I committing sacrilege?" Then he saw himself in the costume of the age—wig, court jacket, lace ruff, breeches and *éscarpins*; heard himself in duet with the one and only Käthe Dorsch; and said yes.

Starting in the provinces in operetta, Käthe Dorsch, Germany's foremost actress of the time, was led in Berlin by the Rotter brothers to straight plays, and now back again to operetta. "Tauber may

[1] Dr Herzer was the last of Lehár's twenty-six librettists. Like Leo Stein and Heinz Reichert, he wrote three books for him. Dr Willner holds the record for Lehár librettists with eight works, Bodanzky is second with six, Léon and Löhner tie for third place with five each. With Bela Jenbach and Julius Bauer Lehár collaborated four times; with Brammer, Grünwald, Knepler and Grünbaum twice; with Mlčoch, Ruthner, Falzari, Gustav Schmidt, Kalbeck, Vincze, Kolhapp, Zasche, Norini, Tann-ßergler, Eger, Lombardo and Forzano once.

serenade me with Lehár melodies free of charge," she said on receiving the *Friederike* offer, "but the two *Bindelbands* will have to pay me a thousand marks an evening for it!"

The two *Bindelbands* were the much-abused and much-slandered Rotter brothers, who now entered Lehár's world. It was thanks to their generosity and theatrical dynamism that his next three works received productions which have gone down in the history of the musical theatre as absolutely flawless. The brothers, Alfred and Fritz, were the sons of a corn-dealer from Leipzig, and as law students at Berlin University had already looked for openings on the stage. During the war they produced the lightest of fare; soon after it their literary adviser, the brilliant Dr Kanehl, directed their attention towards great drama, and was responsible for some of their more ambitious presentations.

(In a spirit of world-weariness he committed suicide, but shortly before had suggested to the brothers that they should take on a college contemporary of his to replace him. Whether the recommended successor called at their offices, and if so whether he was received, put off or shown the door, history does not relate. Five years later this young man, Dr Joseph Goebbels, had become Nazi *Gauleiter* of Berlin, and one of the Rotter brothers' most savage enemies.)

Their enterprises grew: star casts, advertising campaigns and ticket vouchers brought them vast audiences. New theatres were constantly being added to their empire; Alfred's delight in everything connected with the stage and Fritz's shrewd business sense were bearing rich fruit. Now they were in a position to offer Lehár the redecorated Metropoltheater for *Friederike*—and also in Fritz Friedmann-Frederich a reliable *régisseur* who was to fulfil with the utmost fidelity all the work's requirements. Lehár reserved the final decision on any artistic questions. Accepted by all concerned as master of the *métier*, he took the reins in his hands, travelled even to Sesenheim with the stage designers, and looked for authentic décor motifs. He tried to provide perfect casting for even the smallest parts; and he experimented with the orchestra ("by word of mouth"), until he had transformed his score into the most subtle and sublime sound.

While the preparations went on without incident, the great *Friederike* controversy had flared up in the press and also among the public.

Posters called for nationalist protest meetings, left-wing intellectuals screamed in headlines: "End the Rotterization of the Theatre"; liberal papers printed articles, reports and interviews on the "*Friederike* Case"; and cabarets in the Kurfürstendamm put on burlesques in which Goethe himself appeared. Egon Erwin Kisch, the famous roving reporter, outdid everyone. He claimed to have found in a village in Lower Alsace a great-niece of the real Friederike Brion, a very old lady, whom he interviewed to discover whether she could still remember her great-aunt. "Yes, of course," came the answer. "A dear friendly little thing." Had her aunt told her about a young suitor, a student from Strasburg? Indeed she had: ". . . often came to Sesenheim, the young rascal, turned her head—then one day he went off, and nobody ever heard anything of him again".

The Rotters converted to cash value all that happened or was printed. Beda was apprehensive, lost his bravado. He told a friend later about his nervousness on the afternoon and evening of the première,[1] how he walked through the Berlin streets with coat collar turned up, peered into lighted shop windows without seeing anything, turned into Behrenstrasse, and suddenly was standing outside the Metropoltheater with the posters for the world première. How he started in shock, wanted to enter the theatre to look for Lehár; and remembered that his friend would probably be in bed in his hotel having his pre-first-night nap.

He called a taxi, had himself taken to the West End, strolled along the Kurfürstendamm, spoke to two street-walkers, took a drink in the nearest bar, looked again and again at his watch.

Meanwhile the lights of the theatre façade had flashed on in Behrenstrasse, the doors were opened, the first-comers in the audience arrived, the stream of cars began. The Rotters had collected the city's great names: the Crown Prince was there with his brother August Wilhelm, there were Hohenlohes, Henckel-

[1] 4th October 1928.

Donnersmarcks, Mendelssohns, Bleichröders, General von Seekt, Police Chief Weiss, millionaire industrialist Hugenberg, film star Henny Porten, novelist Heinrich Mann, ice-skating champion Sonja Henie, Albert Einstein—and incognito, standing in a quiet corner, the man who had put up the money for the show: the Swedish match king Ivar Kreuger.

At three minutes past seven the house lights went out. Lehár entered the orchestra pit, and with a smile and nod expressed thanks for the applause. The buzz died away; and softly from the dark silence, in flute, clarinet and bassoon octaves, the lilting triplets of the prelude streamed forth.

Showered with a Golden Rain

Thanks to its natural ingredients of poignancy the *Friederieke* story had enjoyed great popularity since the middle of the nineteenth century, as countless novels, plays and operettas written around it, prove. Löhner and Herzer were clever, cultured men of letters, who set about their task with tact and respect, organizing their themes and contrasting effects, and eventually submitting to Lehár the background for a distinguished musical work. In the first act Goethe and Friederike fall in love, in the second Goethe is called to Weimar, and Friederike struggles through the decision to let him go: in the third Goethe comes back after eight years, accompanied by the Grand Duke, for the final parting. Plot and dialogue were reduced to a minimum; characterization, mood, drama and humour were simply to grow out of the music.

How enchantingly Lehár succeeded in this shows in every bar of the score. Of its twenty eight numbers, sixteen go to one or the other or both of the two leads. These numbers are remarkable for the richness of the melodies, their expressiveness and an affinity between words and music which is unique in the whole field of operetta. Friederike's songs have the sense of impending separation brooding over them; they are tender, simple with, the tuneful freshness of folk-songs. As in Paganini's and Elisa's "No one loves you as I do", Friederike's glorious

WA-RUM HAST DU MICH WACH-GE-KÜSST? HAB' NICHT GE-WUSST WAS LIE-BE IST

gives the true heart-beat of a loving heart: not triumphant and proud, as in *Paganini*, but fearful, distracted, resigned. Goethe's five numbers culminate in the Tauber *Lied*:

O Mädchen, mein Mäd-chen, — wie lieb' ich dich!

This time it is not an interpolated *arioso*, no tacked-on serenade, but the great main theme of the work, slowly dawning, constantly growing. We hear it for the first time as a flute solo, then as contrapuntal decoration on the love motif in the prelude; and the moment the curtain rises, in violin octaves to distant organ accompaniment. In the first-act finale it breaks through in its full glory. It is a Lehárian ecstasy of triplet inspiration, with a natural and unaffected vocal line.

Lehár's seven Tauber songs have in common the free, grand melody, vocal forcefulness, sonorous effect and straight rhythm. For all their brilliance and power, however, they fail from the viewpoint of musical drama (except of course "O maiden, my maiden") through their dangerous transfer of weight in favour of the singing star: the action suddenly breaks off, the actor becomes a soloist, the interest of the audience turns away from the dramatic situation to the *Lied*. This tendency did not stop at Tauber and his contrasting encores with their surprising final flourish: it was reproduced by his imitators, who all at once appeared everywhere, and often became part of an annoying cliché. Lehár recognized this early on, and tried to get rid of the habit. In vain: it had grown into an essential part of the evening, and was practised long after Tauber had retired from the scene.

The numbers in the *Friederike* score that are not for the two leads join the general musical picture, and often sound as if Lehár were reverting to the compositions of his pre-operetta period; but as if he had now refined, ennobled and modernized them.

The instrumental structure of the work is worthy of its luxuriant melodic beauty. The orchestration, true to the setting and as sure as ever, with its bewildering abundance of rich *ensemble* sound, pastel tones and glittering ornamentation, represents the technical peak of Lehárian orchestral magic.

It took closed ears, and all the intellectual snobbery and ill-will of the Berlin theatre critics of 1928 to ignore the reverent attitude of the book and the beauty of the music. Hardened cynics among them suddenly felt called on to protect the holy names of Goethe and the other personages on the character list, and fell into a fury which, considering their normal behaviour, bore all too clearly the stamp of hypocrisy. They blamed the librettists for altering the dates of events to suit their own purposes; for tampering with a poetic classic and making Goethe a "whining Willie", Lehár's music they called "detestable", "a trite feast for undemanding ears", "on the level of a cheap romantic novel". One of them went so far as to say: "Puccini is the poor man's Verdi, Lehár is the poor man's Puccini—and such rubbish becomes an international success."

Even Lehár, accustomed to abuse in the press, was not prepared for such outbursts of hate. He paced round his hotel suite for days in great depression, and nothing could cheer him: neither the remark of the respected musicologist Kurt Westermeyer that *Friederike* was one of the crowning glories of his life's work, "the most essential expression of his musical soul and artistic aspirations", nor the rush on the box office of the Metropoltheater.

For *Friederike*, despite the press, had become the theatrical success of the year. Where the hate-filled critics had cried "No!", the public answered them with an enthusiastic "Yes!" Evening after evening Tauber and la Dorsch, as if showered with a golden rain, stood amidst hurricanes of enthusiasm. No one bothered about the fact that each of them was twice as old as the character represented, or that his vocal powers were as superior to hers as her histrionic talents were to his. Never before had a theatrical success spread with such speed over Germany. Suddenly every provincial town had its Tauber, its Dorsch, its malicious critics—and its rush on the box office. Vienna followed with a fine production in which the enchanting Lea Seidl sang the title role; soon there was a production in London too (again with Lea Seidl), in New York, Paris—and the whole world.

In the fourth month of the Berlin run disaster occurred. Tauber had gone to the Rhineland for a short concert tour. On the way back, driving his open car on an icy winter day, he caught a cold. He complained of pain in the neck and chest, but nevertheless appeared every evening. After the celebration of the hundredth performance, when all concerned were receiving the thanks of the audience, Lehár gratefully pressed his right hand. Tauber cried out, convulsed by a stabbing pain: all of a sudden he couldn't move his hand, cold sweat beaded on his forehead. He was wrapped in shawls, taken home and put to bed shivering. A few days later he had recovered; he sang again, discussed plans for a film and for gramophone records, entertained friends. During a lunch party he suddenly fell silent and went deathly pale, with the horrible feeling that his legs and thighs had gone numb.

Specialists were called in, and diagnosed an advanced condition of generalized arthritis. Thus a time of suffering began for poor Schnappula, giving him weeks and weeks of immobility, helplessness and despondency. On 2nd May he was brought by ambulance to Anhalt Station, carried on a stretcher into a special coach, and transported for medical treatment to the famous spa Pistyan in western Slovakia.

XIII
LOVELY, UNLOVELY WORLD

Just Before the Final Curtain

The treatment at Pistyan included burning hot sulphur baths, mud-packs, electro-therapy, fasting; and Tauber bore it all with amazing patience and resignation to fate. Motionless, in agonies of pain, he lay in his bed in the Thermia Palace Hotel. He could no longer laugh as he usually did, and once when he tried voice exercises he had to give up after a few minutes for lack of breath. All that he could expect from the future was to be able to give singing lessons in a wheel-chair, perhaps now and then a *Lieder* recital. The Berlin and Vienna papers came out with headlines

TAUBER WILL NEVER SING AGAIN.

On the radio his old records were played, always followed by expressions of sympathy. The doctors did everything to strengthen the patient's resistance and bring him through the difficult first weeks, which carried with them a constant progression in pain.

Fortunately, however, his heart was equal to the strain, and soon the first small signs of an improvement appeared. Tauber got up occasionally, did hand and foot exercises, phoned old friends, and hobbled around on crutches outside the hotel in the spring sunshine. In the third week of June his nurse heard him give a shout in the middle of the night. "The fly, the fly!" he cried, right arm flailing in the air. "It settled on my nose, and I shooed it off. Shooed off the Schnappula with my hand!" He was laughing and crying at the same time. The sister calmed him down and held his hand till he went to sleep again.

Next morning he was free of pain. He got up cautiously, and cautiously took his first steps. It was three more weeks before he hung up his crutches on the wall in Pistyan's Museum, in the presence of journalists, photographers and radio reporters, and could sing the Prayer of Thanksgiving in a special concert for the poor of the town. His voice resounded through the hall in its old brilliance and on a radiant August morning half Pistyan—doctors, nurses, hotel staff, patients—stood outside the hotel, led by the local band, to say good-bye to Tauber. The same evening he was in Vienna to receive a big hug from Lehár.

Even before the first news of improvement had arrived in Theobaldgasse, the composer had asked the *Friederike* librettists to come and discuss future work. And even before the call reached them, they had agreed on a plan for this, which gained immensely in appeal when they heard there was a good hope of Tauber being back in action.

Among the Lehárians who still admired *The Yellow Jacket*, remembered its beauties and lamented its failure, Beda was the most passionate. He now convinced Lehár, with Herzer's help, that this was the right moment to make it viable through some skilful alterations. Prince Sou Chong, who marries the Viennese girl and takes her to his palace in Peking, was the ideal Tauber role, especially in the circumstances: the Chinese make-up would mask Tauber's facial disfigurement, the long kimonos would conceal a slight limp and the stiffness of the left arm, a legacy of his illness. All that remained was to obtain from Léon, now seventy, a free hand for the modifications to his book (which he readily granted), and persuade Lehár—a more difficult undertaking—to make a partial adaptation of the music.

Here Beda came up with a plan which won the composer's agreement immediately. On page 120 of the 124 pages of the *Yellow Jacket* vocal score, he had discovered sixteen bars which sound for the first and last time just before the final curtain, and which had slipped the memory of Lehár himself. They seemed to him the most beautiful the composer had ever conceived: an inspiration in a thousand, utterly spontaneous, supremely tuneful, perfectly harmonized—the ideal Tauber melody:

Lehár could scarcely grasp it. Beda was right: the brief *arioso*, overlaid by the mass of the rest of the score, contained the main theme of the new work; and on the previous page of the score, also made to measure already, stood the middle section of the new number. Never before had a love song destined for world fame been born more easily.

When Tauber heard it for the first time he was too overjoyed to speak; he picked up the page of music from the piano, looked at it, and softly hummed the tune over to himself. Lehár began to play it again; at the end of the third bar he stopped, and Tauber came in with all his recovered vocal powers.

The same night Alfred Rotter received a telephone call in Berlin, and heard over the phone: "You are my heart's delight". What was the operetta called, he asked enthusiastically. Tauber looked at Lehár, Lehár at Herzer, Herzer at Beda; no one had thought of a title, until Beda now, as if on the spur of the moment, burst out with: "*The Land of Smiles*".

The Transformation

At first glance the differences between *The Yellow Jacket* and *The Land of Smiles* seem negligible and irrelevant. The same characters are involved in the same conflict, appear in the same settings, and express their feelings to the same melodies. Only by a closer examination of words and music can one register the crucial changes which finally transformed failure into triumph.

First and foremost was the omission of all superfluous matter: the wordy dialogue, the social and historical explanations, and the attempts at an operetta humour contradicting the nature of the dramatic action. Herzer and Beda were solely concerned with relating a romance, set in a fairy-tale China, which breaks up on the rocks of traditionalism: the proud Lisa, not created to be one wife among many, has to escape from her Chinese *seraglio*, and like the magnanimous Selim Bassa in Mozart's opera, Sou Chong, having found her out, has to let her go. "He remains alone, deserted, yet smiling," the libretto informs us, "and blessed by his grief, the true conqueror." "But," he sings, "how it feels inside is nobody's concern."

The unhappy ending was decisive for the change in the work's fortunes. It remained, in the words of one newspaper critic, the "beautiful and also brave operetta conclusion, which instead of the hackneyed routine finale" supplied "a worthwhile and psychologically correct solution". The other structural faults in *The Yellow Jacket* were also removed: the shape of the action was reforged, the unnecessary ballast in costumes and décor disappeared, and with it the spun-out chorus and ballet sequences.

Lehár fought for each passage in each *ensemble* number, and Beda had to force him to the stylistic revision bar by bar in protracted debates. There were embarrassing and much-publicized quarrels and explosions at rehearsals; but in the end Tauber's musical and dramatic arguments (and concealed threats to withdraw) succeeded in changing Lehár's mind—very much to his own advantage.

Now at last, augmented by the Tauber song No. 5 and a newly composed *valse lente*—"Who has put the love in our hearts?"—the old numbers, with Beda's revised lyrics, shone radiantly forth: "Your love—my love", "A tea *en deux*"—and "Always smiling", which in both words and music sounds like an expression of Lehár's heart and mind, temperament and character.

Immer nur lä-cheln und immer vergnügt, immer zufrieden, wie s immer sich fügt.

The production[1] resolutely continued the *Friederike* tendencies, concentrating the action and all the musical elements. Orchestral and vocal brilliance were matched, in an attractive setting, with an interesting story, to create a theatrical feast of the first quality.

Tauber had settled down in Berlin in lordly style, and everything—huge salaries, bicycle races, old pals and beautiful women around him—was as it had always been. Until Carlotta suddenly involved him in a discussion of his private life amidst full publicity. The marriage had only lasted two years when rifts appeared (this was before his illness), and now she demanded a divorce. Tauber settled on Carlotta a million marks in cash, a huge monthly allowance, jewellery and the villa in Schöneberg. The financial sacrifices hurt him less than the blow to his pride.

So he left Berlin at the end of the season, and took his Chinese hero on an extended tour. In the autumn he presented him to the Viennese.[2] Marischka had made up his tiff with Lehár: his magnificent production of *The Land of Smiles* was a reconciliation present: the key which after the composer's seven-year absence opened the doors of the Theater an der Wien to him once more.

Some Meditations on Transience

Lehár was sixty. The crisis which may be fatal to other composers at this age, when their critical sense overlays their creative abilities, was something he had surmounted five years before; his graph of success was now back at its *Merry Widow* peak. The previous autumn there had been one day—Sunday, 17th November—when nine performances of Lehár operettas were taking place in Berlin; the Christmas week brought 500 different Lehár productions in central Europe, including 200 of *The Land of Smiles*.

For his sixtieth birthday he retired with Sophie, to escape from festivities and honours, to the peaceful seclusion of Baden-Baden.

[1] Première on 10th October 1929.   [2] On 20th September 1930.

But he was traced, and showered with telegrams of congratulation, decorations, letters, flowers and gifts. A special celebration had been designed by the Deutsche Kappellmeister-Union (German Conductors' Union), of which he was an honorary member: from eight till nine on the evening of 30th April only Lehár music was to be heard on all the radio stations in the country, in all concert halls, music-cafés and night-clubs. Deeply moved, Lehár thanked the organizers in a telegram:

I SHAKE THE HAND OF EVERY SINGLE
COLLEAGUE PROUD BY FAMILY TRADITION
AND PROFESSION TO BE YOURS FOR LIFE

The following day he sat down at his desk to thank every well-wisher in his own hand on the back of a portrait photograph; the mail from Berlin, Vienna and Ischl had meanwhile been forwarded to him. The work took six days, and in the end it was wasted; for something happened that was unique in Lehár's neat and methodical business dealings. The hotel porter, who should have stamped and sent off the post, had by mistake put the whole bundle in the drawer of one of Sophie's wardrobe trunks, where she found it four years later. "To my immeasurable astonishment!" Lehár commented, and went on to philosophize: "I looked through the cards one by one, and could not help observing that in a large number, a very large number of cases, belated forwarding was no longer necessary. Many of the addressees had vanished from my view, many were missing, many dead. I still remembered one or two; but most of the correspondence had settled itself, and I could start meditating on the transience of all earthly things."

The city of Vienna insisted on joining in the birthday festivities. The Bürgermeister invited hundreds of Lehár's friends and admirers—though many captious critics and enviers were also included—to a magnificent dinner in the town hall; and Lehár, to his great discomfort, had to make a speech. In the *Grosse Konzerthaussaal* a celebration concert (with Tauber, Vera Schwarz, the Vienna Philharmonic Orchestra, and the man of the moment on the rostrum) was organized: a two-hour selection of Lehár's *oeuvre*. When Tauber looked through the role assigned to him he refused to take part: it was quite impossible for him to manage twenty solo arias and duets. But directly he heard the G-major introduction to *Paganini*, he jumped to his feet: "What's going on here? 'All my thinking' without Schnappula? Oh no!" Like Bottom in *Midsummer Night's Dream*, he wanted to "play the lion, too", and ended up singing twenty-five numbers.

Operetta Success on an Opera Basis

Everything that came off so completely in *Land of Smiles* missed the mark in *Schön ist die Welt* (How Fair the World). This was the revised version of *Alone at Last*, the next product of the Lehár-Beda-Herzer partnership for Berlin's Metropoltheater.

It would be unfair to hold Lehár wholly responsible for the work's lukewarm reception, but most of the blame must certainly go to him. Against the advice and despite the vehement objections of his partners, he refused to abandon the Mountain scene, his *Urlaut* for *Alone at Last*; and it was only with reluctance that he agreed even to Beda's constructive idea of revitalizing the scene through a Tauber song, to be musically based on those few forgotten bars from *The Stargazer*[1]

The elegant and passionate number always remained a foreign body for him, although with the title waltz it formed the highlight of the score.

The old *Alone at Last* plot was augmented by a few South American elements, but otherwise remained intact in its banality: the story had gained nothing through its elevation into royal circles (it was now set among kings, crown princes and princesses). Alfred Rotter, convinced that the *Yellow Jacket* success was bound to be repeated, had assembled a star cast which besides Tauber included the golden-haired Hungarian Gitta Aplar, coloratura

[1] See musical illustration p. 175.

prima donna of the Berlin State Opera. After the première[1] the critics, with a politeness masking lack of respect, spoke of "an operetta success on an opera basis"—thereby giving a warning signal to the general public.

The success of *The Land of Smiles* had been aided from outside the year before by a constellation of favourable circumstance. Now everything seemed to combine, in a world anything but fair, to belie the optimistic title. Wall Street had in October 1929 suffered the greatest stock exchange disaster of all time; now the repercussions made themselves felt all over Germany: banks collapsed, increasing unemployment led to political disturbances and conflicts; the radical right-wing and left-wing parties had emerged from the general election in triumph; and influential industrial circles began to take an interest in Adolf Hitler—former frequenter of the Theater an der Wien gallery.

The Rotters used all their wiles to keep Lehár's work on the programme. Their methods were criticized in violent press attacks, they themselves were denounced as "art speculators", "croppers of theatres and artistic talents who pushed them this way and that for profit". The crisis they inevitably slid into, however, was averted not by Lehár but by a newcomer among composers and his sensational first operetta.

The Forest Fire

Paul Abraham[2] was a complex character, braggart, epicurean, depressive, hypochondriac: superficial but pedantic, indolent but a firebrand. The sureness of his theatrical and musical instinct and his sense for the popular tune were overwhelming; his flair for orchestral technique was revolutionary, fifteen years ahead of his time. Like a forest fire he swept across the European operetta scene and gave it its last great impetus.

When he appeared for the first time outside Hungary, in a Berlin film studio, he was a tall, thin, dark-haired man in his late thirties. He had been imported from Budapest by a Hungarian film *régisseur*, and the tales of his extraordinary talent soon became

---

[1] On 3rd December 1930.   [2] 1892–1960.

a staple topic in the Berlin cafés. Information about his past was conflicting and dubious. Now he told the reporters he was a former star pupil at the Budapest Academy of Music, now the papers said he had been a successful banker in his native city. He scarcely gave the impression of a man of substance; if anything, he looked feckless, indigent and uprooted. A year later his name appeared in neon lights on a hundred theatre façades and in huge letters on all Germany's poster pillars. *Viktoria und ihr Husar* (Victoria and her Hussar), produced by the Rotters at the Metropoltheater, Berlin, made him world-famous, extremely rich, and the proud owner of a little rococo villa in Berlin's west end.

Basically, it was the old Kálmán operetta with Hungarian girls, gipsy violins and wine festivals. But a fresh breeze could be felt blowing through all of it, and audiences were enchanted.

Lehár was not sure whether to regard Abraham as a true innovator or a successful adventurer. Compared with the music of his tired old friends Eysler, Straus and Kálmán, his score showed a refreshing vigour; compared with his own (he was objective enough to hear this), it lost a good deal of its originality, and owed much to the American operettas of the day. It was an open secret in operetta circles that Abraham, despite his own respectable technical ability, employed arrangers and orchestrators, who brought his ideas into the most super-modern forms and prepared them for production and publication. In Vienna such methods were considered dishonest; and musicians who could not put their melodies down on paper, but could at best play them over on the piano, sing or whistle them to others, were called *Pfeiferlkomponisten* (whistle-composers).[1]

In America, specialization in operetta music had gone so far that a complete score represented the collective work of seven or eight experts, to whom the composer—even if he had a most thorough

Schoenberg and Webern were among those who looked after the hackwork for them. When Arnold Schoenberg was working on the *Gurre-Lieder* at the beginning of the century, an opus on which he was engaged for a decade, he earned his bread and butter as music-teacher—and operetta orchestrator. To complete the 800 pages of his score, he had to write 6,000 pages of scores for operettas, musical comedies and vaudevilles by others.

schooling—would deliver the mere melodic skeleton. The achievement of absolute technical smoothness in a work could no longer be demanded of a single individual. Ballet and chorus arrangements, orchestrations of vocal or dance numbers—everything was entrusted to specialists, whose skill was highly paid and whose names stood out in big letters next to those of the composers on all the posters.

That Abraham used such methods may have had something to do with his indolence, his passion for being in the vanguard of modernity, or his efforts to gain time in order to meet all the calls made on him. Lehár refused such calls, as his upbringing, temperament and artistic convictions demanded. He could always find time for work he wanted to do, but never tackled any for the sake of its financial reward alone. Except in his most intimate circle, he did not express the secret reservations he felt about Abraham's methods. He supported and defended him, and considered it his duty, by protecting him, to protect the whole genre. Abraham was a good musician, as Lehár fully appreciated: "And a good musician can never be good enough for operetta—just as a bad one can do just as little in operetta as anywhere else."

The gossips who connected Lehár's return to Vienna in the spring of 1931 with his disappointment at the Metropoltheater and Abraham's simultaneous rise, were mistaken. They overrated the ambition and underrated the self-assurance of a composer who could look back on five, ten, fifteen world successes.

XIV
DIVERS DISCOURSES

The Place to Retire

In his sixty-second year Lehár returned to Vienna, because he felt it was there and only there he must seek a place to which he and Sophie could retire, and which would be worthy of his world renown. He found it in the Schikaneder-Schlössl, an attractive late-baroque building in Hackhofergasse, between Nussdorf and the old village of Kahlenberg, fell in love with house and garden on sight, and three days later signed the contract to buy it.

The property had not been built (as is often assumed) by Emanuel Schikaneder,[1] the *Magic Flute* librettist, but long before him by a Baron Pilsti. Schikaneder did not acquire it until 1802, selling it three years afterwards, whereafter the house changed hands several times, till a German-American finally sold it to Lehár.

The protracted and expensive conversion, planned by Lehár himself down to the smallest detail, took two years. Meanwhile Sophie saw to the modernization of bathrooms, kitchen, heating system, and the furnishing of the huge rooms.

In June 1933 everything was ready for them to move in. Seen from Hackhofergasse, the house looked modest, almost suburban, as if it wanted to avoid any ostentation. An entrance gate led into a courtyard which separated the front from the main building, and gave a view on the left of Lehár's pride, the chapel. The spacious hall had a double staircase leading to the first floor—the ceiling was decorated with a fresco showing scenes from *The Magic Flute*. Next to the sitting room, dining-room and study were the couple's

---

[1] 1751–1812.

separate bedrooms (with a good distance between them). At the far end of the right wing there was a billiard-room, in which Lehár used to play solitary games, humming away to himself. He had pianos everywhere; and if asked how many there were, would only smile apologetically.

A glance in his library was rewarding, not only for the valuable Italian and French editions on the visual arts in the seventeenth and eighteenth centuries, but because its lavishness showed the universality of Lehár's interests. He read enormously, as long as his eyes were not giving him trouble, and complained that he would like to have done so much oftener, "if only each day had ten hours more"!

The back of the house faced the Danube and the mountains—behind the garden. Here Lehár walked, in summer wearing beret and the Ischl plus-fours, with pruning scissors in hand, in winter wrapped in thick scarves, with ear-flaps, carrying a stick.

The top floor of the house gave storage to the Lehár archives collected over forty years, and transferred from Theobaldgasse. All the Lehár scores starting from *Kukuschka*, in their original writing, with heavy leather bindings, were kept in a safe. One hundred thousand press cuttings, notices, interviews and articles, arranged by date, were stuck in 150 albums: 200 separate volumes contained 200,000 theatre programmes from all over the world. The walls were covered with photographs sent in dedication; special books were reserved for caricatures, letters from famous contemporaries and photographs, special shelves for files with contracts, accounts, business and private correspondence.

The staff who kept the household running smoothly, and looked after the Lehárs' physical well-being, consisted of their devoted butler Karl, a thin, gaunt fellow with a masterly technique for getting rid of uninvited guests; their admirable cook, Anna; and a caretaker couple named Scaja. Franz and Sophie did not entertain lavishly in Nussdorf, any more than they had done at Ischl or in Theobaldgasse. True, there were days when the stream of callers just would not stop; but the house's distance from the centre of the town discouraged mere droppers-in. As years went by the Lehár Schlössl (as it soon became known in Vienna) saw fewer and fewer visitors.

But if there was less human company, Lehár came to take a deep
pleasure in animals: more and more of them inhabited house and
garden. Outside were the squirrels on the trees, the goldfish in the
pond, the tortoise Gretl, fifty years old, on the path—he fed them
all with titbits. Indoors, the canaries Hermann and Mausi fluttered
around, to the annoyance of the two love-birds, who squawked
loudly in their cage. In the study, between the piano and the desk,
a frog lived in its glass case, lazy, comfortable and blown out;
while the white Angora cat Kathi was probably to be found
asleep in some armchair.

The star of this miniature zoo was the tiny brown collie You-
You, "a connoisseur of all my music," Lehár claimed, "except *The
Merry Widow*. He doesn't like that." If his master picked him up
and sang a theme to him from *Luxembourg* or *The Land of Smiles*, he
wagged his head and tail joyfully; but if he heard "Lips are silent"
or Danilo's "Maxim" song, he would open his mouth in a loud
yawn. One day the trick failed: the composer sang "Lips are
silent", and the little dog registered signs of approval. "What's
this, then, You-You?" Lehár demanded. "All of a sudden you
really like that hackneyed thing, do you?"

Drury Lane

At the beginning of 1931 the impresario Stanley H. Scott called on
Lehár in Vienna, hoping to buy *The Land of Smiles* for London:
Tauber was to sing Sou Chong, and the work would be put on at
the Theatre Royal, Drury Lane. Lehár was duly impressed by the
young man's enthusiasm, and no less by evidence of his considerable financial resources. The hope of repeating the *Merry Widow*,
Luxembourg and *Gipsy Love* successes, and of making up for the
disappointments of *The Three Graces, Cloclo, Frasquita* and *The
Blue Mazurka* gave wings to his decision: he accepted, after
receiving from Scott full artistic and financial guarantees. Tauber,
who did not know London and had been trying for months to
expand his sphere of activity westwards, fell in with the idea at
once.

He arrived in England in the middle of April, was met at Dover by Scott and put on a special coach attached to the boat train. The champagne and caviare served to him did little to reduce his disappointment. He had been promised photographers, journalists, big crowds on landing: there was nothing of this to be seen. This made the arrival at Victoria Station all the more surprising. Thousands of people thronged on to the platform, waving their hats, throwing flowers; the station-master in a black top-hat was present with his whole staff, and the cameras whirred. Tauber pressed the monocle into his eye, greeted the crowd proudly—and Scott could scarcely believe his eyes: it looked like the reception of a king.

It *was* the reception of a king. In the train's first coach sat Alfonso XIII of Spain, extremely popular in England, who had abdicated in Madrid the day before, and was now starting his years of exile in London. Schnappula had no inkling of all that. He pushed through the crowd, laughing and waving, nodded to the photographers, climbed into Scott's flower-garlanded white Rolls-Royce, and arrived at the hotel exhausted but highly satisfied. For years he was still talking about the enthusiasm with which he had been welcomed in London, and there is good evidence that to the end of his days he knew nothing of his mistake.[1]

The Drury Lane first night[2] was an event of the most magnificent glamour. Scott had kept his promise, organizing a publicity campaign which raised the public's expectations to the highest pitch.

The first act was received with pleasant anticipation and given friendly applause. Then came the moment in the second when Tauber in his rich silk robe stood alone on the huge stage, held his right arm stretched out before him, and looked provocatively at the audience: "You are my heart's delight". The great melody

---

[1] The episode is reported by W. Macqueen-Pope, Scott's publicity man, in his book written in collaboration with D. L. Murray, *Fortune's Favourite*, London, 1953. This also contains the descriptions given below of the Drury Lane première.

[2] On 8th May 1931.

flooded through the house, and "the great architect of the vocal line" built it up into "a thrilled and thrilling glory".

The last note died away. At first people sat there in utter stillness, as if stunned; then the lock-gates of applause opened. "Winds at gale force, tidal waves dashing against sea walls, surging crowds acclaiming heroic conquerors—that was what it sounded like. The very walls of centuries-old Drury Lane seemed to tremble under the impact of the applause. This was triumph. Tauber bowed and bowed, and the cheering continued. There were almost frantic yells of 'Encore! Encore!' as if he might not do it again, and he must—he must!" He sang the song in five languages, in six variations, seven times; and still the audience demanded more, as though there were no operetta that night, no other actors and actresses, no other music.

The song had "bound the audience in chains. It had crept amongst them, fastening their fetters; it had played with their emotions—and then tossed them about like jetsam in a swell of sound. It had not lured its hearers into sensuousness, as the waltzes had done; it had just made them complete and abject captives."

This climax was so unprecedented that there was fear the enthusiasm might ebb in the third act. Nothing of the kind. The ovations at the end were like those after "the decisive goal, scored just before the referee's whistle at a hard-fought Cup Final. The noise resembled that of Wembley Stadium." It was an unforgettable evening, missing perfection only by the absence of Lehár himself. Scott rang him up in Vienna the same night from the theatre: the triumph was indisputable, a run of one and a half to two years could be reckoned with.

In fact, *The Land of Smiles* ran for seventy-one performances.

The Star is Indisposed

Tauber, unlike his normal self, was both moody and arrogant from the day after the première: he showed star temperament, said he had a sore throat, and was persuaded only with difficulty to appear at the second performance. In the third, a stand-in took over.

People rushed to the box office to ask for their money back, and the papers reported what had happened with big headlines. The fourth night Tauber sang, the fifth he stayed away: no one knew what he wanted, what was wrong with him. Business dropped off, and with it the interest in the new star.

In the third week of May, when it became known that he had returned to Vienna, nobody except the theatre paid any more attention to the affair. Scott tried to save what could be saved. He put a notice in the press saying that a famous tenor was learning the part in Vienna, and would shortly be arriving in London. But Lehár sent word that Tauber had recovered from his indisposition, and that he would himself be accompanying him to London in the middle of June, to conduct the "second first-night" in person.

It equalled the first in brilliance. King George V and Queen Mary were present, Lehár was fêted, a restored Tauber sang more beautifully, a thrilled audience applauded more frantically than ever—but the great sensation would not materialize again. Drury Lane closed its doors on 18th July.

Tauber never gave any explanation for his behaviour, although it caused a conspicuous failure and destroyed the chance of a new Lehár world success. When asked about it in later years, he simply grinned and said: "Schnappula's nerves must have been *schnapping* a bit just then."

He went underground for a time into the Berlin sound-film studios, gave a successful recital of *Lieder* and arias in New York Town Hall in October, sang *How Fair the World* at the Theater an der Wien in December, and early in 1932 returned to London for another brief appearance as Sou Chong.

Films! Films!

The *Land of Smiles* film became one of the first international successes of German sound-films—pacemaker for an endless series of film musicals. Tauber's mastery of microphone technique stood him in good stead, sympathetic direction and camera-work did the rest. Now he was overwhelmed with the most enticing film offers from all sides, but decided to go into production himself, and founded Tauber Tonfilm Ltd. Organizational and financial troubles soon grew too much for him, especially as his next film, *Die grosse Attraktion* (The Great Attraction), with music by Franz Lehár, did not gain the desired public response. So he was glad to climb out of the enterprise after a year without any great loss of money.

Lehár had been a zealous cinemagoer with Sophie since the early days of the movies. He noted with amazement the first *Merry Widows* strip, and in 1917 even appeared, playing himself, in a Lehár film directed by Hubert Marischka: the only condition he made was that he should be allowed to "appear without make-up and act without distortions". Ten years later he again played the part for which he was so well cast. He allowed glances into his daily routine: conducting an orchestral rehearsal, playing the piano, and talking to Beda and Herzer. In the years between, Lehár operettas had become rewarding subjects for the silent film —which may be taken as a compliment to their dramatic treatment or criticism of their *colportage* content. *Das Fürstenkind, The Ideal Wife, Where The Lark Sings* were filmed; and just before the end of the silent film era *The Tsarevich* and *Paganini*.

After *The Great Attraction* Lehár was not really lucky with original films either, certainly less so than his friends Robert Stolz and Oscar Straus. In the classic *Zwei Herzen im Dreivierteltakt* (Two Hearts in Waltz Time) Stolz provided the success formula for the light musical film for years ahead; Straus, though in his eighties, could still participate in a delectable piece of cinematic art like *La Ronde*. Lehár's second film, *Es war einmal ein Walzer* (There was once a Waltz) proved threadbare; the third, *Grossfürstin Alexandra* (Grand-Duchess Alexandra), starring Marie Jeritza, failed so completely that it was decided to destroy all copies.

With the filming of his stage works Lehár was more successful, although none of them (always excepting Lubitsch's *Merry Widow*) proved outstanding. Tauber refused to take part in *Friederike, Paganini* and *The Tsarevich* because he was too clever to expose himself, in his forties, to close-ups in lover roles—and because the *Giuditta* plan was slowly maturing, banishing all other ideas for him as it did for Lehár.

The Moods of Two Capitals

On 23rd December two operettas had first nights, one in Vienna, the other in Berlin, which could not have been more characteristic of the moods of the two capitals at that time. At Berlin's Grosse Schauspielhaus the Rotters put on Abraham's *Ball im Savoy* (Ball at the Savoy), a bombastic spectacle with a lack of inspiration not to be concealed by any tricks of production or staging. The neo-romantic eroticism of the book was based too obviously on old *Fledermaus* and *Ideal Wife* situations; the contrived synthesis of Venetian-Turkish-Spanish-American-Viennese-Hungarian musical colouring indicated all too clearly the composer's diminished powers of invention.

At the Theater an der Wien, under Marischka's aegis, the old biographical operetta enjoyed a happy resurrection. Fritz Kreisler's *Sissy* (English title The King Steps Out) was a jewel of the genre: in an attractive form it told the story of the wooing of Princess Elisabeth of Bavaria by the young Emperor Franz Joseph, framed in the famous violinist's famous melodies.

The effect of the two works on the public was diametrically opposed: in Berlin it led to explosions of hatred from all sides against anyone who could be identified with the production; in Vienna to a surprising wave of general monarchist and Habsburg sentiment.

Marischka, who had been in financial difficulties for months, was enabled by the success to put off disaster for another two years; for the Rotters, this time with Abraham as the fatal agent, it came immediately. Christmas was celebrated at their Grunewald villa; in the middle of January, even before an investigation of their accounts could throw light on the business affairs of their theatrical combine, the brothers lost their heads and fled to Liechtenstein.

A few weeks later they became victims of their indestructible stage enthusiasm. A resident who had hobnobbed with them talked about a farmer's boy in the neighbourhood with an unusually fine tenor voice, just waiting to be discovered. Unable to resist the temptation of giving him an audition, Alfred, his wife and brother, got into the man's car on the morning of 5th April 1933. When they realized it was a kidnapping coup organized by a Gestapo spy, they tried to jump out of the vehicle as it raced towards Germany. Alfred and his wife were killed on the spot, Fritz managed to escape and struggle through to Paris.

Hitler had come to power.

A Finely Conceived Work

Whether *Giuditta* is an operetta, an opera or a musical comedy, whether the weak passages in its score overshadow the strong ones, whether it has fallen into oblivion rightly or wrongly, may remain debatable. As a finely conceived work, elaborated down to the smallest detail, it claims respect and consideration. To call it artless, dismal and trivial would be out of place; to admire it as unique, incomparable, the noblest thing in the realm of music, would be silly. Perhaps Lehár himself set the tone for critics and eulogists, provoking the resistance of the former and the obsequiousness of the latter, when he said of it: "*Guiditta* is my favourite child; I have been able to put into it something created from my innermost being. With it I have given of my best."[1]

Although he had been dreaming for years, even after *Frasquita*, of putting on the stage a "Carmen-like character", his first impression of the *Giuditta* book was unfavourable. Beda and Knepler had written it for him: an undramatic affair, trailing from one contrived situation to another, the story of an Italian officer who leaves the service out of love for a *cocotte* and ends as a night-club pianist. The theme, far from gripping him at once, left him cold; but he was too obliging to reject it out of hand. The librettists became impatient and offered it to various other composers in Vienna, while Lehár was considering other books.

Now and then he looked at his *Giuditta* notebook, sketched out a series of motifs, and asked Beda to write words for them. In the end it was once more Tauber who brought about the decision.

---

[1] On the other hand, he declared two years later in a letter to the New York Theatre manager J. J. Shubert, dated Berlin 28th September 1936, concerning *The Land of Smiles*: "This operetta is the best work I have ever written, surpassing *The Merry Widow* in theatrical effectiveness."

During his first visit to the Schikaneder Schlössl, Lehár suggested revising *Das Fürstenkind* for him.[1] Tauber hesitated: why not something new? After all, three years had passed since *Friederike*, his last original work: and "when are you at last going to let me hear something from this mysterious *Giuditta*?"

Lehár played the first phrase of Tauber's entrance song, one of the most impressive that had ever occurred to him; and Tauber fell for it on the spot. He read the book, listened to other numbers in the score, finished and unfinished, emerging finally with the fatal idea: "*Giuditta* must have its first production at the Vienna State Opera!"

This had never occurred to Lehár: the work had always been designed specifically for the Theater an der Wien. Now he succumbed to auto-suggestion: *Giuditta* should sound forth in the sacred old house, and he would conduct it himself from Gustav Mahler's rostrum—the climax of his life. His ambition was roused, and led him even further astray, to a second lapse of judgement. Completely absurd even then, it sounds today as though poor Lehár had become the victim of a practical joke played by an old friend.

The old friend was Geza Herczeg, who had known Mussolini, now the Italian head of state, in the days of his early journalistic beginnings, and had become his unofficial liaison officer in Vienna. The Duce at that time enjoyed high respect in the country as Austria's protector, guarantor of its frontiers and chief opponent of its Nazi enemies: Herczeg suggested *Giuditta* should be dedicated to him. Lehár seized on the idea, already picturing himself at Toscanini's desk in the Scala. Book and vocal score were magnificently bound, and forwarded to the Palazzo Venezia in Rome with expressions of deepest devotion. A week later they came back.

---

[1] On 25th September 1932 it was produced in Berlin in the revised version: *Der Fürst der Berge* (The Prince of the Mountains).

The covering letter from a secretary stated that His Excellency rejected with disgust the absurd idea of a dedication: the leading character, an Italian officer who left the colours for a woman, was quite unthinkable in Fascist Italy.

The brusque rejection resulted in Lehár making an even stronger effort to arrange *Giuditta* in a style fit for the Vienna Staatsoper. The hope of having it performed there overawed him, and he co-ordinated all his creative and working processes towards it; but rather than encouraging, this inhibited his inspiration. Respect for the famous Philharmonic Orchestra made his orchestration unusually thick, his natural melodic sense became artificial through his desire to win over the opera critics. It was only when he gave free rein to his innate musicality, in Giuditta's waltz,

and in the Tauber-*Lied*

that Lehár's old lyrical genius, the beauty of *Gipsy Love, Paganini* and *Friederike* sang again. And though *Giuditta* does not possess the power and richness of Lehár's great masterpieces, it rises well above the level of many other of his works. Taken as a whole, it was unfairly treated: by the Staatsoper, which regarded it as a necessary but regrettable source of income; by the critics, who because of the setting judged it by *Tristan* standards; by the public, for whom it was only one of many not-to-be-missed daily sensations; and by Lehár himself, who once again saw a chance to redeem an unforgotten blow, Mahler's rejection of *Kukuschka* in 1897.

For good or ill this striving to retrieve failures recurs like a *Leitmotif* all through his life, making it a snakes-and-ladders board of disappointments and triumphs, producing lucky throws like *The Land of Smiles* and failures like *How Fair The World*. Despite various suggestions there was never any question for him of revising *Giuditta*. He considered the book satisfactory, the music faultless, the whole work inviolable. And he proved his faith in his creation by giving it a permanent form unique in the whole history of operetta: at his own expense he had a full-size engraving made of the whole orchestral score—all 388 pages.

Théâtre paré

Directly the State Opera's intention of putting on Lehár's new work became known, it caused a debate in Vienna which put the Berlin *Friederike* controversy in the shade, and made people forget, as in old Girardi times, the most burning political questions of the day. The management, criticized for accepting *Giuditta*, revealed that they had been directed by higher authorities. The responsible Minister, a bibulous provincial, was rumoured to have ordered the production after a drinking bout given in his honour. When the papers asked whether this was true, he replied with indignation that he had acted purely in the interests of the financially distressed Opera House. Whereupon one journalist suggested that in that case it would be far more profitable to hire out the boxes to amorous couples as *chambres separées*—and at the same time to play *Fidelio* so as to maintain the theatre's prestige.

This storm in an Austrian teacup had undertones recalling the country's great humorists, from Nestroy[1] back to the original *Hanswurst*[2] and the old Augustine monk Abraham a Sancta Clara[3] with his "Viennese stories, verse, whims, caprices and divers discourses". Lehár hated the undignified squabbles, but was powerless to prevent them. He had to endure the slings and arrows, waiting till his work could speak for itself.

The evening[4] on which it was finally staged left nothing to be desired as far as externals were concerned. The most elegant *théâtre paré*, tickets three times the usual price, the Federal President and the Government in the boxes, all Society in the stalls, the microphones of 120 radio companies at the footlights, Lehár conducting, Tauber and Jarmila Novotna on the stage; cheering, encores, flowers, laurel wreaths, ovations. A first-class funeral, not only for an unsuccessful idea, but for a whole genre which, after a glorious though often hectic life, had died, tired and worn out, in its eightieth year; while on the other side of the Atlantic, reshaped and revived, it was about to reconquer the world.

The Viennese press gave *Giuditta* its *coup de grâce*. The hatred, scorn and crude denigration poured on Lehár by the papers were equal to anything that Wagner, Bruckner, Hugo Wolf, Mahler and Schoenberg ever had to put up with in Vienna.

It was painful, though not surprising, for the composer to find his friend Ernst Decsey setting the tone. A little while earlier the biographer had written in his notice of *The Land of Smiles*: "Lehár's *oeuvre* extends as far as here. What is still to come is uncertain, probably a surprise. For the artist is always a surprise-giver." Then came the change. Decsey suddenly found that "Lehár's ecstatic, erotic music, in its charm, elegant fascination and delicate feeling leaves out one thing: spirit and rigour". (As if *Die Fledermaus*, *La Belle Heléne* and *The Mikado* were rigorous, *The Merry Widow* and *The Count of Luxembourg* lacking in spirit!) In his otherwise

[1] Johann Nestroy (1801–62).
[2] Josef Anton Stranitzky (1674–1726), the Viennese "Merry Andrew".
[3] Abraham a Sancta Clara (1644–1709), popular preacher, homely philosopher and wit.
[4] 20th January 1934.

quite friendly analyses he allowed small taunts and innuendos to creep in, which grew more and more menacing; until his criticisms became vehement condemnation.

The fact was that Decsey hankered after dramatic laurels, and like many other influential Viennese journalists hoped to gain some personal advantage between the lines. He had submitted operetta drafts to his "revered Master", the revered Master had declined them with thanks, and the librettist *manqué* made no bones about retailing his grudge with full publicity, forsaking the man he had sedulously flattered. Lehár's great hour found him at the peak of his malice and disloyalty: "*Giuditta*", his notice finished, "is a wretched concoction, out of place at the Staatsoper."

The forty-two sold-out houses it achieved there do not refute him, nor is his case proved by its partial rejection everywere else.

Amicable Arrangement

Three weeks after the great première the political end of Austria came into sight with machine-guns rattling everywhere, heavy guns roaring. Democracy had been defeated. While court-martials raged all over Austria, Chancellor Dollfuss marched down the Ringstrasse in triumph at the head of the *Heimwehr*. Five months later he was assassinated by the Nazis; Dr Kurt Schuschnigg succeeded him as Chancellor.

An hour before his death Dolfuss had been ready to approve in cabinet a State subsidy to restore the fortunes of the Theater an der Wien. Marischka had approached him, referring to the theatre's history and importance, the high municipal taxes, the shortage of new works, the public's apathy, rivalry from the cinema; and had finally proved that without State assistance he would have to close down. What he did not mention was his own questionable part in the situation: his lack of flair in the choice of new operettas, and his princely standard of living, which he did not reduce even in critical times. The Karczag Verlag, with its massive collection of copyrights, and the international income therefrom, had to pay for the theatre's losses; consequently it, too, fell into debt, and its authors remained unpaid.

On 1st March 1935 Hubert Marischka was obliged to abandon his management and close the theatre's doors. At the same time alarming rumours spread about the imminent collapse of the publishing company. Lehár, its most important client, detected malpractices exceeding his worst fears. His lawyer advised him, considering his friendship with Marischka, to temper justice with mercy, especially as any lawsuit would "necessarily bring about the company's bankruptcy"; he recommended an amicable arrangement, to include partial compensation. Unofficial negotiations with Marischka took place, and eventually there was a settlement: Lehár refrained from starting proceedings, and Marischka returned to him "the copyright of all his works published by the Karczag Verlag, together with the stock of all musical material in the company's possession".[1]

So one day in April three huge vans came to the stage door of the Theater an der Wien, and loaded up with all Lehár's piano scores, sheet music, orchestral parts, selections, dance arrangements and libretti, took them to near-by Theobaldgasse, and there deposited them in the store-room of the newly founded Glocken–Verlag.

Lehár was asked by friends why he called his company the Glocken-Verlag (the Publishing House of the Bells). He gave a sly smile: "Perhaps because I heard the bells toll for the Theater an der Wien." Through his lifelong experience in all musical activities, he understood the publishing business admirably. Having the necessary capital and the necessary enthusiasm, he became a zealous publisher, too zealous, some thought, for a composer of his importance. Every morning he was driven from Hackhofergasse to the firm's offices, read business correspondence, haggled over royalties with municipal theatres in Germany, Czechoslovakia and Switzerland, organized the packing and dispatch, and kept a careful watch on the details of sheet music sold. When the shop bell rang, announcing the arrival of a customer, he would jump up from his desk, and listen at the door to find out which work was asked for and how many copies were being sold. If the assistant

[1] From the official declaration by Dr Siegfried Fraenkel, Lehár's lawyer, made on 16th August 1950—fifteen years later.

succeeded in selling more than had been originally required, Lehár was delighted and would express effusive thanks.

Frau L. and Frau W.

That *Giuditta* would remain his last work[1] was something Lehár would never have credited when he was tackling it. The obstructions he faced after it did not arise in the sphere of music. They burst upon him from outside and overwhelmed him, in the form of two endless and complicated lawsuits. Both could have been easily avoided, especially as their absurdity was patent to everyone except Lehár himself.

The roots of the first lay in his obligingness. A year before the *Giuditta* première the managing director of the Austrian Performing Rights Society[2] approached him: "Would you mind reading a libretto by a lady I know, with a view to possibly setting it to music?" It was a dramatization of a fairy-tale by the Brothers Grimm. Lehár, who often boasted that he could judge libretti from outside appearances, by their paper, binding and script, at once noticed its amateurishness. Although he did not care much for the intermediary, he hadn't the energy to say "No, thank you", but handed the book, unread, to the faithful Karl, who as usual put it away with dozens of others submitted. After a while the composer was asked for news. Karl got out the manuscript, and Lehár, according to the old routine, returned it with a friendly covering letter.

In March 1934 Frau L., authoress of the fairy-tale piece, came forward with the assertion that Lehár was guilty of plagiarism, as he had asked his librettists to use certain passages in her work. Beda laughed at the idea, and suggested she should go to law: he knew there was not the slightest reason to accept the financial

---

1 Apart from a trifle, the musical numbers for a serialized radio novel, *Die Gefährten des Odysseus* (The Companions of Odysseus), by Pierre Benoît.

2 *Gesellschaft der Autoren, Komponisten und Musikverleger* (Society of Authors, Composers and Music-Publishers), known by its initials as A.K.M., which like the British Performing Right Society (P.R.S.) protects its members' copyrights (in concert, radio and other public performances) based on legal contracts.

demands she was now making. Lehár was puzzled when letters arrived in the next few weeks, cancelling performances for *Giuditta* already fixed. In every case the grounds given were solicitors' letters with Frau L.'s charges of plagiarism and threats of claims for damages. An end must be made to the mischief, Lehár decided, though Beda was against it.

That, to the lawyers' delight, meant the start of lawsuits, charges, writs, hearings, negotiations, interrogations, all of which dragged on for five years, with the whole of Vienna taking sides. The people involved spread to wider and wider circles. Thus seventeen well-known Austrian musicians, men of letters and artists were among those who confirmed Frau L.'s accusations by signing a document which described *Giuditta* as a plagiarism. At the head of the list was Austria's Grand Old Man of Music, Wilhelm Kienzl, now in his late seventies, who could not get over the fact that the State Opera had ignored him, the creator of *Der Evangelimann* (The Evangelist), and had honoured the composer of *The Merry Widow*. Neither tact nor musicianship nor being joint honorary president of the A.K.M. with Lehár stopped him calling the *Giuditta* score "music of the gutter", and persisting in his view that the work was pilfered. It was three years before he admitted, under pressure from the court, that he had never read Frau L.'s book. She had elicited from him the signature and a promise to induce others to sign. He had naïvely believed her foolish assurance, but now offered to make a written withdrawal of all accusations with expressions of his deepest regret. He also promised to get his sixteen fellow signatories (not one of whom had ever seen Frau L.'s book) to do the same.

Out of consideration for Kienzl's age Lehár did not make use of his right to publish the letter. He was content with a brief newspaper notice, and accused Frau L. (although her charges referred to the text of *Giuditta*, not the music) of slander and defamation. Further legal proceedings started, which again dragged on from one hearing to the next, ending with Lehár's complete rehabilitation and a fine for the defendant. At the same time, although there was no connection between the two events, her protégé, who had brought the fatal book to Theobaldgasse, was dismissed from the A.K.M. on grounds of embezzlement, convicted and sent to prison.

"I can't describe these things to you in detail," Lehár wrote to a friend fourteen years later,[1] looking back on what had happened. "The fact is that my nerves were too much on edge all this time to write any new work, as blackmail followed blackmail."

He was here alluding to the second case, running simultaneously with that of Frau L. Its basis was another pronounced Lehár characteristic, his love of respectability, or rather his efforts to conceal behind an inbred love of respectability an innate *psyche erotica*. Through one of his former leading ladies Lehár had come into the circle of Frau W., a fashionable figure in Viennese society. She was in the habit of arranging gay little *divertissements* which appealed to her select guests. Lehár went to them now and then, and found the lady of the house and her parties amusing and stimulating. Until he received a visit one day from a polite elderly gentleman, who introduced himself as Frau W.'s cousin: he was just for the moment financially embarrassed through no fault of his own; could the Master not help him perhaps with a short-term loan? The Master helped; and a fortnight later the man was there again, accompanied by his cousin, Frau W., and a legal adviser. His behaviour was no longer quite so polite, the sum he demanded far higher than the first. He also produced photographs taken during the *divertissements* which if published could be detrimental to the Master's reputation and position . . .

Lehár had fallen into the hands of blackmailers. He informed his lawyer, and demanded that a prosecution should be set in motion. The ringleader was arrested, but the impending trial did not silence the gang. The resulting publicity caused Lehár much anxiety and annoyance. Sophie maintained her calm, while he let himself fall further and further under the thumb of his persecutors. Friends tried to assure him that none of the details of his private life which might possibly be referred to in court were disgraceful. In vain: his solicitor was instructed to adjourn the date fixed for the trial; whereupon the case blew over for the time being. Years later it was to have bitter consequences.

[1] 12th March 1948.

Gleichschaltung

The two lawsuits, and the worry connected with them, made Lehár prematurely old. He lost his suppleness of gait and look of contentment, spoke more softly and faster than before, wrote in tiny letters—generally (because of his bad eyes) under a magnifying-glass—grew suspicious, gave up old friendships, and became more and more dependent on Sophie. Many of his friends, colleagues or collaborators were dead: Josef Weinberger, Smareglia, Dr Willner, Robert Bodanzky, Ivar Kreuger, Poincaré, Pallenberg—and the lovable Oskar Nedbal, who had jumped out of a window on Christmas Eve in a fit of melancholia.

In Nazi Germany the great Gleichschaltung ("unification") took place: uniform abandonment of all human values, bankruptcy of justice, destruction of culture, corruption of morals. Race mania raged, sweeping everything with it, from the lofty to the light-hearted.

Tauber had settled in London. After the outbursts of temperament at Drury Lane he soon regained his old serenity, and with it his star status. He had married the beautiful young film actress Diana Napier; had achieved considerable success at the Royal Opera House, Covent Garden, and also with a production of *Lilac Time*.

The Londoners liked him less as Paganini. The Cochran production of the operetta[1] was taken off after sixty performances. But Schnappula enjoyed going back to Vienna again for a while. At the Staatsoper he sang his repertoire, at the Theater an der Wien the lead in his own operetta *Der singende Traum*[2] (The Singing Dream). That in Germany he had suddenly become *persona non grata* was something he refused to recognize: even when he read in black and white[3] that at last "the people with its healthy instinct had come awake", and were "fed up with his smarmy Jewish way of singing, typically un-Teutonic."

[1] Première at the Lyceum Theatre on 20th May 1937.
[2] Première on 31st August 1934.
[3] *Deutsche Kultur-Wacht*, 1933, No. 7, quoted in Joseph Wulf's *Musik im Dritten Reich* (Music in the Third Reich), Gütersloh, 1963.

Käthe Dorsch had once told him that Goering possessed many of his records and often played them in his circle of friends. Could things really be so bad? He decided to find out for himself. One August morning he drove from Salzburg to Munich, into the lion's den. He arrived at noon at his favourite hotel, and walked through the foyer naïvely unsuspecting, to his favourite restaurant. The head waiter greeted him with all obsequiousness, and led him through the rows of uniformed S.A. and S.S. officials to his old regular table. The great tenor looked round, smiled amiably in all directions, and ordered a gourmet's meal with champagne. Directly after the hors-d'oeuvre had been brought, the manager appeared and implored him in a half whisper, if he didn't want to land up in a concentration camp that same afternoon, to get away as quickly as possible. In answer to a soft "Why?" the manager merely gave a look round his clientele without saying anything.

It was not till an hour later, on the other side of the frontier, that Tauber dared to breathe again. It was his last appearance in public in Germany.

In the view of Goebbels's Propaganda Ministry[1] Lehár represented "a debatable problem for the cultural policy of the Third Reich". The foreign currency his work brought in ran to millions of marks, and the Führer, astonishingly enough, showed an ever-increasing predilection for *The Merry Widow*. On the other hand, the composer's librettists were without exception Jews, he himself moved in Vienna "exclusively in Jewish circles", and wasted his "talents on culturally regrettable subjects".

What alternative was there for the Ministry but to stick its head in the sand, keep quiet and continue to allow Lehár productions, while omitting the names of his librettists?

On Friday, 11th March 1938, an old "Lehárian" came to afternoon coffee at the Schikaneder Schlössl: an operetta composer who in his early days had received encouragement from Lehár, and was now working successfully in England. He had come to Vienna to warn Lehár of the threat of a Nazi invasion of Austria, recommend emigration to him, and assure him, on behalf of influential admirers

[1] File CXLV-604, quoted in Wulf's documentation.

how welcome he and his wife would be in England. Lehár expressed his thanks for the message, but "at the age of sixty-eight", he said, "emigration is no joke". What was he to live on? Who was there to collaborate with? Who would fulfil his obligations in Vienna? Moreover, Austria's independence was a matter for the world's conscience, and guaranteed by many imponderables. No, his London friends doubtless meant well, and he appreciated their solicitude; but things here were not really as black as they looked from abroad, and who would ever hurt *him*, let alone Sophie?

At six o'clock he accompanied his visitor to the tram-stop. "Well then, *auf Wiedersehen*," were his parting words; "don't be such a pessimist". Then, as an afterthought, he added a catchphrase of typical Viennese irony: "Everything will turn out all wrong, you know!"

Two hours later Federal Chancellor Schuschnigg went to the microphone and announced his resignation. When he closed with the words: "I yield to force. May God preserve Austria!" the first swastika flags were already flying from Viennese roofs.

XV
ALLES GEBEN DIE GÖTTER...

The Final Consequence

The "flower campaign", as the Nazi propagandists called Hitler's march into Austria, began in the early hours of Saturday, 12th March. About 8 a.m. Himmler landed at Vienna's aerodrome, and in the first forty-eight hours of his stay could claim credit for 86,000 arrests, 6,000 dismissals from the Civil Service and 200 assassination victims. Schuschnigg, his cabinet and generals; Baron Rothschild; Franz Ferdinand's son Prince Hohenberg, leader of the monarchists; members of the old Austrian aristocracy; Beda, Fritz Grünbaum, Louis Treumann; and everyone else uncongenial to the new masters, down to the poorest Jewish café waiter, disappeared into prisons and concentration camps. Thousands, justifiably frightened and unjustly threatened, left the country: Catholics, Jews, socialists, capitalists, monarchists, republicans: an élite which Austria sorely missed, and could never replace. It included Franz Werfel and his wife Alma Maria (Mahler's widow), Carl Zuckmayer, Oscar Straus, Emmerich Kálmán, Brammer and Grünwald; and also those who could have stayed but didn't want to: the writer Franz Theodor Csokor, the singers Alfred Piccaver, Lotte Lehmann, Jarmila Novotna, the composers Robert Stolz and Ralph Benatzky.

On Hitler's entry the bells rang in all churches, by order of Vienna's Cardinal Archbishop, Dr Theodor Innitzer, and 97.3 per cent of all Austrians entitled to vote said Yes to the *Anschluss* in a plebiscite.

The 0.27 per cent who answered No included the noble

Augustine monk Roman Karl Scholz. During those days, in the quiet of his cell in the monastery at Klosterneuburg, he and a handful of like-minded people established the first Austrian resistance group. Two years later (at the age of only twenty-eight) he was betrayed, and hanged by the Nazis.

Where did Lehár stand amidst all this hell and butchery? When the brown cacophony had finished, the old man was faced by three accusations, which filled his friends with horrified sadness, his enemies with vindictive fury.

The first concerned a waltz dedication to Hitler. On 5th March 1945 a captain of the Second French Tank Division (later a lawyer at the appeals court in Colmar), who had occupied the Obersalzberg near Berchtesgaden, found in Hitler's mountain retreat, the Berghof, a small file bound in red Morocco leather. In its top right corner it bore a silver swastika; below was a silver badge with Lehár's signature and dedication to the Führer. The interior consisted of a booklet entitled:

SOUVENIR OF THE 50TH PERFORMANCE

OF THE OPERETTA

THE MERRY WIDOW

ON 17TH FEBRUARY 1906

To the two numbers printed therein Lehár had added the manuscript, copied in his own hand, of the waltz "Lips are silent, violins whisper", and his signature.

Nine years later Lehár gave the following explanation: "Secretary of State Walter Funk told me that Hitler loved my music, and that when he was in Vienna and had no money he was always in the upper circle (of the Theater an der Wien) to hear *The Merry Widow*. He said Hitler specially remembered the first jubilee celebration, on the 50th performance. Had I still got a programme of this? 'Do send it to him, he'll be so pleased. It's his birthday on 20th April.' He advised me to have it bound, and a swastika put on the top corner. How inexperienced I was then, is shown by the fact that on the cover there was a picture of Mizzi Günther and Louis Treumann (a Jew!) . . .'[1]

[1] This and the following quotation are an extract from a statement by Lehár dated Zurich, 14th March 1947.

At the end of 1938 the unfortunate Frau W. case blew up again, leading to the second charge against Lehár. The postponed hearing was fixed anew, and the blackmailers sent their solicitor to Sophie: one final payment, and they were ready to disappear from the scene. Lehár could see the old aggravations returning, and in his despair asked a Nazi official to have the trial suppressed. In his written application he referred to the fact that the ringleaders were Jews.

"I could see no way out except to approach *Kulturrat* Hinkel in Berlin and ask him to free me from them. I admit that this was careless. Of course I did not mean Jewry as a whole, but was only speaking of the two blackmailers."

Finally the Beda case. On 4th December 1942, after four and a half years of tortures and humiliations in the concentration camps of Dachau, Buchenwald and Auschwitz, Fritz Löhner went to the gas-chamber. Fellow inmates of the camps report that he often thought of Lehár, and talked about him: "Has he forgotten me?" He had not! A letter written, four years after the tragedy,[1] contains undertones of tormenting self-accusation: "I am, as it were, accused of being responsible for Beda's death." Till his last hour he was oppressed by the thought of whether anybody in the Nazi hierarchy approachable by him, would or could have saved his friend, that most hated and outspoken enemy of the Nazis. And how, and when? "Questions (one who heard them declares) full of endless pangs of conscience!"

"One does not enjoy reporting these things . . ." They are lamentable; but to keep quiet about them would be to condone them. They represent the final consequence of Lehár's character: an obliging character that considered itself just "inexperienced", "careless", and for a sin of ommission only "as it were, responsible" —when complications occurred.

Marlene Dietrich, Thomas Mann, Hindemith, Fritz Busch, Remarque, Bassermann and many other courageously left Germany, although Hitler would have used them only too gladly as advertisements for his Third Reich. Lehár stayed because emigration was no "joke".

[1] Dated 20th November 1946.

In the conflict of creeds he remained mute: neutral towards the murderers, because he was naïve enough to believe he was thereby showing the world the great distance between them and him.

Just like Richard Strauss.

Both were approaching their seventieth birthday when Hitler came, and they were regarded in the world as Germany's two most famous composers for the stage. Strauss was still in the midst of his creative process, Lehár had finished his. Both were immersed in their daily routine, and did not recognize the full extent of the horror which the Nazis were still to unleash; both wanted to "do good" by their attitude and "avoid greater misfortune". Neither of them was ever a Party member, and both had Jewish family and librettist connections. The *Rosenkavalier* composer was despised, the *Merry Widow* composer esteemed, by the Führer. Nevertheless, Lehár never received any official musical appointments from the regime, whereas Strauss was given the very highest ones. Strauss the German deplored Nazi rule because a creative artist of his class had to "ask a little squirt of a minister (Goebbels) for permission as to what he might compose"; Lehár the Austrian deplored it because he saw his country, which "could have led the quiet happy life of a second Switzerland", languishing behind the barbed wire of the Reich.

Richard Strauss's friend and publisher, Ernst Roth, has subjected to sympathetic analysis the composer's relations with the Hitler State;[1] it may be applied almost word for word to Lehár. "He did not become involved in public argument with the regime, nor did he make his peace with it . . . he defended himself, his music, his family, and so came in conflict with authority and with his friends, but never with himself. One cannot justify such egoism, but it is one sign more that in Strauss's (and Lehár's) life, with its accent on respectability, art exercised a more dominant influence than superficial observers could recognise."

With the *Anschluss* began the last ten years, the saddest in Lehár's life: years in which he was persecuted, abused, sabotaged and reduced to silence; years in which he was charged with every

[1] Ernst Roth, *Musik als Kunst und Ware* (Music as Art and Commodity), Zürich, 1966.

dishonour under the sun, venality, cowardice, opportunism and desertion; years of waste and frustration, fear and distress, sickness and gradual decline.

"My Strong Will to Live"

Tauber received the news of the rape of Austria in Milan, where a throat specialist was to cure him of an obstinate hoarseness. He broke down; his first impulse was to go back, then he heeded Diana's warnings, stayed locked in his hotel room for three days, playing the piano, looking through Mozart scores, listening to the news on the radio. He tried unsuccessfully to reach Lehár on the phone and persuade him to leave, sent telegrams and letters, but was unable to make contact. In the autumn of 1938, after guest appearances at Covent Garden, he visited Australia on a tour arranged months before. In Sydney at the end of June he received, in answer to another letter to Vienna, the first sign of life from Lehár:

"Dear Richard,
    I was deeply touched by your letter, but find it very difficult to answer you. I can only write that when I hear *Paganini*, *Frasquita*, *Tsarevich*, *Friederike*, *Land of Smiles*, *How Fair the World* and *Giuditta*, the music is inseparably linked with your voice. At each note I hear you! I imagine you are now absorbing a mass of glorious impressions. To see the great beautiful world was once my dream too, but I don't think the dream will be fulfilled now. I am trying to write something new—but have so far not found any suitable libretto. Have received incredibly favourable offers from America. I would once have accepted them immediately, but now I go on changing my mind. Am keeping myself busy on the publishing side, preparing absolutely perfect stage material of *Land of Smiles*, *Gipsy Love*, *Tsarevich*, *Luxembourg*, so that nobody can mess around with them in the future . . ."

    That *The Merry Widow* was nevertheless messed around with throughout Germany, even at the most exclusive theatres, in over-loaded, overdesigned, overcostumed productions, and split up into thirty or forty scenes, was something he could not prevent. The producers were justified by hundreds of sold-out houses, arousing the impotent fury of Richard Strauss. At seventy-five he could still "go raving mad" at the *Merry Widow* waltzes, and during the work on *Capriccio* told the librettist Clemens Krauss "not to miss any chance of denouncing the theatrical sewage". Strauss's wish was fulfilled in the words of theatre manager La Roche:[1]

> "Just look at the low farces
> in which our capital delights.
> The grimace is their emblem,
> Parody their element—
> Their content immoral impudence!
> Clownish and coarse are their jokes . . ."

The Führer, unlike the President of his Reich Chamber of Music, enjoyed the immoral impudence and clownish-coarse jokes of *The Merry Widow*, and received its composer in the Chancellory. Lehár was also received in Rome. The business of the *Giuditta* dedication was forgotten, the Duce had a violin brought in, and entertained the composer with a solo rendering of the *Frasquita* Serenade. It is unfortunate that there were no photographers there to preserve a visual record of the occurrence.

With the Nazi occupation of Austria, *Giuditta* and *Land of Smiles* disappeared from the Vienna Opera. Despite Hitler's patronage their reinstatement on the repertoire could not be achieved. To clarify the position Lehár invited to supper at Nussdorf the *Leiter des Kulturreferates für die Staatstheater in Wien* (Head of the Cultural Office for the State Theatres in Vienna). The young man put down in his diary[2] the conversation, and the thoughts which went on in his head during it.

So there he stands before "the advocate of sickly-sweet simplicity, the Olympian of banality", who "lives on intriguing and intimate terms with the Muses and may here and there give them a little pinch under their short silk skirts"; strolling through his

[1] As pointed out by Walter Panofsky in his Strauss Biography, Munich, 1965.
[2] Quoted from Stan Czech, p. 287 at seq., *Schön ist die Welt*.

house, "an extremely curious mixture of past and present, tradition and souvenirs, Mozart and Lehár". The host does not waste any time: "he works his way round, proceeds diplomatically. One more pounce, and the victim can't escape:

" 'What do you actually feel on the question—whether the classical operetta, that is, let's say, *Fledermaus*, *Gypsy Baron* or my *Merry Widow*, has domiciliary rights in a house where *Fidelio*, *Tristan*, *Parsifal*, *Elektra* are performed?' "

The representative of Nazi culture frankly admits he would be unhappy "if in the same place where the great love-union of Isolde and Tristan has been portrayed, the dashing lover should proclaim to his beloved a few hours later in melting *bel canto* that he belongs only to her, to her alone." Lehár: " 'Of course I know that however much the world may shout encore, my works are branded frivolous: stepchildren of true art. And yet all my life I've tried to write more than mere popular-entertainment pieces. I certainly can't be lumped together with the ragtag and bobtail. Operetta—after all, what does that mean? If it's supposed to describe something inferior, then *Die Fledermaus* is a master opera, like *The Magic Flute* or *Der Rosenkavalier*. Let Richard Strauss turn up his nose: after all, I too have an artistic conscience.' "

The talk came to nothing, and Lehár once more found the doors of the Wiener Oper closed to him. Until his seventieth birthday.

Meanwhile he and Sophie had moved to Ischl with their almost complete zoo, led by You-You's successor, Jeani. The German Army invaded Poland and the war started. Brother Anton, prophesying a rapid end, was wrong this time again: with millions of others.

In the belief that she would thereby protect her husband from attacks, Sophie (still of the Jewish faith) reluctantly had herself baptized. The Nazis did not bother about her for the time being, except for an arrogant Viennese bigwig called Frauenfeld, who pursued her with outbursts of personal hatred. In fear of him she carried a poison phial with her till the end of the war. Despite lingering heart trouble she took a nursing course, as she realized that Lehár's health was gradually deteriorating.

On 30th April 1940 the city of Vienna awarded him the Ring of Honour, and Hitler the Goethe Medal; Party bosses offered congratulations, and the Opera House at long last put on *The Land of Smiles*.

The "total war" began once more, Churchill became British Prime Minister, France surrendered, the Luftwaffe covered London with bombs, the old Kaiser Wilhelm II died at Doorn, the Germans marched into Russia, the Japanese bombed Pearl Harbour, Rommel's Afrikakorps was at the gates of Alexandria, and at a secret conference at Wannsee near Berlin Himmler, Heydrich and Eichmann decided on their tactics for the "final solution of the Jewish question".

Three old Lehárians—Victor Léon, Bela Jenbach and Julius Wilhelm—died in Vienna hide-outs; in London and New York there were two new productions of *The Merry Widow*; both had immensely long runs. Now and then (as in the First World War) Lehár played or conducted for the troops; on 20th February 1943 the Budapest Opera put on a revised version of *Gipsy Love*, the opera *Garaboncias* (Travelling Singers). The new dramatic-romantic book (by Ernö Innocent Vincze) told a passionate love story with the war of 1848 as background. It dispensed with dialogue, skilfully built in the beautiful old melodies, and framed the action with ballet sequences. One of these, a *Feentanz* (Fairy Dance), written down on 16th January 1943, represents Lehár's last composition. While he was writing there was so little coal in Budapest that the hotel could scarcely heat his apartment: "But I would only put down the pen for a bit when my hands were almost frozen."

The rehearsals took six weeks, taxing to the utmost the energy of the seventy-three-year-old. He conducted the première, sat with friends afterwards for an hour at his old regular Budapest café; then his physical strength broke down. For the second performance he was still on the rostrum despite severe kidney pains and against doctor's orders. On 22nd February he was rushed off to Vienna, then taken to Ischl during a brief improvement in his condition.

Here he stayed with short breaks for two years. He often remained in bed for two or three months at a time, suffering from 'flu, pneumonia, a gland ailment and various colics. In addition, his vision was reduced by a clouding of the vitreous body, which sometimes made reading and writing impossible. Yet he always rallied. "I'm slowly recovering," he wrote to a friend, "but my prospects were certainly bad. So bad that many good friends were already condoling with my wife. Still, the doctors' skill and my own strong will to live have enabled me to survive the difficult days. At present, after an interval of a year and a half, I can again sit at the piano for a little while every day—which is the best assurance that things are on the up-grade."

Sophie recalled how in the severe winter of 1943/4 the snow lay so high round the villa that nobody could get through, while the ice on the roads made walking so difficult that Lehár could leave the house only with heavy snow-boots. "I was worried something might happen to him; so whenever he went out, I always sent the caretaker and the chambermaid after him, to keep an eye on him. He never noticed his retinue!"

Meanwhile Himmler's Wannsee programme for the Final Solution had become gruesome reality. Mass deportations and gassings had started. The Lehárs learnt with horror that the victims included Helene Löhner, Beda's young wife, and their two children. In her despair she had applied for help to a Nazi official, a former small-time composer of Viennese songs, who owed his only success to her husband; he had thrown her out of his office.

Lehár and Sophie lived at Ischl in continual fear of death: "One day (he remembered) we had two men knocking at the door. They were members of the Gestapo.[1] 'We are to fetch your wife.' Sophie, who was present, naturally fainted. I was in a desperate state, so it occurred to me that I could ring up Bürkel, the Nazi *Gauleiter* at the time, though I didn't know him personally. I described the situation in excited words. He said: 'Send one of the men to the telephone.' The man talked to him for a longish time, then turned to me and said: 'We are to go.' If I hadn't happened to be at home, I should never have seen my wife again . . ."

The war went on: El Alamein, Stalingrad, the fall of Mussolini, the landings in Normandy, Count Stauffenberg's abortive attempt

[1] Statement of 14th March 1947, op. cit.

on Hitler's life, German rockets over England, air-raids on
Germany—and then 1945: scorched-earth policy and collapse of
the Nazi Reich. In Vienna the mob broke into the Nussdorf
Schlössl and despite Anton's intervention looted all there was to
loot: furniture, mementoes, books, archives. "What are others to
say," the composer asked in crushed resignation, "who have lost
their fathers, sons and wives?"

The last days of battle brought new dangers for the Lehárs. The
bridge over the River Traun, fifty yards from the Lehár villa, had
been mined by the Nazis and was to be blown up on the enemy's
approach. "Our house," Lehár recalled later, "would certainly
have gone up in smoke if some S.S. fanatic had lit the demolition
charge. Sophie talked about it in confidence to her fishmonger.
Although he was in the Party, everyone knew he only used it as a
camouflage. 'Don't you worry, Ma'm,' he told her. 'The bridge
will never be blown up, I'll take care of that. I've got a pair of
scissors in the shop, and the moment things get dangerous, I'll just
cut through the high-tension wire.'"

Austria was Austria once more.

A Soothing Atmosphere

The bridge was not blown up; the entry of the United States
troops into Ischl was carried out in good order and without
resistance in the week of Lehár's seventy-fifth birthday. "As in
every other place" (a soldier in the Rainbow Division recalled on
American radio in December 1947) "our men went from house to
house, questioning, checking, securing. When they came to the
villa on the other side of the river, the door was opened to them
by an old gentleman, short in height, with a deathly white face
which showed no sign of bitterness but a smile of welcome. When
the men began putting their questions, he took them into the
drawing-room and asked them politely to take a seat. Then he
walked to the piano without saying anything; his eyes stared into
the distance, his hands trembled . . ."

Directly the news got around among the GIs that the man who
wrote *The Merry Widow* was living in the town his house was

besieged, the doorbell rang repeatedly, and the troops invited themselves in. They photographed the famous composer, approached him for pictures and autographs, and honoured him in the most naïve manner. The Lehárs enjoyed the young people, the freedom regained, and the bloom of spring.

The Vienna State Opera (destroyed by bombs on 12th March 1945) had taken over the Theater an der Wien for its grand opera repertoire, the Volksoper for its light repertoire. Lehár read of plans for Strauss and Offenbach operettas to be staged; his own remained unmentioned. In answer to a direct inquiry he was informed that the old décor had been overpainted and that productions at the moment were not desirable. Lehár not wanted after forty years in Vienna! There was no point, then, in an undesirable remaining there any longer.

As soon as it became known, however, that the Lehárs wanted to go to Switzerland for treatment by Zürich doctors, a storm broke in the press, Abuse, sneers, threats poured over them, the composer was accused of being cowardly, crafty, ungrateful. "And not a single friend turns up to defend me," he complained. "I wouldn't have thought that all I had achieved in and for Vienna was now forgotten."

On 23rd January 1946, completely emaciated, he arrived in Zürich with Sophie, who was seriously ill. They found a comfortable suite prepared for them in the Hotel Baur au Lac. It had a view on to the lake, the snow-covered Alps and the peaceful lateral canal with swans slowly gliding over it. (Lehár fed them every day, and christened one of them Lohengrin.)

To secure the couple's privacy, the hotel management erected a partition cutting off the rooms which faced the corridor; there was a piano there, deep comfortable chairs, and a fireproof cupboard for the manuscripts of all his scores, which he had brought with him. "A soothing atmosphere in which I can relax, and relive the friendly times of yesteryear." Often with those who had been part of them. Immediately the travel restrictions were lifted, Paul Knepler came from London: "To my surprise and delight I found Franz in good spirits, and eager for work. Yes, after a long break he wanted to be at it again, and the new piece must be more beautiful than anything he had composed before. 'Believe me,' he said, 'I'm not yet written out, I have so much music in me still. So much music! Perhaps now a time *will* come when How Fair the World can be sung again.' And the same evening we discussed the possibility of a new operetta."

Somebody had proposed that he should write one with himself as leading character. "Me—an operetta hero?" he laughed. "Tenor or comedian? Nonsense!" Other stories were suggested: on the life of the Hungarian freedom-fighter Kossuth; another, called *Lavinia*, by Rudolf Bernauer; and a third, *Louisa*, by Knepler himself.

Slowly all the ideas were discarded in turn. "It doesn't work! My creative powers are crippled, my pleasure in writing is gone. I've become an embittered old man . . ."

As far as health went, the couple soon felt better. Sophie's blood pressure was normal, the pain in her left shoulder abated; Lehár put on a stone and a half. In the mirror he could observe with satisfaction that his suits no longer hung loose around him. Their new circle of friends, besides Zürich musical and theatrical people, included two very helpful leading citizens of Zürich, Federal Councillor Häberlin and Municipal Councillor Rüegg, and doctors and healers of every kind and faculty: internal specialists, dentists, homoeopaths and magnetopaths, urologists, gynaecologists; above all, the brilliant ophthalmologist Harry Bollag, whose skill succeeded in bringing about a 50 per cent improvement in Lehár's sight.

Now Tauber's American début in *The Land of Smiles* was approaching, and the composer, like the singer, set high hopes on the event. Apart from periodical concerts, it was months since Tauber had sung. His voice was well rested, and a success in New York at this juncture might have had the most beneficial consequences for him, as well as for Lehár. But *The Land of Smiles*, or *Yours is my Heart*, as it was renamed, became one of the classic Broadway flops. An incompetent management decided to give the well-tried work to hacks who were to adapt book and music "for American taste". Lehár did not learn of the damage until it was done and he was unable to rectify it.

Doubts started for him with Tauber's first night-telegram:

MUSIC MADE FANTASTIC IMPRESSION STOP
THEY LIKED ME TREMENDOUSLY

That didn't sound good; music can't be the only thing in an operetta to make an impression, a tenor—even Tauber—the only thing the audience like. The whole work and the whole production must stand up. From the papers, he gathered the full extent of the disaster—reading about the "stupid libretto", "old-fashioned and tasteless sets", "repellent humour, except when unintentional", a "painful assortment of actors": an "incredibly vulgar, infantile operetta".

How could it have been otherwise in this disgraceful New York production? "Genuine theatrical music," Lehár declared, "arises out of the action. It is written to quite definite words for a quite definite atmosphere. If this atmosphere is taken away, such music becomes no longer part of the scene it was designed for. That my *Land of Smiles*, which achieved thousands of performances all over the world, should have failed on Broadway, surprised me only while I was ignorant of the ill-treatment it had received. The Viennese background had to give way to a Parisian one, the Austrian general's daughter became a French opera star, and 'You are my heart's delight' was sung facing the Eiffel Tower. No one would dare change the Egyptians of *Aida* into Frenchmen, the heroine into a daughter of Louis XIV, with the Nile act transferred to a boudoir! The world would with full justification protest against such a blasphemy."[1]

Tauber became furious during the rehearsals: "This is not the dialogue of *Land of Smiles*! I refuse to utter such nonsense." He was soothed, but an hour later had another fit of rage. The press called his voice "impressive", "astonishing" and "specially beautiful"; but all such eulogies could not avert the calamity, and Schnappula had to take refuge in a throat indisposition. Diana bravely came before the curtain to tell the audience of his withdrawal. "Please forgive him," she added in tears.

[1] The world did nothing of the kind when—*horribile dictu*—someone, in fact, dared! Years later Broadway saw the production of a musical set in the Civil War, called *My Darlin' Aida*, which used story and music from Verdi's opera.

After a distressing three weeks the theatre closed. "Lehár will never forgive me for this," was Tauber's epitaph on the venture.

The various artistic, commercial and copyright matters connected with the *Yours is my Heart* episode, and the first signs of a Lehár renaissance starting all over Europe, hastened the realization of a plan which the composer had long been contemplating. It became absolutely clear to him that his work, business undertakings, he himself and his future estate, needed a first-class man whose loyalty and honesty would be beyond doubt.

He found such a man in Dr Otto Blau, a music publisher of great acumen, expertise and absolute integrity. Originally a lawyer by profession, Dr Blau was a nephew of the celebrated "Herr Rat", under whose guidance he learned the business, and on whose death he took over the firm of Josef Weinberger. At the time when the Glocken-Verlag was founded, Lehár had wanted him to become head of it, and had made him flattering offers; but Blau's old family ties proved too strong. After the war the two men met again in Zürich; acquaintance and mutual esteem ripened into friendship, then into community of interest and a father-son relationship.

The prudent Lehár could not have provided better for his old age and posthumous fame.

Weep With Me, Friends!

When Lehár and Tauber saw one another again in May 1947, nine years had passed since their last meeting. After nine minutes, when each of the "brothers without the luxury of blood relationship" had recovered from the first shock of the other's wasted appearance, and had told him how little he had changed, it seemed to both as if the gap had been only nine days. They listened to each other's reports on war, bombs, and starvation rations, Lehár played numbers from *Garaboncias* and Tauber from *Old Chelsea*, the musical comedy he had appeared in from 1942 to 1945 in England. Otherwise they talked—as if there were no longer any future for them—mostly of the great decade of their partnership. When they walked along the Bahnhofstrasse arm in arm, they were always followed by a crowd of admirers; now and then someone addressed them, congratulated them on the reunion. The photographs from this time make Lehár look older, Tauber younger, than they were.

The composer had secretly arranged an evening with Radio Beromünster, but the singer hesitated: he had come to Zürich to spend a few nice days with his friend, not to work. So Lehár resorted to one of the oldest tricks: "I told him there were rumours current in Europe about his voice: it had declined, lost its brilliance. And Schnappula promptly fell for this—the concert turned out to be the finest we ever gave!" Before they parted, Tauber talked of common plans—now that theatrical and musical life was stirring again in Germany. Lehár looked at him with a resigned smile: a younger partner could no doubt render him better service. . . .

Perhaps one or both of them may have thought of the famous parting scene,[1] when Haydn at fifty-eight was leaving Vienna for distant London, and Mozart at thirty-four said in tears, seeing him off: "Oh my dear, good Papa, this will be our last kiss." And when the older man heard, only a few months afterwards, of the younger man's death.

On his return to London, Tauber set about organizing his coming season: the idea of a new musical came up, an interesting offer to conduct, a series of popular concerts; but somehow he lacked the will to concentrate. "I sit here in my hotel room," he wrote to Diana, "gaze up at the sky, and like Pedro in *Tiefland* wish I 'were back in the mountains whence I came'."

He was tired and restless, and his huskiness grew worse and worse. He had fits of coughing day and night, producing a horrible racking sound. The doctors couldn't make up their minds whether it was a bronchial catarrh or an asthmatic cold; a thorough X-ray examination was to settle the matter.

At the beginning of August, Tauber received a letter from Vienna, saying that the entire ensemble of the Staatsoper had been invited over by the Covent Garden Opera, and would consider it an honour if he, as an honorary member of the famous old house, would appear with the company in any role of his choice.

[1] On 15th December 1790.

Immediately his mood changed. He was as gay and energetic as ever, tiredness and huskiness had vanished. Of course he was ready to sing, he told the Viennese. The role? There was only one worth considering, the one in which he believed he had always given of his best vocally and artistically—Don Ottavio in Mozart's *Don Giovanni*. A shock for Vienna: it had long ceased to be a secret that Tauber's voice had passed its peak. Don Ottavio is considered one of the most difficult tenor parts in all opera. But there was no going back.

On 27th September 1947, when Tauber put on his old Ottavio costume in the star's dressing-room at the Royal Opera House, he was dismayed to find how thin he had become. "Beads of sweat appeared on his brow," Diana relates. "Anxiety and depression could be read in his eyes. He rallied all his powers, and with a pale smile walked towards the stage."

What happened then can never be thought of by anyone in the audience that night as anything but a miracle. From the powerful *"Tutto il mio sangue"* to the *"Or che tutti"* at the end, the voice sounded as it had not done since its great opera days: sublimely beautiful, captivating, and unmistakably Tauber. The jubilation of the crammed house knew no bounds, and Ottavio had to appear before the curtain about thirty times. "I made it! I made it!" he cried over and over again, back in the dressing-room with his wife. "And if I never sing another note, it was a glorious exit."

An emergency operation a few days later showed that he had sung with one of his lungs almost completely decayed. His unshakable, dynamic nature kept him alive for another three months. On Wednesday, 7th January, at 4 p.m., huddled in his armchair and breathing with difficulty, he heard a broadcast in which a tenor was blaring out "You are my heart's delight". Quite cheerfully Tauber asked Diana to give him a piece of cotton wool to block his ears. Then all of a sudden he said: "I feel very bad, please get me to hospital."

The doctors gave him an oxygen apparatus. "Is it better now?" Diana asked. He removed the cylinder. "Well, I never—yes!" he answered. And he began his old-accustomed singing exercises: "Mimimimi—Mimi—Mimimi . . ."

In the evening Eric and Blanche Glass, his devoted friends and business advisers, came to ask whether they could help him in any way, whether there was anything he wanted. Yes, he would like a big helping of *spaghetti Bolognese*. It was produced, and he swallowed it with the best of appetites. It was Schnappula's last meal. In the early hours of the 8th he breathed his last.

Well might Lehár, like Haydn, have lamented, on receiving the news: "Weep with me, friends, for the world will never see his like again."

Four months earlier Sophie had died, suddenly and unexpectedly. One evening at the hotel, chatting to her husband and two friends, one of them a doctor, she got up to go into the next room. Just after she closed the door, a cry was heard: "My heart!" Lehár and the doctor dashed in to her. It was too late.

Since his friend and physician, Dr Wurnig, had drawn his attention, when they left Ischl, to the seriousness of Sophie's condition, Lehár had been obsessed by fear of this happening. Now he broke down. For two days he scarcely stopped sobbing, or moved from the deep chair in his darkened room. It took all his powers to attend the cremation. As from a distance his friend Häberlin's funeral address sounded in his ear: "Fate has granted her a fine and easy departure from life. Only a week ago she was in a box at the Stadttheater with her husband, for the first night of *Paganini*, hearing the frenzied applause of a thrilled audience breaking round them once again. Yes, even on the evening which was to be her last, she was in high spirits. But then her tired heart suddenly stopped . . . Her death leaves a gap in Lehár's life which will never be filled."

Late Autumn in Ischl

Paul Knepler visited him again in those days: "I found an old, sick man, and I knew the melodies which slumbered within him would never again be awakened to life. 'No,' he said. 'I don't want any more . . .' And he quietly spoke the words which remained his life's confession of purpose: 'I wanted to conquer people's hearts, and if I have succeeded, I know I have not lived in vain, nor worked in vain.'"

A month after Tauber's death Lehár conducted a concert devoted to their work together, in the Zürich Kongresshaus. It was to be his last.

Meanwhile his sister Emmy, youngest child of the old Lehár household at Budapest, had been called to Zürich. Thirty-five years before, when she was twenty, she had married one of Anton's fellow officers, Stefan Paphazay, who had a unique reputation in the army for his remarkable linguistic ability, and had risen to the rank of major-general. In 1946 the intelligent, practical and attractive woman had been widowed, and as her son Ferenc had established his own household, she found a new purpose in life through looking after her great brother.

A general examination carried out at Zürich Hospital in early June confirmed a slight improvement in Lehár's condition, but his restlessness became visibly worse. To stay in the hotel suite, in which every corner reminded him of his dead wife, grew unbearable: he longed for Ischl, where he could rest, sleep, die.

At the end of June the doctors gave their permission for the move. Emmy was apprehensive about the expedition, but everything went smoothly: with the Arlberg Express to Salzburg, then by car home, in deepest sadness.

Directly he entered the hall a round ball of a thing came dashing down the stairs: Jeani. Faithful as ever, wagging her little tail like mad for joy, the old dog jumped up, round and all over him. (Jeani survived her master by only a fortnight.)

Ischl greeted its returned honorary freeman with bands, choral societies, serenades and deputations—all the pomp it could muster. The Nazi time was forgotten like a bad dream. Word spread that he had not long to live, and an unusually solemn atmosphere surrounded him when he walked down the Pfarrgasse or along the Esplanade. People made way for him reverently, or took their hats off without speaking. "Understanding eyes, a trace of superiority round the mouth, sternness and kindness alike strongly marked"— this was the impression he made on Maria von Peteani. Often he walked through the house, "even up to the second floor, to linger a while in his old study and look round him in silence. There was his piano, his harmonium, and the old desk with the pencil-sharpener on it. Sun shone through the balcony door. He did not utter a word. When his sister invited him to come into the little *salon* next door and relax there amidst old memories, he only shook his head, turned away, and slowly went downstairs again."

He remained well groomed and careful of his appearance, as he had always been. Every morning a girl from the near-by hair-dressers appeared to shave and manicure him and do his hair. Lady visitors still had to be tactfully turned away, love-letters answered with thanks, proposals of marriage with regrets. The treasure Emmy attended to everything.

Sophie's mortal remains, which had been brought in their urn from Zürich, were laid to their last rest next to Mama Lehár. On 1st September, the anniversary of her death, Lehár wanted to go out to the grave; but his legs failed him, he suddenly fainted, and had to be put to bed.

A few days after him, his friend Oscar Straus had also returned to Ischl (from American emigration). Three weeks older than Lehár, Straus looked far younger, fresher and healthier. He had much to tell about what was going on in New York's light-musical theatre. There was a new musical, *Oklahoma*, by Richard Rodgers and Oscar Hammerstein; it had been running now for five years on Broadway, and had reached 2,000 performances: a powerful folkloristic operetta with glorious music and quite new methods of production and choreography. And *Carousel*, by the same partners: a brilliant transposition of Molnar's *Liliom* into a setting of New England in 1870. Then there was Irving Berlin's *Annie Get Your Gun*, in its third year already, also with an American background and also produced with great originality. Yes—and this might interest Lehár particularly—the latest Broadway musi-cal was *Brigadoon*, a sort of fairy-tale; it had a splendid musical score by Frederick Loewe, son of that Edmund Löwe who sang Danilo in the early days of *The Merry Widow* when Treumann was indisposed.

"Doesn't all this activity, with such a lot of talent around, remind you of our own beginnings—with Fall and Eysler?" Straus asked. Lehár agreed, showing keen interest: so his prophecy had come true that one day "qualified composers would appear who of their own initiative would offer their gifts to operetta, and with these gifts and their strong dedication would lead the old genre upwards once more to glorious heights."

They talked often of their art, their achievements, their hopes fulfilled and unfulfilled; and Straus afterwards gave a summary of the conversations. "We agreed about operetta, despite our stylistic differences. It must always be an excuse for producing beautiful music: music right from the heart; and it must give singers the chance for full vocal play, audiences for unalloyed pleasure."

At the end of September, Lehár's condition deteriorated. Dr Wurnig came three or four times a day, a blood transfusion was given, Viennese specialists were called in. The old man knew he was dying. He asked for the last sacraments to be administered; and with a clear mind drew up his will, in which apart from legal flourishes his own voice can be heard unmistakably: the voice of simplicity, lucidity and order.

First he expresses the wish to be buried near his "devoted mother and beloved Sophie in the family vault at Bad Ischl", with the stipulation "that this vault be maintained in permanency". Then follows the naming of his sister Emmy as sole heir, with all earlier "testamentary dispositions of whatever nature" thereby revoked. Brother Anton, "who through no fault of his own was torn from a brilliant career, and has been deprived of the adequate pension due to him for services to his country, should as far as possible remain relieved for life from financial worries"; he was to receive the Schikaneder-Schlössl, the interest on the house in Theobaldgasse, a large monthly allowance, Lehár's car, watch, clothes and various other articles. The villa was left to the town of Ischl, on condition it was turned into a *Franz Lehár Museum* and preserved as such. The will contained other legacies to his nephew Ferenc, Emmy's son, to his servants, and to the A.K.M. (Society of Authors, Composers and Music Publishers); also the appointment of Dr Blau, "who knows exactly my artistic and business intentions", as head of all his publishing enterprises and, together with two lawyer friends, as his executor. "I wish, moreover, that my works be produced and published in the way I conceived them . . . and that my testament be respected by all the persons remembered. Should any of these persons dispute it, I disinherit him and revoke the legacy made to him."

It was late autumn in Ischl, and the sun went down early. "We put the canaries in Franz's bathroom," Emmy wrote, "because they were freezing downstairs. He had remembered them himself." And: "For me the thought of my own death has nothing frightening about it, but somehow I cannot help thinking of his death as if it were the end of the world. And it moves relentlessly nearer and nearer."

The final struggle lasted a week. Lehár could no longer take in any food, and went almost blind. On the evening of 23rd October he said: "Now I have done with all earthly things", and breathing quietly, fell slowly asleep.

At 3 p.m. the following day his heart stopped.

The Monument in Sound

Within an hour the news of his death spread round the earth, and at once a huge pile of messages of sympathy arrived from all sides. The same evening the big radio corporations of the world arranged memorial broadcasts and memorial concerts. Oscar Straus sat in his study on the other side of the Traun and turned the knobs of his radio. In an endless stream his friend's old songs reached his ear, mingling with the muffled peals of Ischl's church bells.

The black flag went up over the house of mourning, and soon there were black flags showing on all the other buildings in the town, hanging from windows and lamp-posts. The body, in tails, white waistcoat and tie, and patent leather shoes, lay in state in the *Pfarrkirche* between high burning candles. For a week the people of Ischl filed past, saying a prayer, bringing a little bouquet.

On 30th October, after a solemn requiem, the procession, led by the miners' band and a dozen cars full of wreaths and flowers, moved past the Lehár theatre and the Lehár villa to the small cemetry. Ministers, regional governors and Bürgermeisters followed the coffin, with officers of the occupation army, generals from the former imperial army, representatives of writers', musicians' and actors' societies, deputations from Zürich, Berlin, London; friends, strangers—and perhaps, invisibly, the hundreds of characters to whom his music gave life: Danilo, René, Sou Chong, Nechledil, Pfefferkorn, Alexei, Angèle, Eva, Margit, Frasquita, Anna Elisa, Friederike—and masses of gipsies, boyars, mandarins, cavaliers, *grisettes*, *mannequins*, peasant girls, court ladies and tinker-boys.

Lehár had asked to have the Volga-*Lied* from *The Tsarevich* as funeral song: the lament of the lonely soul yearning for love. As the coffin was lowered into the earth, it sounded forth in its solemn G-minor, G-major notes.

"They have laid him to rest like a king," said his friend Otto Blau, who was now left with the gigantic task of looking after the dead composer's artistic heritage, prestige and survival. With mature, careful deliberation, but also boldness and energy where necessary, he set about fulfilling this assignment. There was no musical estate: Lehár had not left any uncompleted work. What he felt worthy of publication, he had published in his lifetime.

Ten years after his death the number of performances of his works at German, Swiss and Austrian theatres surpassed that of all other composers, living or dead. *The Merry Widow*, *Paganini* and *The Land of Smiles* reached about 1,000 each a year, *The Count of Luxembourg*, *Tsarevich* and *Gipsy Love* about 500, and five of his other operettas from 250 to 350 each. The trend continued in the sixties with fluctuations up and down. In the official list of musical productions during the 1964/5 season at all German, Swiss and Austrian theatres, *The Merry Widow* is far ahead of the second and third most popular works, *The Magic Flute* and *Die Fledermaus* respectively. (The first Richard Strauss entry, *Der Rosenkavalier*, comes sixty-first.) Outside the German-speaking countries, too, *The Merry Widow*, *The Land of Smiles*, *The Count of Luxembourg* and *Gipsy Love* are firmly anchored in the repertoire of musical theatres all over the world: a monument in sound instead of the marble ones which Karczag had once predicted. Ischl alone erected such a tangible memorial.

Little over a year later Richard Strauss followed his musical *bête noire* into eternity. He, too, had done with all earthly things, and ordered his burial music (the Finale Trio from *Rosenkavalier*). In his last hours he said with wry humour that dying was exactly as he had composed it sixty years before in *Death and Transfiguration*.

The cheerful Mundi Eysler died, the daring Kurt Weill, soon Kálmán, Künnecke and Oscar Straus; also Benatzky, Marischka, Abraham, Knepler—and on 12th November 1962, aged eighty-seven, Anton Lehár. From her home in Zürich, Emmy acted as trustee to her brother's memory. And on a flowery meadow outside a country house in Berkshire her grandchildren played, the sons and daughters of her son Ferenc—Franz Lehár's seventeen great-nephews and great-nieces: Esther, Alexandra, Susan, Philip, Elisabeth, Agnes, Steven, Cecilie, Catherine, Emeric, Eva, Mary, Anne, Thomas, Sarah, Joseph and Sophie.

The chronicle of Lehár's life closes: a chronicle of a child of fortune, a darling of the gods in Goethe's sense. For

> '*Alles geben die Götter, die unendlichen,*
> *Ihren Lieblingen ganz,*
> *Alle Freuden, die unendlichen,*
> *Alle Schmerzen, die unendlichen, ganz.*'[1]

They gave him sadness and adversity, distress and decline—and they gave him all he ever dreamed of, gold and silver, the ideal wife, all the thinking, all the feeling, highest joy and deepest pain.

---

[1] Written in June 1777, after the news of his sister Cornelie's death.

> The cup's poured full by the gods everlasting
> For their darlings, to the brim,
> All the joys everlasting,
> All the pain everlasting, to the brim.

POSTSCRIPT

in the form of a letter from the author
to his friend, Dr Otto Blau,
the administrator of Franz Lehár's work.

My dear Otto,

In the spring of 1964, when I received the invitation from yourself and the Lehár family to write a comprehensive Lehár biography
for the centenary of the Master's birth, I scarcely anticipated that
it would take me five full years to complete the task: that in its
course I should have to look for material in 50 libraries all over
the world, interview 500 people and examine 5,000 letters, documents, manuscripts, reviews, photographs and newspaper clip-
pings.

And often during all this time the idea occurred to me: I
wonder what *he* would have said, wanted or felt in this or that
context.

I knew him since the *Yellow Jacket* days, and received a great
deal of personal kindness and artistic stimulation from him. After
Giuditta we spoke once or twice about the possibility of a biography. He hesitated: his life was still going on, he said, his work
was by no means finished, and: "After all, I have told people
through my music everything about me they need to know."

Did he not wish to bring to light the *chiaroscuro* of his private
existence? Was he afraid of the harsh colours in the sympathies and
antipathies which surrounded him? Or did he find it embarrassing
to be seen by all the world as "Lord Lehár, sweet Lehár, most anything Lehár, almost most absolute Lehár?"[1]

My book answers some of the questions, and raises others which

[1] *Antony and Cleopatra*, Act One, Scene Two.

are hard to answer. "A man must choose (W. B. Yeats once said) between perfection of the life or of the work." For Lehár this choice never existed. He was not aware of any dilemma between moral action and creative impulse. Inspiration and its full use were alone decisive for him—which may explain the magnitude of his achievements. So many of his melodies immediately formed part of our daily life—and still do so. He adorned the age that shaped him: this is my *apologia* for the many fragments and particles of history in the narrative—for mentioning the black-and-gold canopy and the brown cacophony, the *Ausgleich* and the *Anschluss*, Karl Kraus's Day-of-Judgment speech and Himmler's Final Solution Programme, Sarajevo and St Petersburg, Theodore Roosevelt and Theodor Innitzer . . .

They all belong to Lehár's world, in kind if not in degree, as much as his music—and his partners: producers, managers, librettists, leading ladies, tenors and comedians. As a young composer (under the patronage of your own firm, Otto, the publishing house of Weinberger) I lived and worked through the last decade of the Viennese operetta; and today I still do not know whether the play we acted then was (in Oscar Wilde's sense) "a trivial comedy for serious people" or "a serious comedy for trivial people". The protagonists of the genre were my friends, colleagues, interpreters, critics and rivals. I have observed them in retrospect with as much objectivity as I could muster, often with sympathy or amusement, and have grouped them here round Lehár—as minor characters or "supers".

There is such a profusion of stories that I heard from them, often too good to be true: I have always taken cognizance of these, but only conditionally. Yet some of the stories found their way into the present volume. Because, as old Herodotus said,[1] "It is my duty to relate what is being related, but it is not always my duty to believe it. And this would be my principle in everything I relate."

Whatever I relate is based on my personal experience, or what I have read or been told, more especially on sources which till now have remained unpublished—and which you, together with

[1] Book Eight, 152.

Madame Emmy Paphazay, Lehár's sister, have made available to
me and allowed me to use. Thus my very first thanks are due to
you and to her, who have replied so patiently to all my questions,
who have advised and helped and stimulated me.

I know that there was nothing Franz Lehár hated more, apart
from malicious criticism, than extravagant eulogies. I know, too,
that on this you all agree with him, so that you will have no
objection to any "roughness" painted into the picture. His
recommendation and yours would doubtless be the same as
Oliver Cromwell's to Sir Peter Lely:[1] "I desire you would use all
your skill to paint my picture truly like me: roughness, pimples,
warts and everything . . ."

And this was my aim: to bring Franz Lehár's nature just as truly
and fully to life—as his melodies will always remain.

In sincere devotion

Yours, as ever,

B.

[1] Sir Peter Lely (1618–80), Dutch-English portrait painter.

LEHÁR'S PRINCIPAL WORKS

1896
Kukuschka (1906 revised as *Tatjana*)

1902
Wiener Frauen (Viennese Women)
Der Rastelbinder (The Tinker)

1904
Der Göttergatte (The Husband God) Revised 1913 as *Die ideale Gattin* (The Ideal Wife), and again 1921 as *Die Tangokönigin* (The Tango Queen)
Die Juxheirat (The Mock Marriage)

1905
Die lustige Witwe (The Merry Widow)

1908
Der Mann mit den drei Frauen (The Man with the Three Wives)

1909
Das Fürstenkind (The Prince's Child) Revised 1932 as *Der Fürst der Berge* (The Prince of the Mountains)
Der Graf von Luxemburg (The Count of Luxembourg)

1910
Zigeunerliebe (Gipsy Love) Revised 1943 as *Garaboncíás*

1911
Eva

1914
Endlich allein (Alone at Last) Revised 1930 as *Schön ist die Welt* (How Fair the World)

1916
Der Sterngucker (The Stargazer) Revised 1922 as *La Danza delle Libellule* (The Three Graces), and again 1926 as *Gigolette*
1918
Wo die Lerche singt (Where the Lark Sings)
1920
Die blaue Mazur (The Blue Mazurka)
1922
Frühling (Spring) Revised 1928 as *Frühlingsmädel* (Spring Girl)
Frasquita
1923
Die gelbe Jacke (The Yellow Jacket) Revised 1929 as *Das Land des Lächelns* (The Land of Smiles)
1924
Cloclo
1925
Paganini
1927
Der Zarewitsch (The Tsarevich)
1928
Friederike (Frederica)
1934
Giuditta

INDEX